The Plant Kingdom

The Plant Kingdom

HAROLD C. BOLD

*C. L. Lundell Professor Emeritus
of Systematic Botany
The University of Texas at Austin*

JOHN W. LA CLAIRE II

*Associate Professor of Botany
The University of Texas at Austin*

Prentice-Hall, Inc., Englewood Cliffs, New Jersey 07632

Library of Congress Cataloging-in-Publication Data

Bold, Harold Charles, (date)
 The plant kingdom.

 Bibliography.
 Includes index.
 1. Botany. I. La Claire, John W., (date).
II. Title.
QK47.B73 1987   581   86–17009
ISBN   0–13–680398–9

Editorial/production supervision
  and interior design: *Kathleen M. Lafferty*
Cover design: *Bruce Kenselaar*
Manufacturing buyer: *John B. Hall*

Printed in the United States of America

10 9 8 7 6 5 4 3 2 1

ISBN   0-13-680398-9   01

Prentice-Hall International (UK) Limited, *London*
Prentice-Hall of Australia Pty. Limited, *Sydney*
Prentice-Hall Canada Inc., *Toronto*
Prentice-Hall Hispanoamericana, S.A., *Mexico*
Prentice-Hall of India Private Limited, *New Delhi*
Prentice-Hall of Japan, Inc., *Tokyo*
Prentice-Hall of Southeast Asia Pte. Ltd., *Singapore*
Editora Prentice-Hall do Brasil, Ltda., *Rio de Janeiro*

Contents

CHAPTER FOUR

Nonvascular Land Plants: Liverworts, Hornworts, and Mosses   70

CHAPTER FIVE

Organization of Vascular Plants   96

CHAPTER SIX

Seedless Vascular Plants I: Divisions Psilotophyta, Microphyllophyta, and Arthrophyta   119

CHAPTER ELEVEN

Conclusion   269

Glossary   278

Selected Readings   294

Index   297

Preface

The present (fifth) edition of *The Plant Kingdom* has been prepared to update the material and to improve the text and illustrations in the interests of clarity and lucidity for the benefit of the reader. This edition follows the original plan, an orderly presentation of basic facts regarding the organization and reproduction of representative members of the plant kingdom. In addition to these basic facts, discussions of certain basic concepts have been included, such as plant evolution and phylogeny, types of life cycle, and brief accounts of fossil precursors of extant plants.

The Plant Kingdom remains a small book for use in one-semester and/or one-quarter courses or as a supplement to some textbooks of general biology that are often superficial in their discussion of plants.

In the present edition, the prokaryotic blue-green algae and bacteria are discussed together in a separate chapter. The chapters on slime molds and fungi have been shifted toward the end of the book because, although they are classified according to the International Rules of Botanical Nomenclature and studied by botanists, some biologists question their supposed membership in the plant kingdom.

The treatment of all the groups has been somewhat expanded, and some of the illustrations have been improved and a number of new ones added. Once again, the discussion of the anatomy of the vegetative organs of vascular plants has been consolidated in a separate chapter. The treatment of the flowering plants has been augmented by a brief discussion of several important floral types. Every effort has been expended to modify the text in accordance with new data uncovered by botanical investigators since the fourth edition appeared.

The inclusion of review or discussion questions at the ends of all but the first and last chapters is designed to aid the student in testing his or her own understanding of the topics discussed. Once again, we would emphasize that the student's understanding will be the more secure if he or she has been able to study the plants discussed in the living condition in the laboratory, or *at the very least,* if he or she has had access to appropriate colored transparencies illustrating them.

We would reaffirm the conviction that, although we do not share Thomas Gradgrind's philosophy of education,[1] current emphasis in some writing and teaching on "discovery, concepts, and principles" may have provided students with shadow instead of substance, with a superstructure lacking adequate foundation, or with stones instead of bread. We hope, on the contrary, that the reader, in some cases on his or her own initiative, but in most instances with the instructor's guidance, will be able to formulate concepts and make syntheses more successfully on the basis of an encounter with substantial data.

Once again, we wish to express our gratitude for the reception accorded the earlier editions of *The Plant Kingdom* and for the helpful comments of the many students and teachers who have written about it. We also wish to acknowledge helpful suggestions from Theodore Delevoryas, James D. Mauseth, and Richard C. Starr of the University of Texas at Austin, and Gibbes Patton of Wofford College. We are grateful to Dianne O'Neil for some of the artwork and to Frances Denny and John Allensworth for help with the proof and indexing. We are indebted also to three reviewers of the manuscript of this edition: Robinson S. Abbott, University of Minnesota-Morris; Edward F. Anderson, Whitman College; and Om P. Madhok, Minot State College. We appreciate these reviewers' careful scrutiny and many helpful suggestions.

Harold C. Bold
John W. La Claire II

[1]In Charles Dickens' *Hard Times:* "Now, what I want is, Facts. Teach these boys and girls nothing but facts. Facts alone are wanted in life. Plant nothing else, and root out everything else . . . stick to facts, Sir!"

CHAPTER ONE

Unity and Diversity of Plants

INTRODUCTION

The title of this book, *The Plant Kingdom,* conveys different meanings to different people. To many, "plants" signify trees, shrubs, herbs (as they did to Aristotle); these are mostly organisms that produce seeds. However, although such seed-bearing plants, especially those that have flowers, are most common in the experience of most people, there exist many other types of green (chlorophyll-containing)[1] *seedless* plants, such as algae, liverworts, mosses, and ferns.

Our environment is characterized by richly diversified plant life on which we depend for our very existence. The air we breathe contains a consistently adequate level of oxygen only because it is continually replenished by green, chlorophyllous plants. Furthermore, plants, both aquatic and terrestrial, are the foundation of the food chain for the animal kingdom. Plants of the past and/or their products supply us with fuels (oil, coal, and peat), while the abundant water-conducting and supporting tissues of woody plants provide lumber for furniture and construction. Plant protoplasm and its products are the basic sources of the energy and the building blocks with which animal protoplasm is synthesized.

Existence of the populations of a number of countries is based on nutrition supplied by grain-forming plants (rice, corn, barley, wheat, and oats) or those producing fleshy, underground storage organs (potatoes, sweet po-

---

[1]Some biologists have classified fungi (although they lack chlorophyll) in the plant kingdom. In this book, they are assigned to a kingdom of their own.

tatoes, sugar beets, and turnips). Plant fibers are the basis of many textiles and of rope and some kinds of furniture.

The widely diverse activities of such achlorophyllous organisms as bacteria and fungi are also of great significance to the biological world, especially to human beings (see Chapters 2 and 10).

As we become familiar with representatives of *all* the groups of plants that populate the earth, we will probably be impressed with their diversity. The green scum on certain ponds, the duckweed on others, the lichens, fungi, liverworts, mosses, ferns, conifers, and flowering plants—some representatives of which populate even the most inhospitable areas of the earth, both land and sea—are all elements of this diversity and form the subject matter of the present volume. We shall survey this diversity and emphasize the various important biological principles that are particularly well illustrated by each of the several plant groups. Such questions as the origin of life, the great variety of living organisms, and the nature of their interrelationships will also be considered. We shall devote some attention as well to extinct plants known to us only as fossil remains. One topic, however, the classification of plants, requires immediate consideration.

CLASSIFICATION OF PLANTS

Classifications of organisms are created by humans; they do not exist in nature. There are two types of classification systems of living organisms. In the first and oldest type, **artificial systems,** organisms are grouped together for convenience of identification. Such groupings do not imply actual kinship and hence are not phylogenetic. Examples of this type of classification are the division of plants into beneficial and harmful, into herbaceous and woody, or into evergreen and deciduous. As students of plant structure, called **morphologists,** became impressed with the basic similarity in the body plans of certain plants, they began to group them into systems or categories; after the impact of Charles Darwin's exposition of organic evolution, the categories of these systems were interpreted to be phylogenetic. **Phylogenetic classifications,** which are designed to emphasize genetic relationships among living organisms, are based on carefully evaluated evidence of several types. The more important types of evidence are fossil records, geographical distributions, and comparative studies of living plant structure, function, biochemistry, development, and chromosomal and genetic constitution.

Darwin's publication of *The Origin of Species* in 1859 gave great impetus to phylogenetic classification systems, and a number of new schemes purporting to show phylogenetic relationships were proposed. However, classifications differ with the classifiers' appraisals of available evidence of relationship, sought in the comparative study of both living and fossil plants.

Our knowledge of the latter, of course, will be at best always incomplete. Classifications of plants (and animals), therefore, are in a constant state of flux and are subject to continuing criticism and disagreement, for they represent only approximations. Classifications continually are being modified as new evidence for or against a postulated relationship between groups is discovered. Several systems of plant classification are summarized comparatively in Table 1.1. In addition, the table lists common, anglicized names for the several groups, and estimates the number of species in each. The three systems of classification shown in Table 1.1 are in themselves good evidence that agreement has not yet been reached regarding the lines of relationship among plants. Like science itself, classification of plants is not static but subject to modification as new data emerge. Of course, this table is not meant for memorization but for reference to alternative schemes of classification of the organisms that are discussed in Chapters 1 to 11 and in other books.

As Table 1.1 indicates, certain groups of plants have vernacular names, such as algae, fungi, bacteria, liverworts, mosses, ferns, seed plants, and flowering plants. Examples of these are illustrated in the chapters that follow. In considering such an assemblage of plants, one is at once impressed by their differences in habitat and structure, and by their seeming diversity of function.

Categorization of organisms not only groups together similar and supposedly genetically related types, but in so doing categorization is divisive for it excludes some organisms from each of the categories. Probably the greatest discontinuity among living organisms is that between those that are prokaryotic and those that are eukaryotic (Table 1.1). The former are considered to be the earliest organisms to have developed on the earth and, accordingly, the most primitive. They represent only a small segment of living organisms and are discussed in Chapter 2.

Although the diversity of these organisms is indeed the subject matter of this volume, there are also common attributes that are shared nearly universally by living organisms. Some of these unifying attributes of plants (and animals) are (1) cellular organization, (2) metabolic phenomena, (3) genetic phenomena, (4) sexual reproduction, and (5) adaptation.

1. *Cellular Organization.* In 1838 and 1839, botanist M. J. Schleiden and zoologist Theodor Schwann published their theory that the cell (Figure 1.1) is the universal unit of organization in plants and animals. They arrived at this conclusion as a result of numerous studies by themselves and by other investigators who had been working with the light microscope from the time of its invention in 1590. This basic cell theory has become the generally accepted explanation of the organization of living organisms. Furthermore, with the exception of blue-green algae and bacteria, such cellular components as nuclei, nuclear membranes, cytoplasm, mitochondria, Golgi bodies, and the endoplasmic reticulum (Figures 1.1. and 1.2) are present in almost all plant and animal cells.

TABLE 1.1 A Comparative Summary of Some Classifications of the Plant Kingdom[a]

Eichler, 1883 (with modifications)		Tippo, 1942	
Plant kingdom		Plant kingdom	
A Cryptogamae			
Division 1	Thallophyta	Subkingdom 1	Thallophyta
Class 1	Algae		
	Cyanophyceae	Phylum 1	Cyanophyta
	Chlorophyceae	Phylum 2	Chlorophyta
		Phylum 3	Euglenophyta
	Phaeophyceae	Phylum 4	Phaeophyta
	Rhodophyceae	Phylum 5	Rhodophyta
	Diatomeae	Phylum 6	Chrysophyta
		Phylum 7	Pyrrhophyta
Class 2	Fungi		
	Schizomycetes	Phylum 8	Schizomycophyta
		Phylum 9	Myxomycophyta
		Phylum 10	Eumycophyta
	Eumycetes	Class 1	Phycomycetes
	Lichens	Class 2	Ascomycetes
		Class 3	Basidiomycetes
		Subkingdom 2	Embryophyta
Division 2	Bryophyta	Phylum 11	Bryophyta
Class 1	Hepaticae	Class 1	Hepaticae
Class 2	Musci	Class 2	Musci
Division 3	Pteridophyta		
		Phylum 12	Tracheophyta
		Subphylum 1	Psilopsida
Class 1	Lycopodinae	Subphylum 2	Lycopsida
Class 2	Equisetinae	Subphylum 3	Sphenopsida

[a]Only groups with currently living plants are included. When the name of a group is used later at a higher rank, as is Chlorophyceae, the name of the lower groups is usually retained as a subsidiary under the higher. Although approximately equal to "Division," "Phylum" is not recognized as a category by the International Code of Botanical Nomenclature.

Bold and La Claire, 1987[b]	Common name	Approximate number of living species
Superkingdom Prokaryota		
Kingdom A Monera		
Division 1 Schizonta	Bacteria	4,000
Division 2 Cyanophyta[c]	Blue-green algae[d]	
Division 3 Prochlorophyta[c]	None	
Superkingdom Eukaryota		
Kingdom A Phyta (Plants)		
Division 1 Chlorophyta	Green algae	
Division 2 Charophyta	Charophytes	25,000
Division 3 Euglenophyta	Euglenids	
Division 4 Chrysophyta	Golden algae	
Division 5 Phaeophyta	Brown algae	
Division 6 Pyrrhophyta	Dinoflagellates	
Division 7 Rhodophyta	Red algae	
Division 8 Hepatophyta	Liverworts	8,000
Division 9 Anthocerotophyta	Hornworts	100
Division 10 Bryophyta	Mosses	10,000–12,000
Division 11 Psilotophyta	Psilophytes	8
Division 12 Microphyllophyta	Club and spike "mosses"	1,000
Division 13 Arthrophyta	Horsetails and sphenopsids	10–25
Division 14 Pteridophyta	Ferns	9,500
Division 15 Cycadophyta	Cycads	100
Division 16 Ginkgophyta	Maidenhair tree (Ginkgo)	1
Division 17 Coniferophyta	Conifers	550
Division 18 Gnetophyta	None	71
Division 19 Anthophyta	Flowering plants	250,000
Kingdom B Mycetae (Fungi)		
Division 1 Myxomycota	Slime molds	⎫
Division 2 Acrasiomycota	Cellular slime molds	
Division 3 Chytridiomycota		
Division 4 Oomycota	Posteriorly uniflagellate fungi	⎬ 50,000
Division 5 Zygomycota	Bread molds and others	
Division 6 Ascomycota	Sac fungi	
Division 7 Basidiomycota	Club fungi	
Division 8 Deuteromycota	Imperfect fungi	⎭

[b]This book.

[c]Ending is "phyta" because the organisms in these divisions are named according to the International Code of Botanical Nomenclature.

[d]Numbers included in algae; sometimes called "Cyanobacteria."

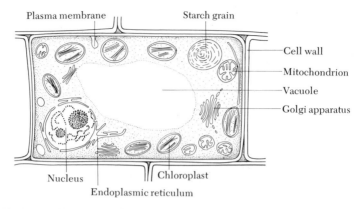

Plasma membrane   Starch grain

Cell wall
Mitochondrion
Vacuole
Golgi apparatus

Nucleus   Chloroplast
Endoplasmic reticulum

Figure 1.1   Generalized diagram of a plant cell. [Modified from W. T. Keeton.]

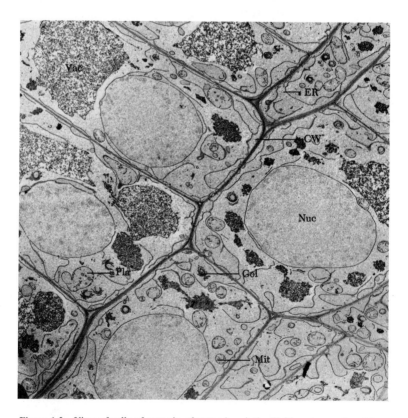

Figure 1.2   View of cells of root tip of water hyacinth, *Eichhornia crassipes* (electron micrograph, × 1770). ER, endoplasmic reticulum; Gol, Golgi apparatus; Mit, mitochondrion; Nuc, nucleus; Pla, plastid; Vac, vacuole; CW, cell wall. [Courtesy of Professor H. J. Arnott.]

2. *Metabolism.* In living organisms, the many chemical activities carried on, collectively called metabolism, offer additional evidence of unity. Such processes as energy release in respiration seem to be universally the same in living organisms, as do many of the pathways of chemical synthesis and degradation. Further, many enzymes (the catalysts of metabolic processes in living organisms) are similar in various types of protoplasm.

3. *Genetic and Developmental Phenomena.* The life of each individual cell, the differentiation of cells in the development of complex multicellular organisms, and, finally, the transmission of hereditary traits are governed—in all organisms—by deoxyribonucleic acid (DNA) in interaction with the cytoplasm through the agency of ribonucleic acid (RNA). The specific pattern of genetic organization is responsible for the structural and functional attributes of the cell as it develops in a given environment.

4. *Sexual Reproduction.* No matter how diverse organisms may be— algae, elephants, daffodils, or human beings—four phenomena are almost always involved in sexual reproduction: (1) union of cells, (2) union of their nuclei, (3) intermingling of two sets of nuclear components (chromosomes with their genetic materials), and (4) reassortment of genes at **meiosis** (reduction division).

There are in addition alternate modes of interchange of genetic material, such as transformation and transduction. Transformation occurs among certain bacteria in which DNA from one strain may enter cells of another and replicates there. In transduction, DNA of viruses may become incorporated in living bacteria and multiply there (see p. 16). These phenomena are connected with another unifying principle, the phenomenon of inheritance, the laws of which are the province of genetics. In the plant kingdom only the euglenids seem to lack sexual reproduction.

5. *Adaptation.* Another manifestation of the unity of living organisms is adaptation, the capacity of organisms, both as individuals and as continuing, sexually reproducing populations, to survive in their changing environment. Adaptations are both morphological (structural) and physiological (functional), two aspects of organisms that usually are intimately connected. Living things must be attuned to their environment; those that are not become extinct.

EVOLUTION OF PLANTS

How, then, are the diversities among living organisms to be reconciled with the equally apparent and striking similarities just enumerated? Modern biology answers this seeming paradox with the concept of **organic evolution**. According to this explanation, diversity has arisen secondarily. It is deviation from original unity and has occurred throughout the more than 3 billion years during which life has existed on this planet. The living organisms we see about us are the present actors on an ancient stage. With passage of time, the settings have changed and so have the actors. They have become transformed by incorporation into the population of genetic changes, called **mutations**, that, upon selection or inbreeding, produced divergent progeny in which the changes became fixed. Many have dropped out; many others have become so changed over the ages through selection and incorporation of new combinations of mutations as to be scarcely recognizably related to their ancestors. We are thus driven to speculation regarding their origin. That such spontaneously occurring changes, or mutations, have occurred and are occurring in living organisms is no longer subject to question. We can observe them taking place in nature at present, and we can induce their occurrence with suitable stimuli, such as irradiation and chemical agents. During many generations of sexually breeding populations, certain combinations of mutations were selected and became dominant, and in time the species changed, while others became extinct. This, it is postulated through extrapolation, is the fundamental explanation of all the diversity of present-day organisms and the cause of their modification from their ancestors. Since the sequence of occurrence and inheritance of many of the changes cannot be followed completely and unequivocally, the story of the *course* of organic evolution in the past will probably remain incomplete. The point to be emphasized here is that a survey of diverse types of plants may tend to obscure the fact that *present diversity sprang from earlier unity.*

What, then, are some of the evidences that organic evolution has occurred and is occurring? First, one may cite the incontrovertible evidence of artificial selection and resultant change in organisms during recorded history. The effects of such selection by man have resulted in the domestication and changes in many animals and plants from their wild ancestors. Examples of this are currently available varieties of such fruits as strawberries, peaches, and apples; the numerous varieties of cattle for meat and milk production; and the various kinds of dogs and cats, all different from their wild precursors, yet clearly related to them.

Second, one may cite the occurrence of spontaneous mutants—genetically changed individuals such as the navel orange and Boston fern—and the production of mutants in many organisms by man, using various mutagenic agents such as irradiation and chemicals.

Third is the important evidence from the fossil record. Most plants and animals living on earth today are different from those that lived in past ages, as they have been recorded in fragmentary fashion by their remains in sedimentary rocks. Furthermore, there is a certain order in the fossil record so that, in general, a progression from simple types to those more complex and specialized has been revealed. However, a number of ancient organisms, such as blue-green algae and bacteria, seemingly have persisted with little change from the time of their first appearance on earth. Finally, with respect to the fossil record, a number of organisms that lived in earlier periods of the earth's history are no longer extant.

A fourth line of evidence for the evolutionary development of living organisms is their similarity at different levels of organization. For example, various kinds of ferns have the same plan of organization as do various flowering plants, and members of a given group are more similar to each other than they are to other groups. Furthermore, on the basis of similarity of organization, different groups of species can be grouped or classified together as genera; these can be grouped into families, the families into orders, the orders into classes, and the classes into divisions or phyla. These categories or groupings seem to represent patterns of organization at various levels, which can best be explained as manifestations of kinship through descent with modification. The evidence of common origin appears to be especially convincing at the cellular and subcellular level where, for example, throughout the eukaryotic groups of plants and animals, one sees upon analysis repetition of the same cellular organelles and biochemical activities.

A fifth type of evidence, more abundant in the animal kingdom than in the plant, is the occurrence of nonfunctional or vestigial organs, clearly homologous, that are fundamentally similar to functional ones in other animals. An example of this type of vestige is the presence of vestigial bones for hind limbs in the bodies of certain reptiles.

In such considerations, we are finally brought face to face with the ultimate question of the origin of life itself. Did it arise but once, or more than once? How was the first life organized? What was the nature of its nutritive and metabolic processes? For a long time, it was taken for granted that answers to these questions must be relegated to the realm of speculation, but significant experiments some years ago indicated that the origin of life was subject to experimental analyses. In a series of investigations wherein various mixtures of gases—methane, ammonia, hydrogen, and water vapor—were enclosed in chambers in which electricity was discharged, the production of amino acids, which are building units in the proteins of living organisms, was achieved in entirely nonliving systems. Thus the distinction between the inorganic and organic has become irrelevant.

Early speculators usually postulated that the most primitive living organisms must have been those that could thrive in an environment containing only inorganic, low-energy compounds; according to this, such organisms must have possessed a tremendous range of enzymes, enabling them to convert such low-energy compounds into protoplasm. Quite the opposite view is now more widely accepted. This postulates that the first organisms lived in a medium supplied with complex, high-energy molecules that they could utilize directly or with a minimum of change to synthesize and repair their protoplasm. As the supply of these complex substances became critically low, alternate pathways of protoplasmic synthesis evolved. These enabled primitive, surviving organisms to build up their substance from increasingly less complex building units.

According to this point of view, chlorophyllous, photosynthetic organisms are less primitive than achlorophyllous organisms like most bacteria, fungi, and animals. On the other hand, it is quite possible that some achlorophyllous organisms evolved from green organisms by losing their ability to produce chlorophyll. Such a change can be experimentally produced in certain unicellular algae like *Euglena* (see p. 50) by high temperature or by immersion in the antibiotic streptomycin.

It has also been hypothesized that chlorophyllous organisms arose by the incorporation of certain primitive photosynthetic cells within originally colorless cells in a sort of symbiosis. It has been suggested that the subsequent modification of these imprisoned cells may have resulted in the photosynthetic organelles called **chloroplasts**.

Comparative studies of the nutrition of microorganisms are shedding a good deal of light on these questions. The origin and relationships of diverse living organisms and of their variations in structure, nutrition, and metabolism constitute the subject matter of organic evolution, which postulates that living things are related to one another through common ancestry. It is the purpose of the present volume to survey these diversities in orderly fashion and thus, hopefully, to provide some insight into the range and activities of members of the plant kingdom.

CHAPTER TWO

Bacteria
and Blue-Green Algae
(Kingdom Monera)

Long after their discovery, the bacteria and blue-green algae were often classified as members of the plant kingdom. With the advent of electron microscopy, it became evident that they differ significantly from plants (and animals and fungi) in cellular organization. They lack membrane-bounded nuclei, mitochondria, Golgi bodies, endoplasmic reticulum, and membrane-bounded plastids, all of which are present in the cells of plants, animals, and fungi.

Why, then have the authors continued, in this edition, to include the Monera in a book called "The Plant Kingdom"? The Cyanophyta, blue-green algae, are in their unicellular, colonial and filamentous organization, and photosynthetic pigments algalike and autotrophic: in fact, their photosynthetic system is virtually like that of green plants. The bacteria, unpigmented or having a different type of photosynthetic pigments and mechanism, have been included because they illustrate fundamental biological principles, and in many ways play important roles in plant life.

Members of two divisions of the superkingdom Prokaryota, and Kingdom Monera, the Schizonta, and Cyanophyta, will be discussed in this chapter.

THE BACTERIA (DIVISION SCHIZONTA)

Patterns of Nutrition

Chlorophyllous plants, as well as some bacteria, using light energy, are able to convert low-energy compounds—namely, carbon dioxide and water—into energy-rich carbohydrates in the process of photosynthesis. From simple sugars or fragments of them as basic units, with the addition of inorganic materials absorbed from the soil or the water in which they are bathed, green plants are able to synthesize their protoplasm. They are said to be **photoautotrophic** because they use light energy to build living matter from inorganic substances. The great majority of organisms lacking chlorophyll are dependent on the complex substances manufactured by green plants for the materials with which to build their bodies; these organisms are **heterotrophic.** The distinction between these groups is not absolute. Certain green plants can live heterotrophically in light and darkness when supplied with appropriate organic compounds.

Some heterotrophic organisms, called **parasites,** require the living protoplasm of their hosts or grow upon them, sharing their metabolites. Others are **saprobic,** requiring either nonliving protoplasm or the nonliving products of protoplasm. Saprobes occur in soil, in water-containing organic matter, and upon inadequately protected wood, textiles, and foods. The saprobic heterotrophs are the main agents in degrading the complex products of other organisms and in causing decay of their bodies after death. Thus, decaying organic materials are broken down in many stages to carbon dioxide, water, and numerous other inorganic compounds, a common pool of substances that can be incorporated anew into the bodies of other organisms. The processes of degradation are especially striking as one digs down carefully through layers of undisturbed forest litter. Were it not for the activity of heterotrophs making available elements bound up in other organisms, life would be limited by a grave shortage of certain materials, especially available nitrogen.

A third group of heterotrophic organisms, which includes most animals, ingests protoplasm or its products; these are called **phagotrophic, phagocytotic,** or, sometimes, **holozoic.** Animals, certain flagellates, and slime molds are examples of these.

A few bacteria, although lacking chlorophyll, can synthesize their protoplasm from low-energy inorganic compounds by using the chemical energy released in oxidation of these compounds (see p. 17) and by obtaining their carbon from carbon dioxide (CO_2). Organisms of this type are said to be **chemoautotrophic** or **chemosynthetic.** It should be emphasized that the same essential major chemical elements—carbon (C), hydrogen (H), oxygen (O), phosphorus (P), potassium (K), nitrogen (N), sulfur (S), calcium (Ca), iron (Fe), and magnesium (Mg)—are present in the protoplasm of most living organisms. Differences, however, prevail in the degree of complexity of carbon and nitrogen compounds required for the synthesis of protoplasm. Autotrophic organisms start with simple compounds of these substances—carbon dioxide (CO_2), water (H_2O), ammonia (NH_3), and nitrates (NO_3^-)—using light energy or that available from oxidizing reduced compounds. In summary, autotrophs may be photoautotrophic or chemoautotrophic, depending on the primary source of their energy.

In the preceding paragraphs, we have, in effect, classified living organisms on the basis of their nutrition. Heterotrophic organisms described in this book are the bacteria, slime molds, and fungi (Table 1.1). Most of these organisms are structurally as simple as or even simpler than the algae. Certain biologists suggest that some of the fungi may have derived from algae by loss of chlorophyll. Others consider protozoa as ancestral to fungi, for some fungi, like protozoa, are phagotrophic.

Although they are united by a common lack of chlorophyll and consequent lack of photoautotrophic nutrition (except in the case of certain bacteria), considerable diversity exists among the bacteria, slime molds, and fungi, which accordingly are classified as separate groups (see Table 1.1).

Cellular Organization

The increasingly long list of common attributes shared by bacteria and blue-green algae has impelled some to classify these organisms together in a group, Prokaryota, an allusion to their lack of membrane-bounded nuclei and of (in the blue-green algae) plastids. Bacteria are probably the most simple and minute living organisms with cellular organization. Bacterial cells are usually less than 8 micrometers in length and may be as little as 0.25 of a micrometer in width. The cells of bacteria may be of three types: (1) spherical, the **cocci** (singular, *coccus*); (2) rod-shaped, the **bacilli** (singular, *bacillus*); or (3) spiral, the **spirilla** (singular, *spirillum*) (Figure 2.1*a–d*). The first two may be joined to form clusters or filaments. The individual cells, like those of blue-green algae, differ from other plants in nuclear organization and in lacking large aqueous vacuoles (Figure 2.2). Bacterial cells contain DNA, the universal basis of heredity, but it is not localized within a nuclear membrane, although it is sometimes called nucleoplasm. Instead, the DNA occurs often in the form of a continuous fibril, which, if extended, would be many times longer than the cell. More than one DNA region may be present in a cell (Figure 2.2*a*). Bacterial cells lack other membrane-bounded organelles such as mitochondria, Golgi apparatus, and endoplasmic reticulum.

The cell wall of the bacterial cell (and of other cells) accounts for the

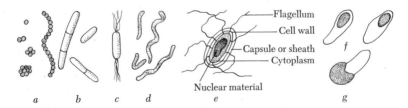

Figure 2.1   Bacteria. (*a*) Cocci. (*b*) Bacilli, two in division. (*c*) Polar-flagellated bacillus type. (*d*) Spirillum. (*e*) Cellular organization of a peritrichous bacterium. [After E. E. Clifton.] (*f*) Spore formation. (*g*) Spore germination.

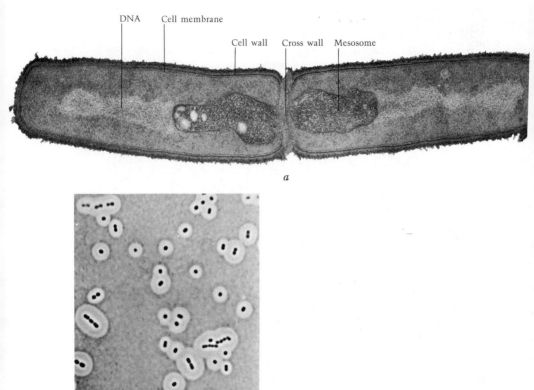

Figure 2.2   (a) *Bacillus subtilis*, electron micrograph. [Courtesy of Stanley C. Holt, after T. D. Brock.] (b) *Acinetobacter* sp., showing capsules. [Courtesy of Elliot Juni.]

rigidity and maintenance of its shape. This is readily demonstrable by lysing the wall with the enzyme **lysozyme,** which digests the nucleopeptides (or peptidoglycan) of the wall so that the protoplast tends to change its form. Bacterial cell walls contain sugars and amino acids, including α,ϵ-diaminopimelic acid, also present in the walls of blue-green algae.

Bacteria may be classified as Gram-positive or Gram-negative on the basis of their reaction to a staining procedure known as the Gram stain, which involves coloring with a dye called crystal violet and with iodine (I_2)–potassium iodide solution (KI). These form a complex within the cells. Gram-positive bacteria are not decolorized when immersed, after staining, in alcohol or acetone, but Gram-negative bacteria are. This reaction depends on a difference in the physical organization of the cell walls: the walls of Gram-positive bacteria, upon dehydration in alcohol or acetone, become impermeable to the stain in the protoplast, the stain being retained; the walls of Gram-negative bacteria are permeable to the stain, which diffuses out.

As in eukaryotic cells, the plasma membrane of bacterial cells is differentially permeable. This means it controls the entrance and egress of solutes from the cell.

In addition to the cell wall itself, some bacteria secrete slimy sheaths about themselves, which are called **capsules** (Figure 2.2*b*). These are analogous to the sheaths of blue-green algae.

Some bacteria have flagella (Figure 2.1*c, e*). These emerge from basal discs within the cellular envelopes. They are composed of the protein **flagellin** and may be variously arranged on the cells, that is, at one or both poles or all over its surface, among other arrangements. Bacterial flagella are much more delicate than the cilia and flagella of eukaryotes and lack their 9 + 2 fibrillar organization (Figure 3.3*b*). Bacterial movement is slow as compared with that of eukaryotic cells. The photosynthetic bacteria exhibit positive phototaxis, while heterotrophic bacteria exhibit positive chemotaxis if motile.

Certain types form thick-walled **spores** (Figure 2.1*f, g*) that are remarkably resistant to desiccation and unfavorable environmental conditions, and are not unlike some blue-green algal spores.

Some spore-forming bacteria, many of which live in soil, must be reckoned with in canning to insure their destruction. *Clostridium tetani,* a spore-producing anaerobe that is the causative agent of tetanus in humans, must be taken into account when soil contaminates deep wounds.

Bacterial Reproduction

Bacteria multiply by cell division that may be repeated rapidly, as often as once every 15 to 20 minutes. It has been estimated that if one bacterial cell and its progeny were to continue multiplying at this rate for 24 hours, the number of individuals produced would be 1×10^{21}, with a total group weight of 8000 pounds! Why, then, is the world not overrun by bacteria? The answer, of course, lies in their requirement for a specialized environment, their competition with other microorganisms—namely algae, fungi, protozoa, and other bacteria—and finally, their accumulation of toxic products. Biologists sometimes lose sight of these facts in applying to natural situations conclusions that are based on pure cultures of microorganisms. At cell division, the DNA replicates, and the two strands are segregated in each of the products of cell division, after which a transverse wall is formed. Some bacteria form resistant spores (Figure 2.1*f, g*) that enable them to survive desiccation.

That certain bacteria also have a mechanism for genetic interchange was first demonstrated in 1946 by Joshua Lederberg and Edward L. Tatum when they cultivated together populations of two mutants of the colon bacillus *Escherichia coli;* each of the mutants was unable to synthesize two (of four) substances required in nutrition and metabolism. One required biotin and methionine, and the other required threonine and leucine; each could synthesize the two substances required by the other. Out of each billion cells from the culture of mixed mutants planted in a medium lacking all four required substances, approximately 100 colonies appeared. This is a clear manifestation that genetic interchange had occurred between individuals in the cultures of mixed mutants.

At present, three different methods are known for transfer of genetic material between bacterial cells. These include (1) conjugation, (2) transformation, and (3) transduction.

Conjugation was demonstrated initially for *Escherichia coli,* as noted above. Certain strains are donors and others recipients, and this is genetically determined. In the process of conjugation, an extension of the donor cell, called a **pilus,** makes connection with a recipient cell (Figure 2.3) and some DNA from the donor is transferred to the recipient. The cells apparently separate after conjugation.

Transformation has been demonstrated in some bacteria. In this process certain cells, called recipients, are capable of incorporating free DNA from their environment into their own DNA, and they thus become changed or transformed. The newly incorporated DNA has been found experimentally to evoke various genetic changes in the cell, such as resistance to antibiotics, changes in chemical composition of the capsules, and in use of various carbohydrates in nutrition. There is good evidence that transformation occurs in nature as well as that induced in the laboratory. It was first demonstrated in *Diplococcus pneumoniae.*

Viruses act as vectors of foreign DNA in the process known as **transduction.** As they penetrate the cell wall in their host bacteria, some of the

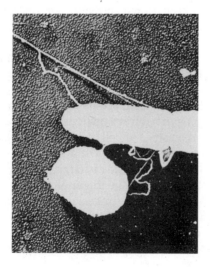

Figure 2.3 Cytological evidence of genetic interchange in the bacterium *Escherichia coli.* Note connection between individuals of morphologically distinct strains. [Courtesy of Dr. Thomas F. Anderson, after F. Jacob and E. L. Wollman.]

DNA of the virus becomes incorporated in that of the host, which, accordingly, becomes different genetically; for example, the host bacterium may become immune, after transduction, to the transducing virus. It has also been shown that viruses released from one bacterium can transfer some of their former hosts' genes to the new bacterial cell that they invade. Transduction, then, is a recombination process. DNA is carried from cell to cell by temperate[1] viruses. A transducing virus transfers not only its own genes, but also some of the genes of the host from which it was derived.

Genetic interchange and combination in bacteria are different from sexual reproduction as it occurs in eukaryotic organisms in that in the former only partial transfer of genetic material occurs, while in the latter the complete genetic complements of two cells are combined in the zygote.

Bacterial Activities

The fact that relatively simple morphology does not preclude physiological and biochemical complexity is strikingly evident in the bacteria. A few are chemoautotrophic and photoautotrophic in nutrition. The former obtain energy from oxidations to build their protoplasm entirely from inorganic units. Two nitrifying bacteria, *Nitrosomonas* and *Nitrobacter*, exemplify chemoautotrophic types; they obtain their energy as indicated in the following reactions.

Nitrosomonas
$$NH_4^+ + 2O_2 \longrightarrow 2H_2O + NO_2^- + energy$$

Nitrobacter
$$NO_2^- + \tfrac{1}{2}O_2 \longrightarrow NO_3^- + energy$$

Photosynthetic bacteria, such as *Rhodospirillum*, although photoautotrophic, carry on a type of photosynthesis quite different from that of plants containing chlorophyll *a*. In photosynthetic bacteria, which contain bacteriochlorophyll, no free oxygen is released, and hydrogen is provided by donor substances other than H_2O, such as hydrogen sulfide (H_2S) or alcohol, with low expenditure of energy. Chlorophyll *a* occurs in all green plants. Certain accessory chlorophylls, such as chlorophyll *b*, differ in their side chains and absorption spectra.

The vast majority of bacteria are heterotrophic, and their widespread chemical activities, catalyzed by myriads of enzymes, constitute the major areas of research in current microbiology and bacteriology. As they affect people directly, bacterial activities are both harmful and beneficial, but the beneficial ones probably exceed the harmful.

---

[1]Temperate viruses are those that penetrate cells without lysing them.

Bacteria cause diseases in both plants and animals. These pathogenic types affect their hosts adversely by robbing them of vital metabolites, by enzymatically destroying host tissues, and sometimes by secreting poisons. It is significant that some bacteria themselves are subject to the ravages of pathogens in the form of bacterial viruses, called **bacteriophages,** which destroy the bacterial cells. Nonpathogenic bacteria can be bothersome too, for they are instrumental in spoiling foods and in causing decay in materials that people desire to preserve.

The activities of bacteria in spoiling foods are only a special example of their universal activities in decay and degradation, processes accomplished by many types of bacteria and fungi through their enzymes. These processes culminate ultimately in the production of CO_2, H_2O, and many other inorganic compounds. The value of such destructive activities in freeing bound metabolites has already been cited (see p. 12).

The importance of bacteria in maintaining soil fertility is paramount, especially in replenishing the element nitrogen, which is an essential part of proteins. Certain bacteria, either living freely in the soil or in the roots of legumes (beans, clover, alfalfa, and so forth) or certain nonlegumes (alder, *Casuarina, Myrica*) fix molecular nitrogen and reduce it in synthesizing their protoplasm, thus tapping a source of nitrogen not available to most other organisms. (A number of blue-green algae function similarly.) Other bacteria, such as *Nitrobacter* and *Nitrosomonas*, oxidize NH_4^+ to nitrates (NO_2^-) and nitrates (NO_3^-), thereby enriching the nitrogen supply in the soil and reducing the escape of gaseous NH_4 from it. By contrast, still other bacteria are denitrifying in that they reduce nitrates to ammonia.

The cheese industry depends on the bacteriological fermentations of lactose, a milk sugar, and the production from it of lactic acid, which coagulates the milk proteins and forms curds (and whey). The formation of acetic acid (in vinegar) is effectively accomplished by other bacteria; this occurs in the souring of cider and wines. Numerous other potentially useful chemical activities of bacteria have been controlled for man's benefit. Not the least important of these is the production by bacteria of antibiotics such as tyrothricin, bacitracin, subtilin, polymyxin B, streptomycin, and terramycin. An antibiotic is a chemical produced by one microorganism that is able to kill or inhibit the growth of other microorganisms.

Bacteria, like algae, are ancient organisms. They have been preserved as fossils, in spite of the delicacy of their cells, in Precambrian strata at least two billion years old (Figure 2.4). Their manifold activities through the ages and at present emphasize their important role in the biological scheme. They were classified as plants largely because botanists made the early studies of bacteria. Later, however, the study of bacteria became a special area of biological science called **bacteriology.**

For a more comprehensive account of the bacteria and their activities,

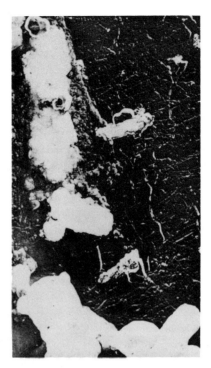

Figure 2.4 Precambrian fossil bacteria (bacilli), approximately 2 billion years old. [After J. W. Schopf, E. S. Barghoorn, M. D. Maser, and R. O. Gordon; micrograph by M. D. Master.]

the reader should consult the microbiological books of Brock (1984) and Stanier et al. (1986).

BLUE-GREEN ALGAE (DIVISION CYANOPHYTA)

Cellular Organization

The Cyanophyta, or blue-green algae, being prokaryotic, differ from all other algae in their cellular organization (Figure 2.5). The differences are the following: they, like bacteria, lack membrane-bounded nuclei; the organization of the pigmented cytoplasm is different; and they lack mitochondria, Golgi apparatus, endoplasmic reticulum, and large, aqueous vacuoles (Figure 2.5). The cell structure is thus much like that of bacteria. The photosynthetic lamellae, or **thylakoids,** are not enclosed by membranes to form plastids, as in the green algae and other plants. The walls of some blue-green algae have been shown to contain various substances such as α,ϵ-diaminopimelic and muramic acids, which are also present in the walls of Gram-negative bacteria. Furthermore, several D-amino acids occur only in the walls of blue-green algae and

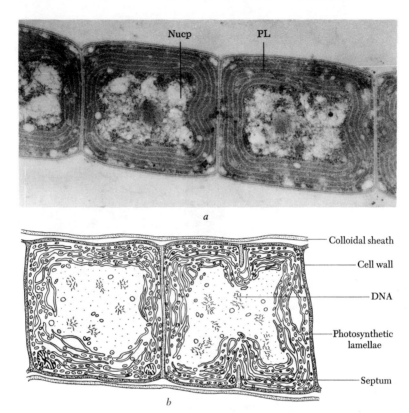

Figure 2.5   Blue-green algae. (*a*) Electron micrograph of a section through several cells of the filamentous alga *Plectonema boryanum*. Note concentric photosynthetic lamellae, PL., and central, diffuse nucleoplasm, Nucp. [After K. M. Smith, R. M. Brown, D. A. Goldstein, and P. L. Walne.] (*b*) Diagram of the organization of a blue-green algal cell as revealed by the electron microscope. Note ingrowing septum of dividing cell, right. [After J. C. McMenamin.]

certain bacteria. The DNA in blue-green algae is dispersed within the cell, which is hence said to be **prokaryotic.**

Unicellular, colonial (noncoenobic), and filamentous blue-green algae are known. *Chroococcus* Figure 2.6*a*) and *Gloeocapsa* (Figure 2.6*b*) are examples of the unicellular type. They reproduce only by cell division. The division products sometimes remain associated to form incipient colonies.

In *Merismopedia* (Figure 2.7) cell divisions regularly in two directions build up a colony consisting of a flat sheet of cells. This reproduces by fragmentation.

Spirulina, Nostoc, and *Anabaena* (Figure 2.8) exemplify filamentous blue-green algae. Here cell division always in the same direction builds up chains of cells. The helical filaments of *Spirulina* are of interest in that one

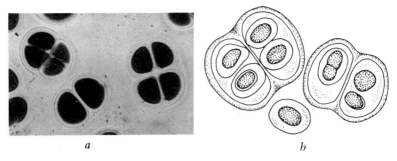

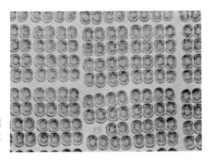

Figure 2.6 (*a*) *Chroococcus turgidus,* a unicellular blue-green alga, in division. (*b*) *Gloeocapsa* sp.

Figure 2.7 *Merismopedia* sp., a colonial blue-green alga. The colony is a flat sheet of cells one layer thick.

of its species, *S. platensis,* has been pressed into algal cakes and sold for food in the Chad Republic, Africa. *Spirulina* is being cultivated in the United States and Mexico and is for sale in health-food stores.[2]

Reproduction

Reproduction by fragmentation occurs also in filamentous forms such as *Oscillatoria, Nostoc,* and *Anabaena.* The filaments of many species of *Oscillatoria* are motile, as are the fragments, called **hormogonia,** of many filamentous blue-green algae. Their pattern of motility has been designated as "gliding movement." Specialized, granular, thick-walled cells, called spores or **akinetes,** are produced by some filamentous genera, many of which also produce **heterocysts,** transparent thick-walled cells (Figure 2.8*d*). There is good evidence that heterocysts are the site of nitrogen fixation in blue-green algae which fix nitrogen in a manner similar to that of certain bacteria (see p. 18).

Although the precise mechanism remains to be elucidated, it is clear that

[2]Additional economic and biological activities of blue-green algae are discussed with those of other algae on p. 25.

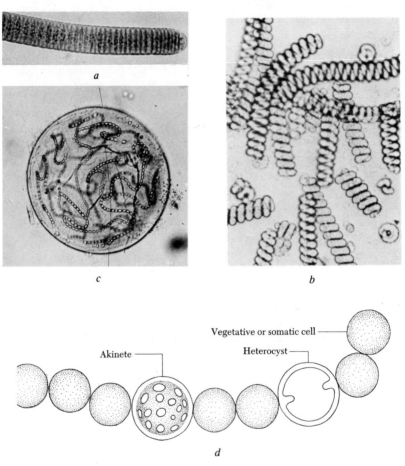

Figure 2.8 Filamentous blue-green algae. (*a*) *Oscillatoria* sp., note lack of differentiation. (*b*) *Spirulina* sp. [After H. C. Bold, C. J. Alexopoulos, and T. Delevoryas.] (*c*) *Nostoc* sp.; filaments within colloidal matrix. (*d*) *Anabaena* sp.; note the thick-walled, dormant spore, or akinete, and heterocyst.

genetic recombination, as in sexual unions, occurs in at least some blue-green algae. It has been shown, for example, that when streptomycin-resistant and polymixin B–resistant strains of a unicellular blue-green alga (*Anacystis nidulans*) are grown together, one can recover strains resistant to both antibiotics. The mechanism probably involves transmittal of DNA, possibly by transformation, as in bacteria (see p. 16). Apparently, the blue-green algae are a group of ancient organisms, some of which possibly were flourishing in Precambrian times about 1 billion years ago (Table 6.1).

QUESTIONS FOR REVIEW

1. How does cellular organization of bacteria and blue-green algae differ from that of eukaryotic organisms?

2. In what respects is bacterial cellular organization similar to that of blue-green algae?

3. Give reasons for and against classifying blue-green algae and bacteria together.

4. What types of nutrition occur in living organisms? Define, giving examples of organisms with each type.

5. Why are bacteria not included with fungi? With slime molds?

6. What kinds of cell form occur among bacteria?

7. Can bacteria be classified solely on the basis of morphology? Explain.

8. What is nitrogen fixation? Where do the nitrogen-fixing bacteria grow?

9. What methods of interchange of genetic materials occur among bacteria?

10. How do bacterial flagella differ from those of eukaryotic cells?

11. List some harmful and some beneficial activities of bacteria.

12. What is the relation of spore formation in bacteria to canning and to deep wounds?

13. What ingredients would you include in a culture medium for heterotrophic bacteria?

14. What does the fossil record indicate regarding bacteria?

15. What characteristics distinguish blue-green algae from bacteria?

16. Define or explain the following: akinete, heterocyst, spore, vegetative, and somatic.

CHAPTER THREE

Algae

INTRODUCTION, GENERAL CHARACTERISTICS, AND CLASSIFICATION

Although no one can describe the organization of primitive life with absolute certainty, the fossil record strongly indicates that organisms much like certain modern algae lived more than 2 billion years ago. This is not to state categorically that algae were the earliest living organisms. The fossil record is incomplete and always will be, but there is every indication that algae, along with bacteria and certain fungi, are extremely ancient organisms; at least some of them have persisted with little modification from their progenitors. For this reason and because of the relative simplicity of most algae, we shall begin our survey of the diversity of the plant kingdom with these plants.[1] Furthermore, algae provide elegant material for laboratory demonstrations of many fundamental biological phenomena.

What are algae? Where do they grow? What do they do and what good do they do? In the following pages we shall attempt to answer these questions about algae (and later about every group of plants we consider). To the layperson, algae are "pond scums," "seaweeds" (even when they grow in freshwater!), and, too often, "mosses." To the biologist, they are chlorophyllous organisms characterized by having one of the following (Figure 3.1): (1) gametes but no specialized sex organs (this is characteristic of certain unicellular algae), (2) unicellular sex organs, or (3) multicellular sex organs in which every

---

[1]Other than blue-green algae (Chapter 2).

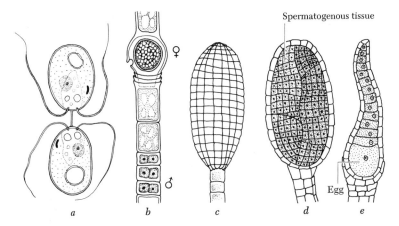

Figure 3.1 Sexual reproduction in algae and nonalgae, diagrammatic. (*a*) *Chlamydomonas* sp.: the organisms themselves function as gametes. (*b*) *Oedogonium* sp., the gametes are borne in special unicellular gametangia (male, below, and female, above). (*c*) Multicellular (plurilocular) gametanigium of *Ectocarpus,* a brown alga; every cell is fertile. (*d, e*) Sex organs of a bryophyte (diagram): (*d*) the male organ or antheridium; (*e*) the female organ or archegonium. Note the sterile cells surrounding the fertile ones in (*d*) and (*e*).

cell forms a gamete. In these respects, they differ from all other green plants. This definition may seem technical, but it is necessary, for science, in its dedication to accuracy, requires strict definition.

Algae live in both marine and fresh waters. They may be floating at the surface, suspended in the water (**planktonic**), or attached to various substrates. They also occur on and within soil and on moist stones and wood, as well as in association with fungi and certain animals such as *Paramecium, Hydra,* sponges, marine worms, and corals. In summary, algae grow everywhere.

With respect to "what they do" and "what they are good for," algae are of paramount importance as primary producers of energy-rich compounds that form the basis of the food cycle of all aquatic animal life. In this connection, the planktonic algae are especially important, since they serve as food for many animals; this is, of course, based on the photosynthetic activity of the algae. Furthermore, algae oxygenate their habitat while they are photosynthesizing, thus increasing the level of dissolved oxygen in their immediate environment. In addition, certain blue-green algae (Chapter 2), like some bacteria but unlike most other plants, can employ gaseous nitrogen from the atmosphere in building their protoplasm and in this way contribute significantly to the nitrogenous compounds in the water and soils where they live. This activity is called **nitrogen fixation.**

In addition to these basic biological activities, algae have proved useful to people in a number of ways. More than 70 species of marine algae (seaweeds) are used for food, mostly by Asian peoples (although several of the red algae are sold as food supplements in the United States). Certain brown and red marine algae produce large amounts of hydrocolloids (water-holding substances) as intercellular secretions. Of these, algin (from brown algae) and agar and carrageenan (both from red algae) are used commercially. These hydrocolloidal substances are extracted from the algae and then dried and powdered. Upon rehydration, they are used as stabilizers and emulsifiers in chocolate milk, ice cream, prepared icings and fillings, toothpaste, and so forth. Agar is used in biological studies to solidify culture media.

Another type of algae, the diatoms (Figure 3.34), which populated ancient seas and occur in lakes and oceans today, are also of economic value. The cells of ancient diatoms, covered with siliceous walls, settled to the sea bottom upon death; the walls were deposited in extensive layers of diatomaceous earth, which is now of use in filtration, insulation, paint (as an ingredient), silver polish (as a fine abrasive), and other areas.

In some instances, however, algae may become noxious, particularly when they are offensive to the eye or nose. The appearance of a great concentration of algae under favorable growth conditions produces **water blooms,** which render reservoirs and recreational bodies of water temporarily unusable. The occurrence of large mats of floating algae may result in the death of many fish from lack of oxygen, since at night the algae not only compete with the fish for this gas but also form a blanket that reduces oxygenation of the water from the atmosphere. Furthermore, toxic products from algae as well as from some bacteria associated with them in water blooms may poison livestock and fish. The phenomenon of the so-called red tides that kill fish and marine invertebrates is associated with the abundance of several algae (dinoflagellates, p. 60). *Lyngbya majuscula,* a marine blue-green alga, causes dermatitis in humans, and *Microcystis aeruginosa,* a freshwater colonial blue-green alga, is poisonous to livestock.

Finally, one further aspect of the use of algae is their importance in basic biological research, in such areas as photosynthesis, reproduction, metabolism, and genetics. The unicellular algae are especially useful here because of their small size and the ease and rapidity with which large populations may be grown under rigidly controlled environmental conditions.

FORM OF THE ALGAL PLANT BODY

The algae range from minute, simple types, as exemplified by unicellular species, to very large and complex ones, for example, the kelps (p. 52). The green algae (Chlorophyta) have the most complete range of body type, for they include not only unicellular but also colonial, filamentous, membranous, and tubular genera. The association of organisms in colonies (Figures 3.6 and 3.9) and filaments (Figures 3.12 and 3.13) probably originated during **ontogeny** (development of the individual) by failure of the cells to separate after their division. These associations often are so loose that a colony may be shaken apart into fragments, even into individual cells. In some instances, however—for example, in certain species of *Volvox*—the individual cells of the colony are bound together by connections that suggest the protoplasmic continuity through the cell walls of the so-called higher plants.[2] The repeated division of a single cell and its descendants in the same direction without separation of the cells produces a **filament,** which may be branched or unbranched. Algae may also be composed of sheets of cells one or more layers thick; these are membranous or leaflike (Figure 3.18). Certain green and yellow-green algae are composed of solitary or interwoven tubes, which are not partitioned into individual cells. In complexity of form and in size, the kelps of the brown algae, Phaeophyta, are probably unsurpassed by any other algae.

Algae differ in growth patterns, too. **Growth** is an irreversible increase in size; it may or may not be accompanied by differentiation. Growth in such algae as *Spirogyra* (Figure 3.16), and *Ulva,* the sea lettuce (Figure 3.18), is **generalized,** or **diffuse,** because increase in cell number and size is not confined to a specific region of the plant. In contrast, growth in other algae, such as *Fucus* (Figure 3.32), and all land plants is **localized,** usually at the apices.

CLASSIFICATION AND REPRESENTATIVES OF ALGAE

Although the algae were once thought to be a cohesive group of closely related organisms, that is, **monophyletic** (Table 1.1), they are currently considered to be **polyphyletic** and classified in seven (or more) separate divisions (Table 3.1). The divisions to be discussed in this book are the Chlorophyta, Charophyta, Euglenophyta, Phaeophyta, Chrysophyta, Pyrrhophyta, and Rhodophyta. Some biologists assign unicellular and colonial algae to the Kingdom Protista, which is composed of all unicellular and colonial organisms that are eukar-

[2]The significance of these connections is often cited in discussions dealing with organizational questions. Do multicellular organisms and their complex activities represent merely the total sum of the individual cells of which they are composed, and their cellular activities? The presence of intercellular connections in multicellular organisms is interpreted by some biologists as evidence that there is supracellular unity and that the organism is the significant biological unit. Multinucleate, nonseptate organisms, such as *Rhizopus,* the black mold (see Figure 10.12), and the tubular green algae (Figure 3.20) support this view. Furthermore, electron microscopy has demonstrated that cellular continuity through nonliving walls is even more extensive than previously observed with the light microscope.

TABLE 3.1 Major Algal Groups and Their Noteworthy Characteristics

Division	Common Name	Pigments[a]	Stored Photosynthate	Major Components of Cell Wall	Flagellar Number, Length, and Position[d]	Habitat[e]
Chlorophyta	Green algae	Chlorophylls a and b	Starch	Cellulose in many plus pectin	1, 2–8, or many; equal; apical	fw, bw, sw, t
Charophyta	Stoneworts	Chlorophylls a and b	Starch	Cellulose plus pectin	2; equal; subapical	fw, bw
Euglenophyta	Euglenids	Chlorophylls a and b	Paramylon	Proteinaceous periplast, ± lorica	1–7; equal; apical or subapical	fw, bw, sw, t
Chrysophyta	Golden algae (including diatoms)	Chlorophylls a and c	Lipids, chrysolaminarin	Silicon dioxide plus pectin; cellulose in some	1–2; unequal or equal; apical	fw, bw, sw, t
Phaeophyta	Brown algae	Chlorophylls a and c	Mannitol, laminarin	Cellulose plus algin	2; unequal; lateral	fw (rare), bw, sw
Pyrrhophyta	Dinoflagellates	Chlorophylls a and c	Starch	Cellulose or no cell wall	2; 1 trailing and 1 girdling	fw, bw, sw
Rhodophyta	Red algae	Chlorophyll a; d (in some) R- and C-phycocyanin, Allophycocyanin R- and B-phycoerythrin	Floridean[b] starch	Cellulose, other polysaccharides (agar, carrageenan)	None	fw (some), bw, sw (most)
Cyanophyta[f]	Blue-green algae	Chlorophyll a, C-phycocyanin, Allophycocyanin, C-phycoerythrin	Cyanophycean[c] starch	Peptidoglycans (mucopolysaccharides)	None	fw, bw, sw, t

[a]In addition to the chlorophylls, phycocyanin, and phycoerythrin listed in the table, all the algae contain carotenes and xanthophylls. The abundance of the latter may mask the chlorophylls in some, such as the Phaeophyta and Chrysophyta.

[b]Stains wine-red with iodine.

[c]Glycogenlike; many algal storage products are polymers of glucose with various types of linkages of the molecules.

[d]In motile cells, when such are produced.

[e]fw, freshwater; bw, brackish water; sw, salt water; t, terrestrial.

[f]Included here for purposes of comparison.

yotic. Hundreds of genera[3] of algae are known, and our knowledge of them is being augmented constantly. It should be apparent from Table 3.1 that the several groups of algae differ in pigmentation, food reserves, wall composition, number and nature of organs of locomotion, and habitat. Representatives of seven divisions of algae are discussed in the following account.

Green Algae (Division Chlorophyta)

Green algae live in both fresh and saline waters and also in terrestrial habitats (in and on soil, and on rocks and woodwork). They illustrate a wide range of plant-body forms, including unicellular, colonial, filamentous, membranous, and tubular organisms (Figures 3.2 and 3.21). This account of representative green algae is longer than that of other algae because they are here used to illustrate certain basic aspects of plant reproduction.

Representatives of two series of these algae are discussed next. In the first group, the organisms are motile, having flagellated cells, while in the second series the organisms are nonmotile, although in some, flagellated reproductive cells are produced.

Motile Green Algae.   Included in the series of motile green algae are organisms that normally have flagellated cells (Figures 3.2 and 3.3). Such algae are either unicellular or colonial and are considered to be primitive organisms.

Chlamydomonas. The species *Chlamydomonas* constitute a large genus and are widespread in water and soil. Figures 3.2 and 3.3 illustrate the cellular organization of one species. The most prominent organelle is the **chloroplast** (a membrane-bounded, chlorophyll-containing structure), which in the species illustrated contains a differentiated body, the **pyrenoid**, the site of starch synthesis. Visible in Figure 3.3*a* is the **stigma**, or "eyespot," thought to be the site of light perception. The uninucleate cells are bounded by cell walls and contain two (or more) **contractile vacuoles** that are thought to regulate the water content of the cells in freshwater algae. The **flagella** are protoplasmic

---

[3]Genus (plural, genera): one of the categories of classification each of which is a taxon prescribed by the International Code of Botanical Nomenclature. The code recognizes the following taxa in ascending order: species, genus, family, order, class, and division. In illustration of these, the alga *Chlamydomonos eugametos* is classified as follows:

Division: Chlorophyta
Class: Chlorophyceae
Order: Volvocales
Family: Chlamydomonadaceae
Genus: *Chlamydomonas*
Species: *Chlamydomonas eugametos*

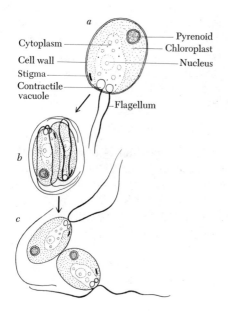

Cytoplasm —
Pyrenoid
Chloroplast
Cell wall —
Nucleus
Stigma —
Contractile —
vacuole
Flagellum

Figure 3.2 The structure and reproduction of *Chlamydomonas*. (*a–c*) Asexual reproduction in *Chlamydomonas moewusii:* (*a*) single individual. (*d–m*) Sexual reproduction in *C. moewusii* (see also Figures 3.3 and 3.4 and text): (*d*) + and − mating types separated along P-P´; (*e*) clump formation after mating types have been mixed; (*f–h*) gamete pairing and union; (*i*) union of gamete nuclei; (*j,k*) zygotes (diploid nucleus visible in *k*); (*l,m*) zygote germination after meiosis. (*n*) *Chlamydomonas* sp., anisogamy. (*o*) *Chlamydomonas* sp., oogamy: nonmotile egg surrounded by sperm.

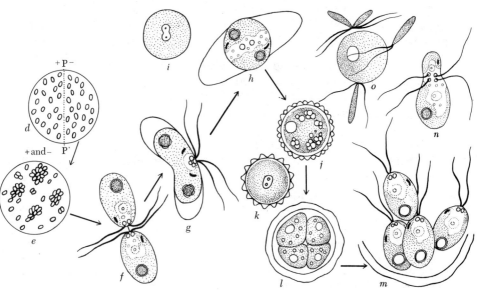

extensions composed of nine peripheral and two central microtubules enclosed in a sheath (Figure 3.3*b*). The electron microscope reveals that the cells contain such other components of eukaryotic cells as endoplasmic reticulum, mitochondria, and Golgi apparatus.

In asexual reproduction (Figure 3.2*b,c*) the cells become nonmotile and, by nuclear and cell division, form two or more juvenile cells, called **zoospores,**

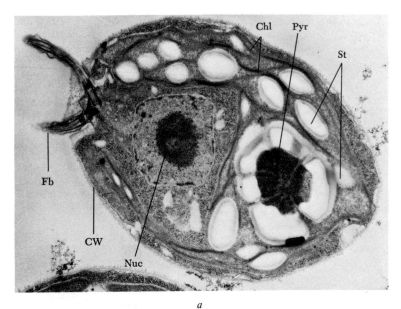

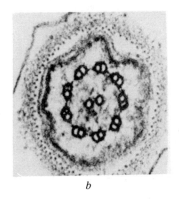

a

b

Figure 3.3 (*a*) *Chlamydomonas reinhardtii* Dangeard. Electron micrograph of median longitudinal section of a cell (× 7190). Chl, chloroplast; CW, cell wall; Fb, flagellum; Nuc, nucleus; Pyr, pyrenoid; St, starch. [After D. L. Ringo.] (*b*) Transection of a flagellum. [Courtesy of D. L. Ringo.]

which, when liberated by enzymatic lysis and breakage of the parent cell wall, swim away and grow into mature cells that repeat asexual reproduction indefinitely.

In populations of *Chlamydomonas* where sexually mature and compatible individuals are present,[4] the sexual process begins with grouping or aggregation (Figures 3.2*e* and 3.4*a, b*) of cells attracted to each other by chemical

[4]When sexually compatible individuals are present in a culture (population) that has developed from one individual (a clonal culture), the culture is said to be homothallic. When the compatible mating types develop only from different clonal cultures or individuals, the cultures are said to be heterothallic.

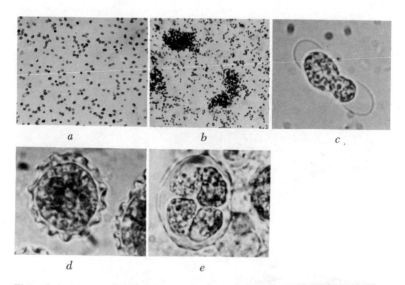

Figure 3.4 The sexual reproduction of *Chlamydomonas moewusii*, micrographs. (*a*) Sexually mature cells of one mating type (−). (*b*) The same shortly after adding + gametes. Note clumps of gametes and free pairs. (*c*) Uniting gametes, enlarged (flagella not shown). (*d*) Dormant zygote. (*e*) Germinating zygote, showing the four cells produced after meiosis (compare with Figure 3.2*l*, *m*).

substances diffusing from their flagella. From these groups paired individuals emerge (Figure 3.2*f*). In some species, each pair is connected by a cytoplasmic strand and is actively propelled by the two flagella of one member of the pair; in others, the uniting cells are not actively motile. Cells that unite in sexual reproduction are called **gametes.** As the sexual process continues, the delicate cell walls are dissolved at the point where the two gametes are closest together, and in a process called **plasmogamy,** the contents of the two cells flow together (Figures 3.2*g–k* and 3.4*c*). Sooner or later, the two nuclei brought together by plasmogamy unite (Figure 3.2*k*); this nuclear union is termed **karyogamy** and culminates in **zygote** formation. In the zygote two sets of parental chromosomes and their genes are thus associated within a single nucleus (**diploid, 2***n*). In the process just described for *Chlamydomonas,* several phenomena are present that characterize almost all sexual reproduction. These are: (1) the union of cells; (2) the union of nuclei; (3) the association of chromosomes and genes; and (4) meiosis. The parental chromosomes, however, retain their identity and do not unite in the fusion nucleus. In some species of *Chlamydomonas,* the uniting gametes are the young organisms themselves (Figure 3.2*f*). In multicellular organisms, by contrast, the gametes are special cells of the mature organism, formed for the specific function of reproduction (Figure 3.1*b, c*).

Several other features of the sexual process in *Chlamydomonas* illustrate important biological principles. A number of species produce gametes that are apparently not distinguishable as "male" and "female" and hence are called **isogamous** (Figure 3.2*f*); other species of *Chlamydomonas* and most other organisms produce gametes that are clearly distinct from each other in size (Figure 3.3*n, o*), and these are designated male (smaller) and female (larger). Such gametes are called **anisogamous,** or **oogamous** if the larger one lacks flagella.

In *Chlamydomonas* the zygote wall becomes thickened (Figures 3.3*j, k;* 3.4*d*) and a period of dormancy ensues that is terminated by germination (Figures 3.21*m;* 3.4*e*). As this process begins, meiosis occurs. **Meiosis** is a special kind of nuclear division in which the diploid (2*n*) number of chromosomes is changed to **haploid** (*n*) and genetic segregation occurs. Thus, the zygote is the only diploid cell in the *Chlamydomonas* life cycle, all the other cells being haploid; meiosis, accordingly, is said to be **zygotic.** The germinating zygote undergoes two (occasionally more) internal divisions, and four flagellated cells emerge as the zygote wall is lysed and fissured (Figures 3.3*m;* 3.4*e*). The reproductive cycle described for *Chlamydomonas,* in which the zygote is the only diploid phase, characterizes a number of other green algae (and certain fungi, p. 253).

Carteria. Carteria (Figure 3.5) is similar to *Chlamydomonas* in cellular organization and in asexual and sexual reproduction. It differs only in having quadriflagellated, rather than biflagellated, cells.

Gonium, Pandorina, and Volvox. Gonium (Figure 3.6*a*), *Pandorina* (Figure 3.6*b*), and *Volvox* (Figure 3.7) are **coenobic** colonial organisms composed of cells with *Chlamydomonas*-like cellular organization. In such colonies (coenobia) the number of cells is fixed at the origin of the young individual and not augmented during its existence. The component cells are embedded in a gelatinous matrix. In these genera asexual reproduction is by formation of **autocolonies,** the latter miniatures of the parent, which arise by repeated divisions of parental cells. The slightly curved colonies of *Gonium* have 16 cells within a matrix; in *Pandorina* the cells are in a colonial spheroid. In *Gonium* and *Pandorina* all the cells of a colony usually give rise to autocolonies at maturity, but in *Volvox* only a small number of the parental cells, called **gonidia,** do so. The autocolonies are liberated from the parental colonies, swim away, and grow to the size characteristic of the species.

Sexual reproduction in *Gonium* and *Pandorina* is isogamous; in *Volvox* it is oogamous (Figure 3.7*b–d*). It has been demonstrated that the male col-

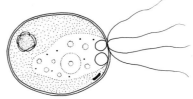

Figure 3.5 *Carteria* sp. Single vegetative cell; structure like that of *Chlamydomonas* except for four flagella.

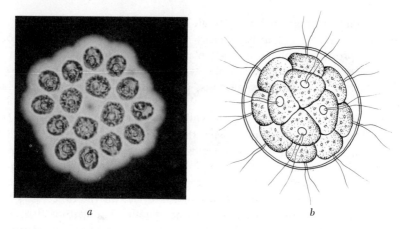

a   *b*

Figure 3.6 (*a*) *Gonium pectorale* (the two flagella on each cell are not visible in this photomicrograph). (*b*) *Pandorina morum* (Coenobic green algae).

onies in some species of *Volvox* produce a substance that causes juvenile colonies to mature as males. The substance is called a sexual inducer. In *Gonium, Pandorina,* and *Volvox,* meiosis is zygotic; it occurs during zygote germination as in *Chlamydomonas* (Figure 3.15*a*).

Nonmotile Green Algae.   Because a number of green algae, although nonmotile throughout most of their existence, can produce flagellated reproductive cells, the latter have often been considered a reversion to the putative primitive flagellated state, exemplified in the organisms previously discussed. However, there are other nonmotile green algae in which flagellated reproductive cells are never (or rarely[5]) produced. Accordingly the nonmotile green algae may be grouped in two series based on their ability or inability to produce flagellated reproductive cells. Flagellated asexual reproductive cells of nonmotile algae have long been called **zoospores,** a reflection of the earlier concept that only animals, not plants, possess the capacity for motility. It has been said that "nature mocks at human categories" and this is supported by unicellular, colonial, and filamentous organisms occurring in both series!

Unicellular and Colonial Representatives.   Representatives of unicellular and colonial organisms to be discussed are *Chlorococcum, Pediastrum, Hydrodictyon, Chlorella, Eremosphaera,* and *Scenedesmus.*

Chlorococcum.   The mature cells of most species of the unicellular *Chlorococcum* (Figure 3.8) are spherical and uninucleate. Under proper conditions, their protoplasm undergoes division to form motile uninucleate cells, **zoospores,** which develop *Chlamydomonas*-like cellular organization (Figure 3.8*b*,

---

[5]Isogamous sexual reproduction by biflagellated gametes occurs in one species of *Scenedesmus,* while oogamy occurs in one strain of *Eremosphaera.*

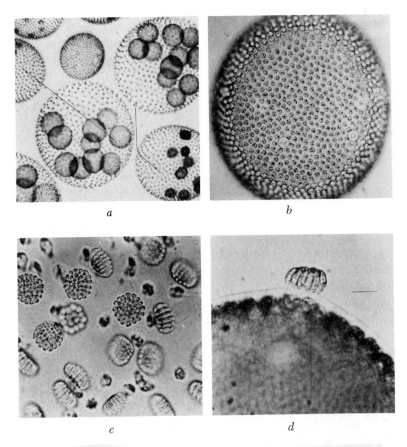

Figure 3.7 (a) *Volvox aureus,* vegetative colonies in asexual reproduction, containing daughter colonies. (b) Female colony with eggs. (c) Sperm packets. (d) Sperm packet at surface of female colony.

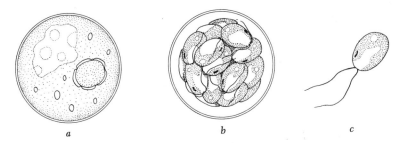

Figure 3.8 Unicellular green algae. (a–c) *Chlorococcum* sp., a zoospore-producing organism: (a) vegetative cell; (b) zoosporangium; (c) zoospore.

c), including two flagella, an eyespot or stigma, two contractile vacuoles, and a chloroplast with a pyrenoid. Following liberation from the parental cell wall, these remain motile for periods up to 24 hours, then lose their flagella and gradually enlarge and become spherical; at maturity they again undergo zoosporogenesis. Under certain conditions the potential zoospores skip the usual flagellated motile phase and grow directly into young cells, being liberated by bursting of the parental cell wall. Such young cells are termed **aplanospores.** A few species of *Chlorococcum* undergo isogamous sexual reproduction.

Pediastrum and Hydrodictyon. Both *Pediastrum* and *Hydrodictyon* (Figure 3.9) are coenobic colonies. In **coenobia** the number of component cells is determined at the time of their origin by the number of zoospores involved in their formation. Once they have formed, no cell divisions occur until those that produce the succeeding generation of zoospores, which form autocolonies.

In *Pediastrum* the cells of the colony are arranged in one plane (Figure 3.9*a*); in *Hydrodictyon* they are joined in a cylindrical netlike configuration (Figure 3.9*b*). In both genera, individual cells of the coenobia at maturity give rise to new individuals by forming zoospores, which arrange themselves, within the parental cells, or cellular vesicles, to form autocolonies (Figure 3.9*c*).

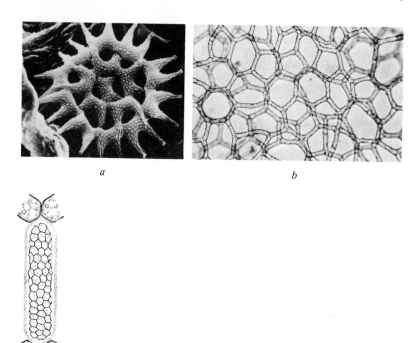

a

b

c

Figure 3.9 (*a*) *Pediastrum boryanum,* coenobium. [Courtesy of Dr. Harvey Marchant.] (*b*) *Hydrodictyon reticulatum,* the "water net," a zoospore producer. (*c*) Young net within parent cell.

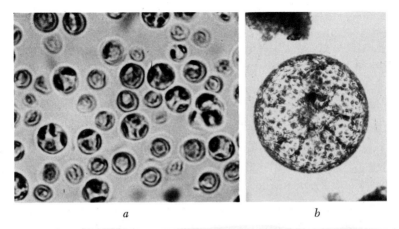

a   *b*

Figure 3.10   (*a*) *Chlorella* sp. and (*b*) *Eremosphaera viridis,* both nonzoospore producers.

Chlorella and Eremosphaera. Both *Chlorella* and *Eremosphaera* are spherical and unicellular, the former about 5 to 7 micrometers in diameter. However, in one species of the latter the cells are up to 250 micrometers in diameter. *Chlorella* (Figure 3.10*a*) is ubiquitous in soil and water, while *Eremosphaera* (Figure 3.10*b*) occurs most frequently in acid waters. Reproduction is exclusively asexual in both, consisting of the division of the cells into two to four (*Eremosphaera*) or more (*Chlorella*) young cells called **autospores.** Upon liberation from the parental cells, the autospores float away and enlarge to the size characteristic of the species, whereupon they repeat the cycle.

Scenedesmus. *Scenedesmus* (Figure 3.11) is widespread in soil and freshwater. Its coenobia consist usually of four or eight elongate cells jointed lat-

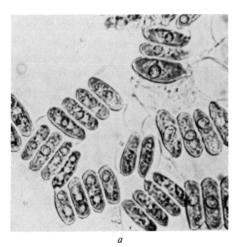

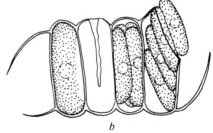

Figure 3.11   *Scenedesmus* sp. (*a*) Coenobia. (*b*) Autocolony formation [*b* after H. C. Bold, C. J. Alexopoulos, and T. Delevoryas.]

a

erally along their long axes. In some species the terminal cells have hornlike processes on their walls. Asexual reproduction is by autocolony formation (Figure 3.11b) in which each component cell divides to form, and subsequently releases, a juvenile colony.

Filamentous Representatives. **Filaments** are chains of cells that arise by repeated division of single cells in one plane and cohesion of the division products. Filaments may be unbranched or branched, and their component cells may be uninucleate or multinucleate. Again, in this group occur representatives of two series: zoospore producers and nonzoospore producers. Of the first group, *Ulothrix, Oedogonium,* and *Cladophora* are discussed below. *Spirogyra* and *Zygnema* illustrate the second series.

Ulothrix and Oedogonium. The filamentous algae *Ulothrix* and *Oedogonium* (Figures 3.12 and 3.13) both produce zoospores; those of *Ulothrix* are bi- or quadriflagellated (Figure 3.12c) and those of *Oedogonium* are multiflagellated (Figure 3.13a). Both *Ulothrix* and *Oedogonium* are unbranched filaments, and both may be attached to the substrate by special cells called **holdfasts** (Figure 3.12a). Species of *Ulothrix* usually grow attached to rocks and wood in fresh and marine waters. Species of *Oedogonium* are restricted to freshwater and are often epiphytic on other algae and aquatic flowering plants.

In asexual reproduction, the zoospores of these plants swim freely and then settle down upon a suitable substrate, form a holdfast, and by nuclear and cell division grow into filaments. Sexual reproduction is isogamous in *Ulothrix* and oogamous in *Oedogonium.* In the latter, the eggs are borne within enlarged cells, called **oogonia** (Figure 3.13b), and the multiflagellated sperms arise in pairs within discoid cells called **antheridia**[6] (Figure 3.13c). Some species of *Oedogonium* are monoecious and others are dioecious. In both *Ulothrix* and *Oedogonium* meiosis is zygotic.

Cladophora. *Cladophora* (Figure 3.14) occurs in both marine and freshwater. The branched filaments are composed of relatively large cells that contain numerous pyrenoids and nuclei (Figure 3.14b). In the various species of *Cladophora* the zoospores may be quadriflagellated or biflagellated. For several species it has been demonstrated that two types of structurally similar plants occur in nature: Some produce quadriflagellated zoospores and others produce biflagellated isogametes. When the zoospores develop into new plants, these form only gametes at maturity; the zygotes, unlike those of green algae discussed up to this point, do not undergo a period of dormancy nor do they thicken their walls. Instead, they grow directly, *without undergoing meiosis,* into plants that produce only zoospores (Figure 3.15c). The gametic plants

---

[6]The term antheridium in algae usually refers to unicellular structures that produce male gametes. In land plants, antheridia are multicellular (Figure 3.1d)

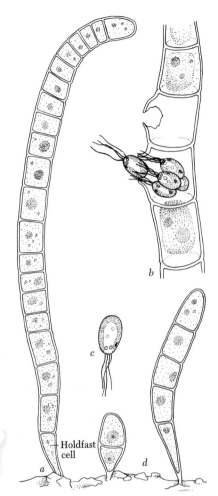

Figure 3.12 *Ulothrix* sp., a filamentous green alga. (*a*) Mature vegetative plant. (*b*) Zoospore formation. (*c*) Zoospore. (*d*) Development of quiescent zoospore into young filament.

may be called **gametophytes,** because they are sexual and produce gametes. On the other hand, the zoospore-producing plants are termed **sporophytes,** because they produce asexual[7] spores. The gametophytes have one set of chromosomes in their nuclei and thus are haploid[8], while the sporophytes, because they develop from zygotes that do not undergo meiosis, are diploid (having two sets of chromosomes in their nuclei). This type of life cycle (Figure 3.15*c*) in which diploid, spore-producing plants alternate with haploid gamete-producing plants is an example of **alternation of generations** or **phases,** a phe-

---

[7]Asexual in the sense that union with other spores in not necessary for further development.

[8]From the Greek *haplos,* "one" (in this usage, having a single set of chromosomes).

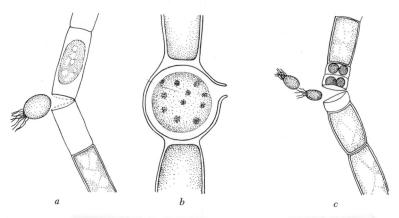

Figure 3.13 *Oedogonium* sp., a filamentous green alga. (*a*) Zoospore formation. (*b*) Female plant with oogonium containing egg. (*c*) Male plant with antheridia liberating sperm.

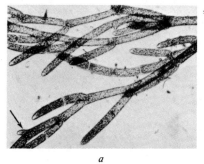

a

s.   m.o.s.

b

Figure 3.14 *Cladophora* sp. (*a*) Habit of growth; note branching filaments. (*b*) Cellular structure. S, surface view; m.o.s., medium optical section. [After H. C. Bold, C. J. Alexopoulos, and T. Delevoryas.]

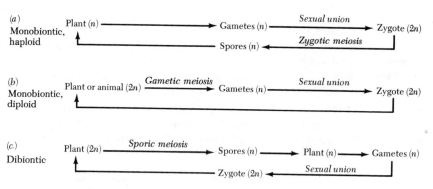

(*a*) Monobiontic, haploid   Plant (*n*) ⟶ Gametes (*n*) — *Sexual union* ⟶ Zygote (2*n*)
                              Spores (*n*) ⟵ *Zygotic meiosis*

(*b*) Monobiontic, diploid   Plant or animal (2*n*) — *Gametic meiosis* ⟶ Gametes (*n*) — *Sexual union* ⟶ Zygote (2*n*)

(*c.*) Dibiontic   Plant (2*n*) — *Sporic meiosis* ⟶ Spores (*n*) ⟶ Plant (*n*) ⟶ Gametes (*n*)
                    Zygote (2*n*) ⟵ *Sexual union*

Figure 3.15 Types of life cycle in algae and other organisms.

nomenon widespread in the plant kingdom. Such a life cycle[9] is sometimes termed **dibiontic,** meaning that two free-living individuals are involved. By contrast, the life cycle in *Chlamydomonas* and the other sexual organisms discussed earlier may be called **monobiontic** (Figure 3.15*a*). In the case of dibiontic life cycles, meiosis is **sporic;** it occurs during sporogenesis; thus, in the case of *Cladophora,* the zoospores are haploid.

In dibiontic life cycles the alternants may be morphologically identical, or they may differ from each other (see *Nemalion,* p. 62). In the first case the dibiontic life cycle is said to be **isomorphic** and in the second, **heteromorphic.**

Spirogyra, Zygnema, and Desmids. The green algae *Spirogyra, Zygnema,* and desmids differ from *Ulothrix, Oedogonium,* and *Cladophora* in that they do not produce flagellated motile cells. They are often called "conjugate algae" because of their sexual reproduction, which involves the pairing of walled individuals and the union of gametes that undergo amoeboid movement.

Spirogyra and *Zygnema,* both unbranched filaments, occur frequently in ditches and freshwater pools. The uninucleate cells of *Spirogyra* (Figure 3.16*a–c*) contain one (or more in some species) spirally twisted, ribbonlike chloroplasts with prominent pyrenoids. In the cells of *Zygnema* (Figure 3.16*d*) there are two star-shaped chloroplasts with a nucleus between them.

In sexual reproduction two individuals become connected by **conjugation papillae,** which open at their areas of contact to form **conjugation tubes.** The amoeboid gamete of one filament moves through the conjugation tube to unite with the protoplast of the connected cell to form a zygote. Meiosis is zygotic, and the life cycle is like that of *Chlamydomonas.* After a period of dormancy, the nucleus of the zygote undergoes meiosis and germination occurs. Only one filament emerges from the zygote (Figure 3.16*c*), because three of the four nuclei, formed by meiosis, degenerate.

The desmids are a group of nonmotile green algae with both unicellular and filamentous members. They are classified with *Spirogyra* and *Zygnema* and discussed at this point because their sexual reproduction parallels that of those organisms, involving as it does, union of amoeboid gametes.

Three unicellular desmids are illustrated in Figure 3.17. The name "desmid" is derived from the Greek *desmos* (bond or bridge) because each cell consists of two mirror-image semicells connected by a bridge of cytoplasm that contains the single nucleus. Cell division (Figure 3.17*b*) is unusual in that, after mitosis, the cytoplasm cleaves between the two nuclei, and each division product regenerates a new semicell. When this reaches its final size, a new wall is

[9]Also designated "life history." Although alternation occurs in land plants, the two phases are physically attached to each other except in ferns and other vascular cryptogams (*Lycopodium, Selaginella, Equisetum,* etc.) and seed plants.

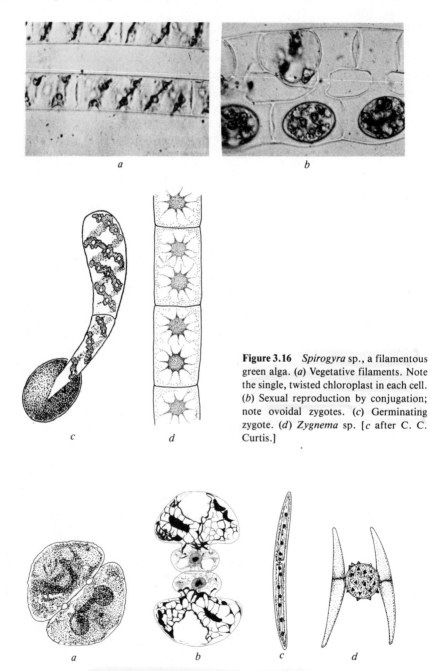

Figure 3.16 *Spirogyra* sp., a filamentous green alga. (*a*) Vegetative filaments. Note the single, twisted chloroplast in each cell. (*b*) Sexual reproduction by conjugation; note ovoidal zygotes. (*c*) Germinating zygote. (*d*) *Zygnema* sp. [*c* after C. C. Curtis.]

Figure 3.17 Desmids. (*a*) *Cosmarium* sp. (*b*) Cell division of *Cosmarium*. (*c*) *Closterium* sp. (*d*) Sexual conjugation in Closterium. [*b* after J. Pickett-Heaps.]

secreted around it. Thus the walls are composed of two portions of unequal age.

In sexual reproduction, cells become paired in a mucilaginous matrix, and each cell may form one or two amoeboid gametes. These unite to form zygotes (Figure 3.17*d*), which—after a period of dormancy—undergo meiosis, and germinate, each giving rise to one or two new vegetative cells. The number depends on the number of nuclei that survive in the zygote after meiosis.

Membranous Representatives.   Examples of membranous green algae are *Ulva* (Figure 3.18*a–c*) and *Enteromorpha* (Figure 3.18*d*), both marine organisms.

Ulva and Enteromorpha.   The marine genus *Ulva,* commonly known as *sea lettuce,* is widespread on most coasts and in estuaries around the world. The bladelike, membranous plants grow attached to rocks or other algae often at such levels that they are exposed to the air at low tide. Some plants of *Ulva* produce only quadriflagellated zoospores (Figure 3.18*b*). After a brief period of motility, these settle down, attach to the substrate, and undergo nuclear and cell division. The latter is at first always in the same direction so that an unbranched, *Ulothrix*-like filament is formed. Subsequently, cell divisions in two additional directions result in the typical membranous plant body two layers of cells thick.

Plants that arise from zoospores produce biflagellated gametes of two different sizes (anisogamy) (Figure 3.18*c*), which occur on different individ-

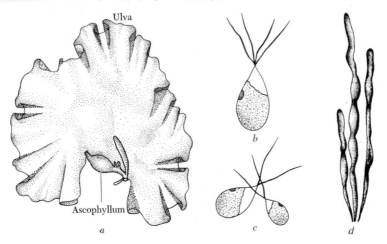

Figure 3.18   (*a*) *Ulva lactuca,* the "sea lettuce," a membranous green alga attached to *Ascophyllum,* a brown alga. (*b*) Zoospore. (*c*) Uniting anisogamous gametes. (*d*) *Enteromorpha* sp. [*d* after H. C. Bold and M. J. Wynne, *Introduction to the Algae* (Englewood Cliffs, N.J.: Prentice-Hall, Inc.), © 1985, p. 196. Reprinted by permission of Prentice-Hall.]

uals. These are periodically released in great numbers into the water in which smaller male gametes unite with female gametes to form motile, quadriflagellated zygotes. Gametes that fail to unite may develop directly into another generation of haploid gametophytes. This phenomenon is called **parthenogenesis**. The zygotes develop into the plants that produce zoospores without undergoing a period of dormancy or meiosis. Meiosis is sporic; it takes place in the cells that produce the zoospores which, accordingly, are haploid. The life cycle of *Ulva* then is dibiontic as in *Cladophora* and the two alternating phases are isomorphic (Figure 3.15c).

The plants of *Enteromorpha* (Figure 3.18d) are tubular and may be constricted at intervals. Some species reproduce only asexually by means of zoospores, while others have dibiontic, isomorphic life cycles as in *Cladophora* and *Ulva*.

Tubular Representatives.

Acetabularia, Codium, and Caulerpa. These three coenocytic organisms are marine green algae chosen here to represent the siphonous or tubular type of plant body. *Acetabularia* (Figure 3.19), the "mermaid's wine goblet," is about 2 inches tall and grows attached to calcareous rocks and shells in tropical and subtropical waters. The plant body of *Codium* (Figure 3.20) consists of interwoven siphonous tubes, some of which become fertile and produce gametes. The large tubes are multinucleate, and such structures are called **coenocytes.** *Codium* has within recent times "invaded" the northern Atlantic coast where its presence is deleterious to certain molluscs like oysters. In *Caulerpa,* the plant body of the numerous species is a continuous tube with prostrate and erect branches (Figure 3.21); the latter suggest fern fronds in some species. In these three plants septa form only in response to injury or when

Figure 3.19 *Acetabularia crenulata.*

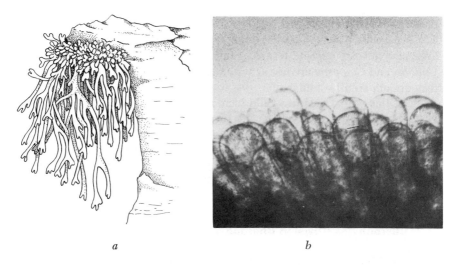

Figure 3.20 (*a*) *Codium* sp. (*b*) Enlarged view of surface of *Codium*.

the reproductive cells are formed. The siphons are multinucleate in *Codium* and *Caulerpa*, since mitoses are repeated without cytokinesis.

In *Acetabularia* the zygote nucleus persists and enlarges through most of the development of the plant body; it is called the primary nucleus. At the time of reproduction it divides repeatedly and rapidly to form thousands of small nuclei that become distributed throughout the plant body. Cleavage occurs in the cup portion of the plant so that many multinucleate cysts are formed. After their release and maturation, these germinate forming isogametes that unite in pairs to form zygotes. Each of the latter has the potentiality of growing into a new plant. The plants are diploid, and meiosis probably occurs when the enlarged primary nucleus divides to form the many small

Figure 3.21 *Caulerpa* sp.

nuclei that are incorporated into the cysts and, ultimately, into the gametes. The life cycle of *Acetabularia* is, therefore, monobiontic; the plants are diploid, and meiosis may be termed **gametic** (Figure 3.15*b*). The life cycles of *Codium* and *Caulerpa* are not as well understood as that of *Acetabularia,* but they are apparently similar.

At this point, then, it would seem appropriate to recall that in the green algae three types of life cycle occur (Figure 3.15): (1) monobiontic, with haploid plants and zygotic meiosis; (2) monobiontic, with diploid plants and gametic meiosis; and (3) dibiontic, with haploid gametophytes and diploid sporophytes and sporic meiosis; in this type of life cycle the alternants may be structurally similar, **isomorphic,** or they may differ; thus the phases are termed **heteromorphic.**

Charophytes (Division Charophyta)

Similar in pigmentation and in their storage of starch to both the Chlorophyta and green land plants, the Charophyta, here exemplified by *Chara* (Figure 3.22), differ considerably in organization from other algae. Stonewort

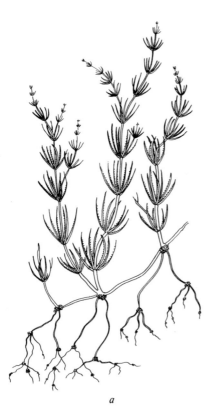

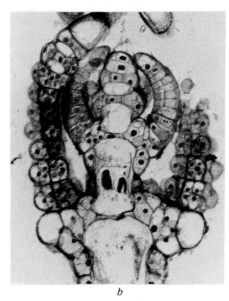

b

a

Figure 3.22 *Chara* sp. (*a*) Habit of growth. Note whorled branching and rhizoidal system. (*b*) Median longisection of branch tip; note apical cell. [Courtesy of Dr. R. C. Starr.]

plants are divided into nodes and internodes, with whorled branches at the nodes. The long internodal cells, in which cytoplasmic streaming may be readily observed, may or may not be surrounded by corticating cells. The plants are recognizable macroscopically and in quiet lakes may be several feet in length.

Growth is apical (Figure 3.22*b*) and may be traced to a prominent, dome-shaped apical cell, which divides at right angles to the long axis of the plant to cut off derivative cells basally. These divide in the same plane into pairs of cells; one elongates and enlarges to form a multinucleate internodal cell and the other, the nodal cell, divides to form branches. The branches, in turn, are organized as nodes and internodes. In most species of *Chara* the internodal cells become surrounded by corticating cells. Cytoplasmic streaming or cyclosis occurs in the internodal cells, which may be several inches long.

The sex organs are borne at the nodes of branches (Figure 3.23*a*), the antheridia slightly below the oogonia. The antheridium is a globular structure, orange-red at maturity, and contains twisted, colorless **antheridial filaments** (Figure 3.23*b*), each cell of which produces a biflagellate sperm. The oogonia (Figure 3.23*a*) consist of an egg cell surrounded by spirally curved tube cells whose tips are segmented to form five **crown cells** (ten in *Nitella*). The zygotes become packed with food and are dark green or black at maturity. After a

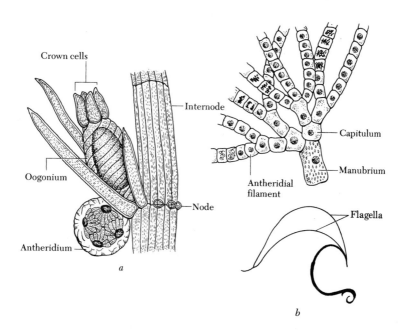

Figure 3.23 *Chara* sp., sex organs. (*a*) Branch with antheridium and oogonium. (*b*) Antheridial filaments and sperm.

period of dormancy, the zygote germinates to form a filamentous precursor on which a new plant is borne. The site of meiosis has not been determined with certainty but it probably occurs as the zygote germinates so that the life cycle is monobiontic (Figure 3.15*a*).

The Charophyta differ profoundly from the green algae in the organization of the plant body and reproductive organs. It has been suggested that they are a group apart from the green algae, a view accepted by the authors.

Euglenids (Division Euglenophyta)

Euglenids (Table 3.1), which are unicellular and colonial flagellates, are well known through such examples as *Euglena* (Figures 3.24, 3.25), *Trachelomonas* (Figure 3.26), and *Phacus* (Figure 3.27). Just beneath the plasma membrane of the unwalled cells of Euglenids there is present a structure called the **pellicle,** which is proteinaceous and composed of ridged and grooved strips. Euglenids exhibit such animallike characteristics as contractile vacuoles and, in some cases, the capacity to change their cellular form. Although they contain chlorophylls *a* and *b*, as do the Chlorophyta (Table 3.1), they store their excess photosynthate in the form of paramylon, a β-1,3–linked glucan. Sexual reproduction is unknown in the Euglenophyta.

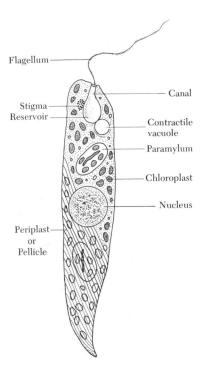

Flagellum

Canal

Stigma
Reservoir

Contractile
vacuole

Paramylum

Chloroplast

Nucleus

Periplast
or
Pellicle

Figure 3.24 *Euglena* sp. Living individual.

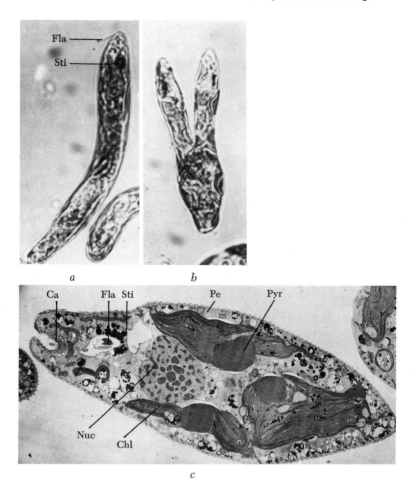

Figure 3.25 *Euglena mesnilii,* a unicellular organism. (*a*) Living individual with short flagellum, Fla, and stigma, Sti, visible. (*b*) Stages in reproduction by cell division, here binary fission. (*c*) *Euglena granulata,* electron micrograph. Chl, chloroplast; Ca, canal; Fla, flagellum; Nuc, nucleus; Pe, pellicle; Pyr, pyrenoid; Sti, stigma. [Courtesy of Professor H. J. Arnott.]

Euglena (Figures 3.24 and 3.25) illustrates most of the attributes of the Euglenophyta. The cells of many species undergo continuous changes in form made possible by the pliable consistency of the surface layer of protoplasm, the pellicle, which often has characteristic spiral markings. The anterior pole of the *Euglena* cell is colorless and contains a flasklike invagination, the **canal** and **reservoir,** at the base of which the two flagella are attached; only one flagellum is emergent. The granular stigma, or eyespot, is prominent at the anterior end of the cell, as is a large contractile vacuole, which empties into

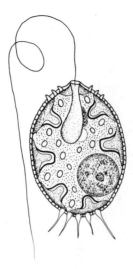

Figure 3.26 *Trachelomonas armata,* euglenid cell within lorica.

the reservoir. The form of the chloroplasts varies in the different species, but in all of them the large nucleus is central. *Euglena* does not ingest food, as some of its colorless and thus more animallike relatives do. *Euglena* reproduces by binary fission and may undergo encystment.

When grown at higher temperatures and in the presence of streptomycin, *Euglena* loses its plastids and grows as a colorless organism if suitable soluble organic food sources are supplied. Mutants resistant to streptomycin also are known.

Trachelomonas is like *Euglena,* but its cells live within a shell-like covering, the **lorica** (Figure 3.26). The cells may undergo changes of form within the lorica. Upon division of the cell, one of the division products emerges through the anterior pore and secretes a new lorica.

Phacus is a flattened euglenid with a rigid cell surface. In other respects, its cellular organization is similar to that of *Euglena* and *Trachelomonas.*

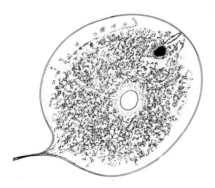

Figure 3.27 *Phacus pleuronectes.*

Brown Algae (Division Phaeophyta)

The brown algae (Table 3.1) are almost entirely marine. The simplest among them are unbranched and branching filaments; unicellular and colonial types are unknown. In this group are also coarse plants such as kelps and rockweeds, which have a complex tissue organization. Both the complexity of organization and the size of the kelps exceed those of other algae and, indeed, those of many land plants. Another common form is that in which the plant body consists of numerous intertwined filaments. Hence the alga may look parenchymatous in section but is really **pseudoparenchymatous.** Growth in brown algae may occur throughout the plant (**diffuse** or **generalized growth**) or the cell divisions may be localized in discrete regions, **meristems**, that can be apical, basal, or somewhere between (intercalary).

The plastids of brown algal cells contain chlorophylls *a* and *c* and some xanthophylls and carotenoids (Table 3.1). One xanthophyll, **fucoxanthin**, is so abundant that it masks the chlorophylls, imparting the brown color to the plants. All the plastids in a cell are completely surrounded by a layer of endoplasmic reticulum, and this **chloroplast endoplasmic reticulum** is continuous with the membranes of the nuclear envelope (Figure 3.28). This unusual feature is found in most other chlorophyll *c*-containing groups (except dinoflagellates). Oddly, all algae with chlorophyll *c* have their photosynthetic membranes (thylakoids) in stacks of threes within the plastids (Figure 3.28). Pyrenoids are common in the chloroplasts. The main storage product is **laminarin,** a glucose polymer that does not stain with iodine. An alcohol polymer, **mannitol,** is also produced by many brown algae; it functions in controlling water balance, as well as being a storage product. There are two laterally attached flagella in motile cells, with the anteriorly directed one bearing tubular projections known as **mastigonemes** (Figures 3.29 and 3.32). The cell walls of many brown algae contain **alginic acid** (or **alginate**), which is commercially valuable: it is used as an emulsifier or thickening agent in many products including ice cream, chocolate milk, and paints, to mention a few.

Ectocarpus. Ectocarpus, a filamentous organism (Figure 3.29) grows attached to coarser marine algae, shells, rocks, and submerged woodwork. Growth of the branching filaments is diffuse. The cells contain brown, band-like plastids. Two kinds of reproductive organs are formed during the dibiontic life history. On the Massachusetts coast, the diploid plants or sporophytes (Figure 3.29*a–c*) produce enlarged, unicellular zoosporangia in which meiosis occurs. Hence, meiosis is sporic. As a result, within these **unilocular zoosporangia** are formed 32 to 64 haploid zoospores. These settle and develop into the haploid plants or gametophytes (Figure 3.29*d*), which, except for their gametangia, are similar to the diploid plants (so they are **isomorphic** phases). The haploid plants develop multicellular (or **plurilocular**) gametangia, which produce gametes (Figure 3.29*d–e*). The gametes are isogamous in *Ec-*

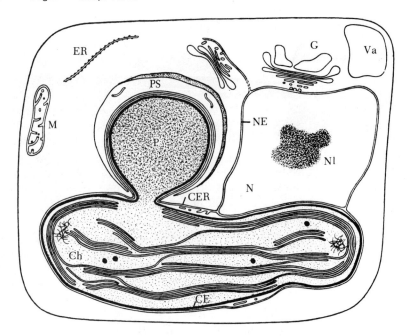

Figure 3.28 Diagram of a brown algal cell as seen with the electron microscope. The chloroplasts (Ch), their envelopes (CE), and pyrenoids (P) are surrounded by an extension of the nuclear envelope (NE) known as the chloroplast endoplasmic reticulum (CER). Note that the photosynthetic lamellae are arranged in stacks of threes. ER, endoplasmic reticulum; G, Golgi apparatus; M, mitochondrion; N, nucleus; Nl, nucleolus; PS, photosynthate; Va, vacuole. [After G. B. Bouck, "Fine Structure and Organelle Association in Brown Algae." Reproduced from *The Journal of Cell Biology,* 1965, Vol. 26, pp. 523–537, figure 165, by copyright permission of the Rockefeller University Press.]

tocarpus, but anisogamy and oogamy occur in other types of brown algae. The zygotes formed develop into the diploid plants. Certain other types of life history have been reported for species of *Ectocarpus* from Naples, Italy, and from the Isle of Man, in the Irish Sea.

Laminaria and Other Kelps. Among the kelps, which are coarser brown algae, *Laminaria* (Figure 3.30*a*), one of the smaller genera, often 3 to 10 feet long, is widely distributed. The plant consists of a flattened blade that may be branched and is connected to a rather massive, branching holdfast that anchors the organism to the rocky bottom. Growth is by an intercalary meristem, occurring at the junction of blade and stipe (stalk), both of which are quite complex internally. The life history of *Laminaria* is dibiontic with sporic meiosis, but in this case the haploid and diploid phases are markedly dissimilar; thus the phases are **heteromorphic** (Figure 3.15). The conspicuous phase is the diploid sporophyte, on the surface of which unilocular zoosporangia

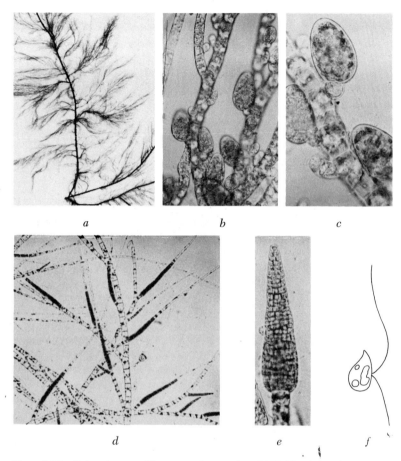

Figure 3.29 *Ectocarpus* sp., filamentous brown alga. (*a*) Habit of growth, natural size. (*b*) Diploid plant (sporophyte) with unilocular zoosporangia. (*c*) Enlarged view of zoosporangia. (*d*) Haploid plant (gametophyte) with plurilocular gametangia. (*e*) Single plurilocular gametangium. (*f*) Gamete (note unequal, lateral flagella).

develop. After meiosis, these liberate 32 to 64 haploid zoospores that settle and develop into microscopic filamentous gametophytes, which, in turn, produce the eggs and sperm (Figure 3.30*b, c*); so reproduction is oogamous. After union of the gametes, the zygotes develop into the larger sporophytes of *Laminaria*. This type of life cycle occurs in all the kelps.

A number of other genera of kelps occur on the Pacific coast of North America. Among them are *Postelsia,* the "sea palm" (Figure 3.31*a*), and such giant kelps as *Nereocystis* (Figure 3.31*b*) and *Macrocystis* (Figure 3.31*c*). In all these organisms, the plant body consists of a massive holdfast, a stipe or stipes, and blades. Species of *Macrocystis* more than 100 feet long are commonly encountered, making them the largest of all the algae—some even sur-

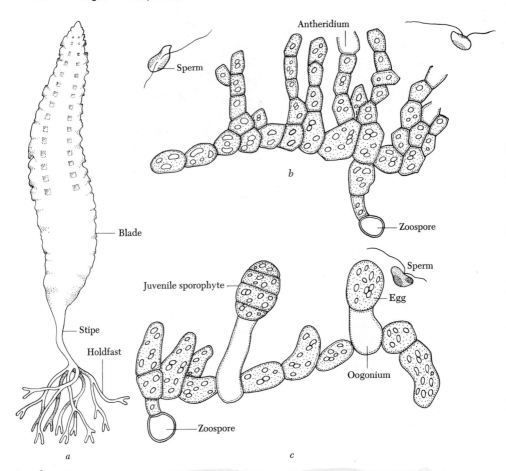

Figure 3.30 *Laminaria agardhii.* (*a*) The sporophyte. (*b*) Male gametophyte. (*c*) Female gametophyte. Note old zoospore walls. The holdfast branches are collectively known as haptera.

passing the majority of land plants in terms of size. In *Macrocystis* sieve-tube-like cells are present, that resemble the phloem (see p. 103) of vascular plants. Indeed, even the overall morphology of the kelps parallels that of many land plants, in bearing rootlike (holdfasts), stemlike (stipes), and leaflike (blades) parts.

Rockweeds. The rockweed, *Fucus* (Figure 3.32), grows attached to rocks in cold ocean waters. Many, but not all, of the plants grow at such levels as to be exposed to the air at low tide. Cell wall polysaccharides that bind water prevent the plants from drying out. The plant body may attain 1 foot or more in length. Plants are straplike, several times dichotomously branched, and they have a discoid holdfast. Growth is strictly apical.

Reproduction is entirely sexual and is oogamous. The plants are diploid

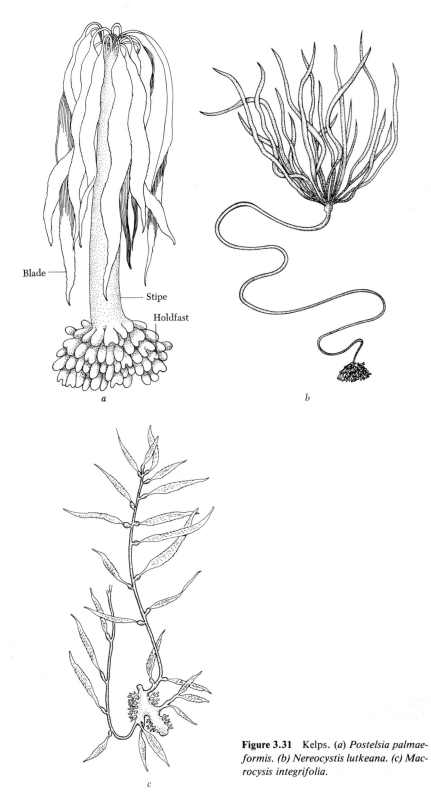

Blade

Stipe

Holdfast

a

b

c

Figure 3.31 Kelps. (*a*) *Postelsia palmae-formis. (b) Nereocystis lutkeana. (c) Macrocysis integrifolia.*

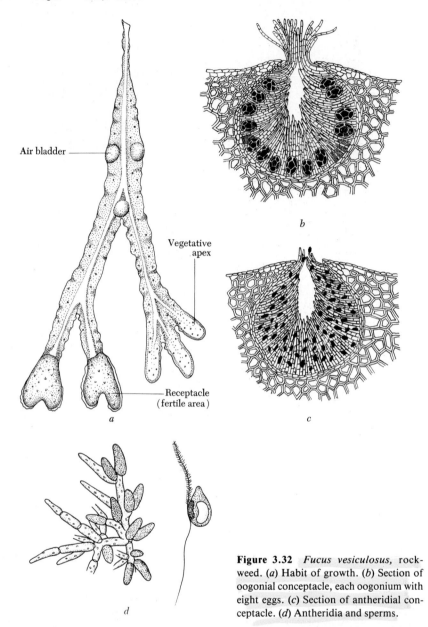

Air bladder

Vegetative
apex

Receptacle
(fertile area)

a

b

c

d

Figure 3.32 *Fucus vesiculosus,* rock-
weed. (*a*) Habit of growth. (*b*) Section of
oogonial conceptacle, each oogonium with
eight eggs. (*c*) Section of antheridial conceptacle. (*d*) Antheridia and sperms.

and produce haploid gametes within special chambers, the **conceptacles,** on
the distal apices (**receptacles**) of mature plants (Figure 3.32*a–c*). The sperms
(Figure 3.32*d*) and eggs develop in antheridia and oogonia, respectively, in
which meiosis occurs. The zygotes grow directly into new *Fucus* plants so the
life cycle is monobiontic with gametic meiosis (Figure 3.15*c*).

Although at least one species of *Sargassum* (Figure 3.33), a type of rock-weed, occurs in colder ocean waters (for example, at Cape Cod), most grow in warmer waters. Great quantities of *Sargassum* may be left stranded by storms on the shores of the Gulf of Mexico. The *Sargassum* plant consists of branching axes with leaflike appendages (Figure 3.33), and air bladders form on special stalks. The reproductive branches, which develop at certain seasons, are contracted as compared with the leaflike appendages. Sexual reproduction, like that in *Fucus,* is oogamous, and the life history is essentially identical.

Golden Algae, Diatoms (Division Chrysophyta)

Like the brown algae, the Chrysophyta contain chlorophylls *a* and *c,* and the xanthophyll pigment, **fucoxanthin** (among others and various carotenoids), partly masks the chlorophylls, giving them their golden brown color. The polysaccharide storage product is also very similar to that found in Phaeophyta, and so it is called **chrysolaminarin.** Lipids are also a major food reserve. Where present, there are typically one to two apical flagella, one of which may bear mastigonemes. A chloroplast endoplasmic reticulum system is also present in the cells of Chrysophyta. There are several classes in this division, but approximately 85 percent of the species are in the class Bacillariophyceae or diatoms, so only this group will be discussed.

Diatoms (Table 3.1, Figures 3.34–3.36) are organisms of great biological interest and economic importance; some are used as indicators of water quality and pollution. Most diatoms are unicellular, although some form chains and

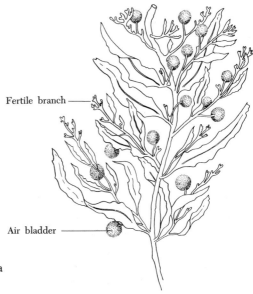

Fertile branch

Air bladder

Figure 3.33 *Sargassum filipendula,* a brown alga related to *Fucus.*

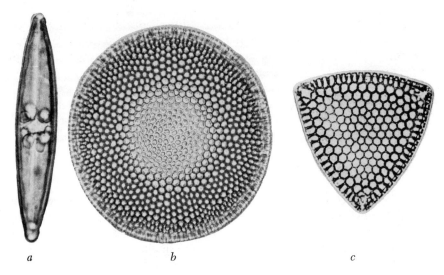

Figure 3.34 Chrysophyta, diatoms. (*a*) *Navicula* sp. (*b*) *Coscinodiscus* sp. (*c*) *Triceratium* sp.

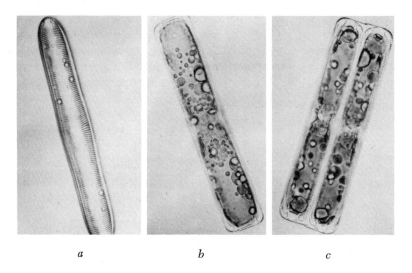

Figure 3.35 *Pinnularia* sp. (*a*) Valve view. (*b*) Girdle view. (*c*) Cell division.

colonies of cells. Two types of diatoms have been distinguished on the basis of their symmetry: (1) the bilaterally symmetrical, or **pennate** types; and (2) the radially symmetrical, or **centric** types. The former are abundant in both fresh and salt water, whereas the latter type is most abundant in marine waters. Some pennate diatoms are capable of gliding across substrates, but no centric ones can do this. The cell walls of diatoms are impregnated with varying

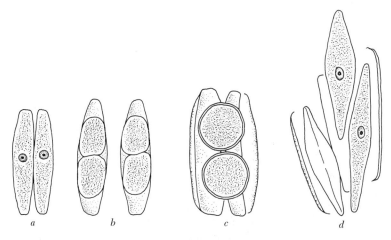

Figure 3.36 *Navicula halophila;* stages in sexual reproduction. (*a*) Pairing of cells.
(*b*) Formation of two gametes in each cell. (*c,d*) Two zygotes or auxospores formed.

amounts of silicon dioxide (the substance of glass and quartz!), which is very
resistant to decay. After the death of the protoplasts within, these walls or
frustules persist, and vast deposits of them from ancient seas today furnish
us with diatomaceous earth, which has many important uses (in filtration and
silver polish, among others). One of the largest of such deposits in Lompoc,
California, is nearly 200 meters deep—an impressive thickness considering the
microscopic size of each cell wall! The fossil record of diatoms indicates that
they have existed for almost 200 million years.

The frustule, which may be elegantly ornamented with spines and other
projections, consists of two slightly overlapping halves, known as **valves** (Figure 3.35). The region of overlap is called the **girdle.** The two valves fit together
somewhat like the cover and bottom of a Petri dish. The cells divide by longitudinal cell division in which one resulting cell uses the slightly smaller valve
as a cover, while the other uses the larger one in the same way. Thus, in most
diatoms, cell division results in diminution of size in part of the population.
The most common means of overcoming this size decrease is by sexual reproduction (see below).

Diatoms are diploid; their life history is monobiontic and meiosis is gametic (Figure 3.15*b*). In most pennate diatoms, the valves are discarded as one
or two amoeboid isogametes from paired individuals conjugate (Figure 3.36).
The resulting zygote enlarges considerably before it secretes entirely new valves.
The enlarged zygote is known as an **auxospore.** In some centric diatoms, reproduction is oogamous; a small uniflagellate sperm unites with another cell's
protoplast, which functions as an egg. After fertilization the zygote of centric
diatoms also enlarges to form an auxospore, which attains the maximum size

characteristic of the species before it forms new walls. Thus, sexual reproduction is the means by which a diatom species maintains its size over time.

Dinoflagellates (Division Pyrrhophyta)

The dinoflagellates are a very diverse group of organisms, so only members of the pigmented class, Dinophyceae, are discussed in the following account. As a group, they occur in both freshwater and marine habitats. Most are motile, but a few are nonmotile unicellular, and some are even filamentous. Similar to the brown algae and diatoms, the plastids contain chlorophylls *a* and *c*. An abundance of xanthophylls and carotenoids masks the chlorophylls, giving the organisms a brown to reddish brown color. The dinoflagellates are the only chlorophyll *c*–containing algae that produce starch and that lack the chloroplast endoplasmic reticulum (Table 3.1).

There are several unusual cytological features of dinoflagellates. Although two flagella are usually present, one encircles the cell transversely, and the other is directed posteriorly as the cell swims. Both lie in furrows of the cell surface. The transverse flagellum imparts a whirling motion that is characteristic of these organisms. The nucleus is also peculiar in that the DNA has nearly no associated histone proteins—something typical of prokaryotes! This and other features have led some biologists to consider the dinoflagellates "mesokaryotes," although the cells are otherwise eukaryotic. Finally, the eyespot is not contained within any of the chloroplasts, as in *Euglena*.

Dinoflagellate cells may be naked (Figure 3.37*a*) or may have a cell wall. This cellulosic wall is unique in being composed of polygonal plates (Figure 3.37*b, c*) that lie beneath the plasma membrane, like the pellicle in *Euglena*. Some forms have highly ornamented and elaborate cell walls.

Sexual reproduction has been observed in dinoflagellates; their life his-

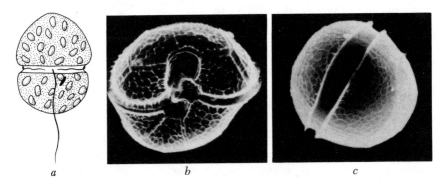

Figure 3.37 Dinoflagellates. (*a*) *Gymnodinium* sp., an unwalled organism. (*b,c*) *Peridinium* sp., covered with cellulosic plates. [*b, c* courtesy of Dr. H. J. Arnott and Dr. E. R. Cox.]

tory is monobiontic and meiosis is zygotic. Both isogamy and anisogamy occur. Asexual reproduction involving mitosis and cell division is the most common mode of reproduction. Cell division may involve a shedding of the cell wall plates (each resulting cell producing a complete set of plates), or a partitioning of the plates between the resulting cells with each synthesizing the ones it lacks. Rapidly reproducing populations may become so abundant that they discolor the water. These "blooms" are known as red tides, and the toxins associated with them frequently kill many fish, invertebrates, and even humans who eat shellfish that have accumulated the poisons. It is not known why the cells produce the poisons, but some of them are extremely potent.

One curious feature of marine dinoflagellates is that most are capable of bioluminescence (the emission of visible light by an organism). Although the function is unknown, the chemical mechanism by which the cells produce the turquoise light is apparently similar to that used by fireflies and other bioluminescent animals.

Red Algae (Division Rhodophyta)

The Rhodophyta, or red algae, are also largely marine, although more than 200 freshwater species have been described. Marine red algae, some of which grow at great depths, are in many cases very beautiful plants; they are often pressed on white paper and used as ornaments. Unicellular, filamentous, and membranous types occur in the Rhodophyta. The pseudoparenchymatous form is especially well developed among the red algae, where the plant consists of numerous interwoven filaments. The plastids contain chlorophyll *a* (and *d* in some), along with various carotenoids and xanthophylls. Additionally, the red algae have the phycobilin pigments **phycoerythrin, phycocyanin,** and **allophycocyanin,** similar to those of the Cyanophyta. In most Rhodophyta, phycoerythrin is the dominant pigment that masks the others and imparts the reddish color to the plants. With the electron microscope, aggregates of the phycobilins, or **phycobilisomes,** are evident as dots on the unstacked, single thylakoids (Figure 3.40). The storage product, which stains red with iodine, is called **floridean starch.** It is an amylopectin, like the starch in land plants. The starch granules occur throughout the cytoplasm. Aside from apical cells and reproductive cells, most cells are multinucleate in the Rhodophyta. Another feature the red algae share with the blue-green algae is the complete absence of any flagellated stages.

The cell walls of Rhodophyta contain a network of cellulose fibrils embedded in a mucilaginous matrix. Both **agar** and **carrageenan** that are of commercial value are examples of polysaccharides composing this matrix. A few species of red algae are harvested for their agar, which is widely used in microbiological culture media. Carrageenan, on the other hand, has many important uses similar to those of alginate. Many red algae have calcium carbonate (lime) in their cell walls, also. One peculiar feature of the red algal cell wall is the **pit connection** (or **septal plug,** Figure 3.38). This structure is deposited between cells after cell division (or secondarily, later on); its function is not known. Reproduction in the red algae is extremely complex, posing quite a challenge to most botany students. Three representatives of the Rhodophyta are described below, in order of increasing reproductive complexity.

Porphyridium. Porphyridium (Figures 3.39 and 3.40) is a unicellular organism, one species of which grows on moist soil where it may form blood red patches. The individual cells are spherical and each contains a single nucleus and starlike chloroplast with a pyrenoid. Reproduction is exclusively by division of the unicells.

Nemalion. Nemalion (Figure 3.41) occurs on intertidal rocks and looks like a mass of dark red worms. Its pseudoparenchymatous construction is evident upon gently squashing the gametophytes: several longitudinal filaments, each with its own apical cell, compose the main axis of the plant, and lateral pigmented branches bear the reproductive structures (Figure 3.41*a*). The life history of *Nemalion* is a modified dibiontic type, with sporic meiosis. The conspicuous gametophytes are monoecious. Male gametangia, the **spermatangia,** are clustered (Figure 3.41*b*), and each liberates a single, colorless male gamete or **spermatium**. The female gametes, **carpogonia,** are borne on short lateral branches with their **trichogynes** emerging from the surface of the ga-

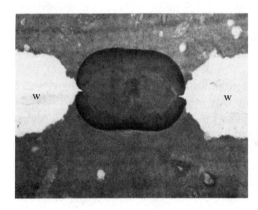

Figure 3.38 Electron micrograph of a septal plug (or pit connection) between two cells in the red alga *Plumaria* (longitudinal section). The cell wall (w) flanks the structure.

Figure 3.39 *Porphyridium purpureum.* Note asteroidal plastid.

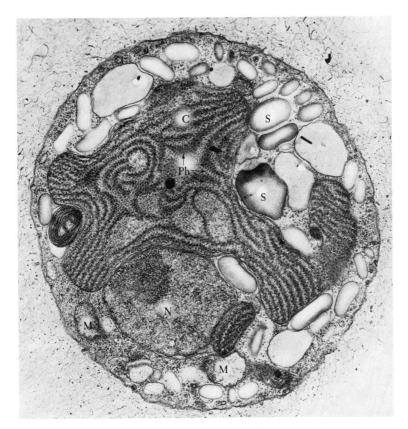

Figure 3.40   Electron micrograph of *Porphyridium*. Phycobilisomes (Ph) inside the stellate chloroplast (C) appear as dots on the unstacked photosynthetic lamellae. M, mitochondria; N, nucleus; S, floridean starch grains. [After E. Gantt and S. F. Conti, in W. A. Jensen and R. B. Park, *Cell Ultrastructure,* © 1967 by Wadsworth Publishing Company, Inc., p. 19, Figure 4–3. Reprinted with permission of the publisher.]

metophyte (Figure 3.41*c*). The aflagellate spermatia may be carried by water currents to the receptive trichogynes with which they unite. A single male nucleus moves down the trichogyne to the egg, where it fuses with the egg nucleus. After the zygote divides transversely (Figure 3.41*d*), the upper cell divides many times longitudinally (Figure 3.41*e*) to produce chains of cells (in a knot) that become **carposporangia** (Figure 3.41*f*). At maturity, each releases a single **carpospore**. The mass of carposporangia represents the **carposporophyte**, a diploid stage that develops upon the haploid gametophyte.

Upon being shed from the carposporophyte, the carpospores develop into diploid plants, called **tetrasporophytes,** that are microscopic filaments. Thus, the gametophytes and tetrasporophytes are heteromorphic in *Nemalion*.

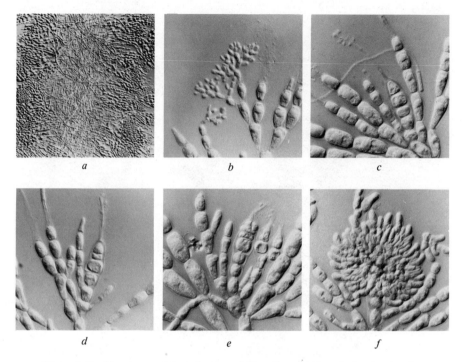

Figure 3.41 Structure and reproduction of *Nemalion*. (*a*) Squash showing longitudinal axis composed of many filaments. Reproductive structures occur in the outer regions, where larger cells are evident. (*b*) Spermatangial branches. (*c*) Carpogonial branch, with several spermatia attached to the trichogyne of the carpogonium. (*d*) Fertilized carpogonium that has cleaved transversely; the upper cell will initiate further development. (*e*) Early carposporophyte development. (*f*) Nearly mature carposporophyte with chains of carposporangia.

Meiosis occurs in the **tetrasporangia,** resulting in four haploid **tetraspores** in each. The tetraspores germinate and develop into the gametophytes. The life cycle of *Nemalion* is summarized in Figure 3.42. It is clear from the diagram that this life history is similar to that of *Ulva* except for the intercalation of the carposporophyte between the zygote and tetrasporophyte. Therefore, there are three distinct phases instead of two, but only two of them are free-living, whereas the carposporophyte develops attached to the gametophyte.

Polysiphonia. *Polysiphonia* (Figure 3.43) grows in marine waters attached by rhizoidal holdfasts to rocks, to other algae, or to marine angiosperms. Growth is strictly apical and derivatives of the apical cell divide, organizing a central cell (often called a central siphon because of its tubular organization and multinucleate condition) surrounded by a number of pericentral cells. The life history of *Polysiphonia* is slightly different from that of *Nemalion* (Figure 3.42) in that the gametophytes and tetrasporophytes are iso-

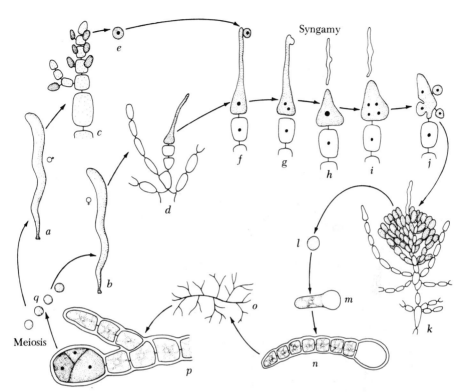

Figure 3.42 Diagram of *Nemalion* life history. Male gametophytes (*a*) produce spermatangia (*c*) that liberate spermatia (*e*). Female gametophytes (*b*) bear carpogonia (*d*) that function as eggs. Fertilization involves plasmogamy (*f–g*) and karyogamy (*h*). The zygote (*h*) proliferates mitotically (*i–j*) to produce chains of carposporangia, comprising the carposporophyte (*k*) that is attached to the female gametophyte. Carpospores (*l*) are liberated, and germinate (*m*) into the filamentous tetrasporophyte (*n–o*). At maturity, the tetrosporophyte develops tetrasporangia (*p*), the site of meiosis, resulting in tetraspores (*q*). Half of the tetraspores develop into male gametophytes, and half into females. [After Scagel et al., *Nonvascular Plants, An Evolutionary Survey*,'' © 1982 by Wadsworth Publishing Company, Inc., p. 435, Figure 11-27. Reprinted by permission of the publisher.]

morphic. The haploid gametophytes are dioecious (Figure 3.43*b*, *f*–g). After fertilization, the diploid zygote nucleus moves to a nearby cell, the **auxiliary cell,** and the latter fuses with other nearby cells to form a multinucleate **placental cell,** which contains both haploid and diploid nuclei. The latter migrate into buds of the placental cell, which mature as carpospores surrounded by a sterile, urnlike container, the **pericarp.** The entire structure, carposporophyte and pericarp, is known as a **cystocarp;** it develops upon the female gametophyte (Figure 3.43*c*, *h*–*j*). The tetrasporophytes are indistinguishable from the gametophytes (isomorphic), except that they produce sporangia in series (Fig-

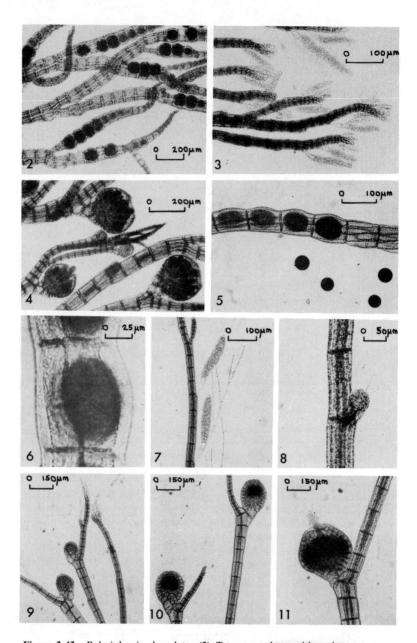

Figure 3.43 *Polysiphonia denudata.* (2) Tetrasporophyte with seriate tetrasporangia. (3) Male gametophyte with colorless branches of spermatia. (4) Female gametophytes with carposporophytes. (5) Tetrasporophyte that has liberated tetraspores from one tetrasporangium. (6) Tetrasporangium, more highly magnified. (7) Male gametophyte grown in laboratory culture. (8) Female gametophyte. Note emergent trichogyne on fertile lateral branch that encloses the carpogonium. (9–11) Successively more advanced stages in development of the carposporophyte. [Courtesy of Dr. Peter Edwards.]

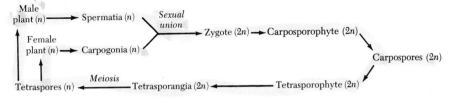

Figure 3.44 Diagrammatic summary of the life cycle of *Polysiphonia*.

ure 3.43*a, d–e*). After meiosis, two members of each tetrad of tetraspores develop into male gametophytes and two into female gametophytes. Like *Nemalion,* the life history here is a modified dibiontic one with sporic meiosis (Figure 3.44).

EVOLUTION OF ALGAE

Chemical analysis of Precambrian shales (see Table 6.1) has provided abundant evidence that the crude oil and other matter present in the shales represent carbon compounds originating from photosynthesis, which may be inferred to have been performed by algae. The fossil record has yielded little evidence regarding the origin, interrelationships, and course of evolution of the algae. There is direct evidence that blue-green, and probably green, algae were among the earliest living organisms, already present on the earth more than three billion years ago. Because of their prokaryotic cellular organization, the blue-green algae are different from all the other groups and most probably are more closely related to bacteria. The resemblance of these ancient fossil algae to currently living (extant) species is remarkable in some cases.

   With respect to the eukaryotic algae, the occurrence of unicellular, flagellated motile stages in many otherwise nonmotile organisms suggests that they evolved from a flagellate ancestry. These flagellates probably diversified during the course of evolution into the variety of organisms discussed in earlier pages. Increase in size sometimes involved cellular differentiation and consequent specialization in the plant body, as in the kelps (for example, *Laminaria*); at other times, tissue differentiation did not occur (for example, in *Ulva,* the sea lettuce). Type of sexual reproduction—isogamy, anisogamy, and oogamy—apparently evolved independently of body form. For example, all three patterns of sexual reproduction occur among the species of the single unicellular genus *Chlamydomonas,* while algae with more complex organization may exhibit isogamy (*Ulothrix, Ectocarpus*) or oogamy (*Oedogonium,* kelps, red algae). The algae also provide examples of increasing specialization and segregation of reproductive tissues from somatic or vegetative tissues. Thus, in unicellular organisms such as *Chlamydomonas* there is seemingly no *morphological* difference between young vegetative cells and gametes (Figure 3.1*a*). By contrast, the reproductive function is localized in special organs (*Oedogonium,* Figures 3.1*b*, 3.13) or branches (*Ectocarpus*, Figures 3.1*c* and 3.29*d, e*) in many algae.

Because of fundamental similarities between the Chlorophyta and the land plants (so-called higher plants), especially with respect to pigmentation and stored photosynthate, it is generally considered that the former represent the ancestral line from which the latter evolved. Current evidence indicates that the other divisions of algae did not evolve beyond the algal level, although the Rhodophyta sometimes have been postulated to have given rise to the Ascomycota and Basidiomycota among the fungi.

These pages should give some insight into what algae are and how useful they are, both economically and biologically. The reference works listed under Selected Readings at the end of the book contain more complete accounts of these exceedingly important and interesting members of the plant kingdom.

QUESTIONS FOR REVIEW

1. What does the geologic record show regarding the algae?
2. How may algae be distinguished from other organisms containing chlorophyll?
3. In what habitats do algae occur?
4. In what respects are algae of value to man?
5. What are "red tides"?
6. What types of plant body occur among the algae?
7. What organisms may be included in the group Protista?
8. What is the "stigma" in algae?
9. Distinguish between the terms sexual and asexual reproduction.
10. After you have witnessed it in the laboratory, describe sexual reproduction in *Chlamydomonas.*
11. Define the terms: gamete, zygote, plasmogamy, karyogamy, meiosis, haploid, diploid, monobiontic, dibiontic, parthenogenesis, isomorphic and heteromorphic, mitosis, sporophyte, gametophyte, pyrenoid, zoospore, autocolony, isogamy, heterogamy, oogamy, coenobium, holdfast, oogonium, antheridium, autospore, conjugation.
12. Summarize with the aid of diagrams the three basic types of life cycle that occur in algae.
13. How do the major algal groups—Chlorophyta, Phaeophyta, and Rhodophyta—differ from each other?
14. Define the following in single sentences: plurilocular, zoosporangium, gametangium, kelp, conceptacle, receptacle, carpogonium, spermatium, carpospore, tetrasporophyte, tetrasporangium, trichogyne, pellicle.
15. What are the distinguishing characteristics of diatoms?

16. What is diatomaceous earth?
17. Why is *Euglena* not classified in Chlorophyta?
18. Define the terms prokaryotic and eukaryotic.
19. In what respects do blue-green algae differ from other algae?
20. In what respects are Charophyta different from other algae?
21. If algae are the ancestors of land plants, as is often postulated, which group of algae would you consider most similar to the postulated ancestors?

CHAPTER FOUR

Nonvascular Land Plants: Liverworts, Hornworts, and Mosses

INTRODUCTION

It is generally believed that life first arose in an aquatic environment and that terrestrial plants and animals are the descendants of aquatic ancestors. Accordingly, land plants are considered to be the modified progeny of green algae. In the plants that now populate and have in the past populated the earth, two diverse series are apparent, one possibly derived from haploid and the other from diploid algal ancestors. The plants of the first group, liverworts, hornworts, and mosses, are characterized by a lack of lignified vascular tissue, that is **xylem** and **phloem** (p. 103) which, respectively, conduct water and food. The absence of lignified vascular tissue probably accounts for the relatively small size of liverworts, hornworts, and mosses, as they do not have efficient systems for transporting water and food rapidly over any considerable distance. Plants in the second group, seedless and seed-bearing plants, have vascular tissue; this characteristic probably is correlated with the large size and complexity of many vascular plants, and their ability to live in harsh terrestrial habitats. To this group belong the ferns and other seedless vascular plants, as well as the seed-bearing plants.

All land plants contain chlorophylls *a* and *b*[1] and all synthesize starch. With respect to reproduction, all land plants are oogamous and have gametangia with both sterile and fertile cells. Although not dibiontic like certain algae, all are diphasic, having both gametophytic and sporophytic phases as well as sporic meiosis. The spores of land plants have protective walls which

---

[1]Except, of course, for a few colorless parasite species.

Figure 4.1   Nonvascular fossil plants. (*a*) *Hepaticites kidstonii* Walton, a fossil leafy liverwort from the Carboniferous. [After J. Walton. Reprinted with the permission of the Annals of Botany Company from the original figure in *Ann. Bot.,* Vol. 39.] (*b*) *Hypnites arkansana* Wittlake, a fossil moss from Lower Eocene strata in Arkansas. [After E. B. Wittlake.]

enable them to be dispersed through the air and this involves special mechanisms for their dispersal.

Although Hepatophyta (liverworts), Anthocerotophyta (hornworts), and Bryophyta (mosses) are usually placed before the vascular plants in classifications of the plant kingdom (see Table 1.1), they are not more ancient, according to present evidence from the fossil record (see Table 6.1 on p. 120). Their place in systems of classification is probably inspired by their relative simplicity of form, their small size, and the lack of evidence that they are related to vascular plants. A fossil liverwort and fossil moss are illustrated in Figure 4.1.

LIVERWORTS (DIVISION HEPATOPHYTA)

Liverworts long ago received their rather curious name because the lobing of the plant bodies of some genera is suggestive of an animal liver. A number of botanists consider liverworts and hornworts to be closely related to the mosses and classify them both in the division Bryophyta; others have challenged that view (see Table 1.1) because of differences between liverworts, hornworts, and mosses in the organization of both the gametophytic and sporophytic phases.

Liverworts and hornworts, with a few conspicuous exceptions, seem to require more moist conditions than do mosses, and they grow on moist soil, rocks, and tree bark. The rhizoids of liverworts and hornworts, in contrast to those of mosses, are unicellular. The liverwort sporophyte is less complex than that of mosses and lacks a peristome (see p. 88), which is present in the sporophyte of most mosses.

The essentials of organization of several commonly occurring liverworts—*Ricciocarpus* and *Riccia, Marchantia,* and *Porella*—are presented in this section. The liverworts may be **thallose,** that is, without distinct axes and leaves (Figure 4.2*a*), or **foliose** (Figure 4.8). The plant body of a nonvascular plant is often called the **thallus.**

Thallose Liverworts

Ricciocarpus and Riccia.   The simplest of the thallose liverworts externally, *Ricciocarpus* (Figure 4.2) and *Riccia* (Figure 4.3), are more complex internally than one would expect. *Ricciocarpus natans* grows either floating upon quiet bodies of freshwater or on their muddy shores. *Riccia fluitans* is

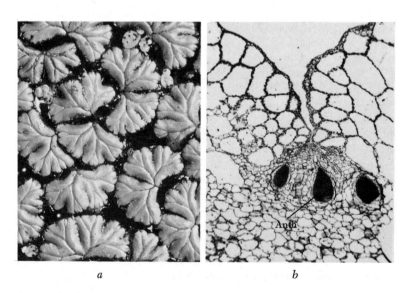

a   *b*

Figure 4.2   *Ricciocarpus natans,* a thallose liverwort. (*a*) Plants floating on water. Note dichotomous lobing and the dorsal furrows. [Courtesy of W. C. Steere.] (*b*) Transection of a plant in region of the antheridia. (*c*) Median longitudinal section (m.l.s.) of single antheridium. (*d*) Transection of plant in the region of archegonia. (*e*) M.l.s. of an immature archegonium. (*f*) M.l.s. of young sporophyte within the enlarging archegonium (calyptra). (*g*) M.l.s. of sporophyte at tetrad stage. Note calptra and archegonial neck. Anth, antheridium; Arch, archegonium; Cal, calyptra.

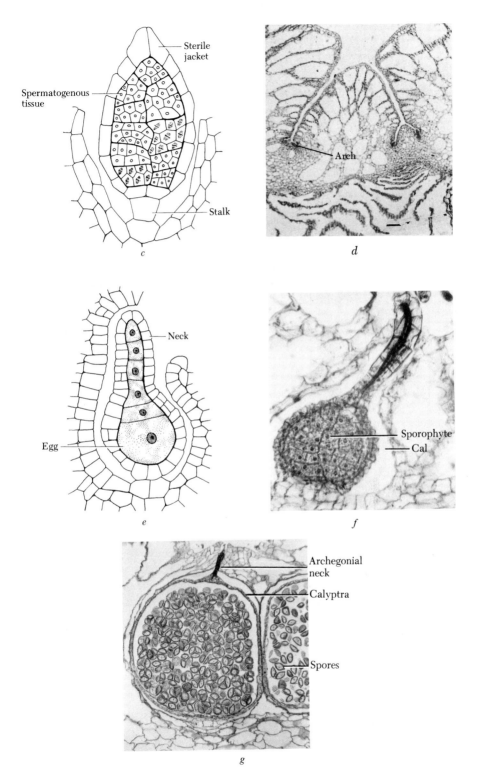

Sterile jacket

Spermatogenous tissue

Stalk

c

Arch

d

Neck

Egg

e

Sporophyte

Cal

f

Archegonial neck

Calyptra

Spores

g

73

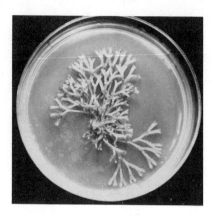

Figure 4.3   *Riccia fluitans* growing on inorganic agar medium.

a submerged aquatic species that grows readily in aquaria and on soil, while most other species of *Riccia* form small rosettes, about 0.5 to 1 inch (2.5 centimeters), on moist soils.

Growth of these plants is strictly apical, and is initiated at their apices by a single apical cell; the pattern of development is *dichotomous*—that is, by equal lobing or branching into two parts. The aquatic plants usually lack rhizoids, but these are present on the ventral surface of plants that grow on soil. The internal tissues are more or less spongy because of fissures and air chambers, but the plants are clearly differentiated into spongy (apparently photosynthetic) tissues and more compact storage tissues (Figure 4.2*b*). We should distinguish among the terms rhizoid, rhizome, and root. **Rhizomes** are elongate, often fleshy, nonvertical stems often growing upon, or slightly below, the surface of the soil. **Rhizoids** are rootlike in performing the functions of anchorage and absorption. They lack root caps and xylem and phloem, which characterize **roots;** they may be unicellular, as in liverworts, hornworts, and ferns, or multicellular, as in mosses (see Chapter 5 for a discussion of rhizomes and roots).

At certain times of the year the *Ricciocarpus* plants become sexually mature, producing clearly distinguishable male and female gametangia on the dorsal surface, which is infolded (Figure 4.2*b, d*) to form the **dorsal furrow.** The male gametangia, which produce minute, biflagellate sperm, are called **antheridia** (Figure 4.2*c*); these consist of a stalk and sterile jacket, which surround the spermatogenous tissue. The female ones, called **archegonia** (Figure 4.2*d, e*), are approximately flask-shaped and at maturity contain single eggs within their bases; the archegonial necks have six rows of **neck cells.** Accordingly, sexual reproduction here, as in all land plants, is oogamous. Unlike the gametangia of algae and fungi, archegonia and antheridia of land plants are composed of gametogenous cells surrounded by somatic ones (compare Figures 3.1 and 4.2*c, e*).

Ricciocarpus plants are bisexual in that archegonia and antheridia are both borne on one individual; this is said to be **monoecious**. Depending on the particular species, *Riccia* plants produce male and female gametes on different individuals. They are therefore, **dioecious**. In either case, the sperm, upon release from the mature antheridia, swim to those archegonia that are also mature. The maturity of the archegonium is evidenced by the disintegration and extrusion of the cells within the archegonial neck, making the egg available for union with the sperm. It is probable that here, too, as demonstrated in *Chlamydomonas, Oedogonium, Achlya* (a fungus), and ferns, a chemical secretion attracts the sperm to the archegonia.

In *Ricciocarpus* and *Riccia,* the zygotes undergo a number of mitoses and cytokineses, resulting in the development of a spherical mass of diploid tissues within the archegonium (Figure 4.2*f*). This spherical structure is the **sporophyte** because it is diploid and ultimately forms spores. The archegonium enlarges and its basal region becomes two-layered by the cell division. After it enlarges, the archegonium is called the **calyptra**. Except for the superficial covering layer, the diploid cells, called **sporocytes** or spore mother cells, undergo two rapidly sequential nuclear divisions in which meiosis occurs, each sporocyte giving rise to a tetrad of haploid cells (Figure 4.2*g*). Accordingly, like the spores of all land plants, these spores are **meiospores**. They develop thick, impervious walls, separate from each other, and are shed by decay of the gametophytic plants. After a period of dormancy they develop into new plants.

This reproductive cycle is basically the same in liverworts, hornworts, and mosses (as well as many algae), in that it consists of two alternating phases, the haploid gametophyte and the diploid sporophyte. In *Ricciocarpus* and *Riccia,* the sporophyte consists of a sphere of diploid cells, located within the enlarged archegonial calyptra and the somatic tissues of the gametophyte. If chlorophyll is present at all within the cells of the sporophyte, it is only in negligible amounts, and the sporophyte is clearly parasitic on the chlorophyllous gametophyte. Although the alternation of generations here is essentially similar to that of certain green algae, it differs in liverworts, hornworts, and mosses in that the sporophytes of these groups are borne *within* and *upon* the gametophytes, and thus are not free-living, or dibiontic.[2] The life cycle of liverworts and hornworts is summarized in Figure 4.4.

Marchantia.   The several species of *Marchantia* (Figure 4.5 to 4.7) occur on soil (especially burned-over soil) or on calcareous rocks. *Marchantia* has a dichotomously branching, lobed plant body that is more complex internally than that of *Riccia* and *Ricciocarpus,* as it has highly specialized air chambers and pores differentiated from the compact storage tissue (Figure 4.5*b*). This is somewhat similar to the organization of leaves in vascular plants (p. 114). Specialized, budlike branches, the **gemmae** (Figure 4.6*b*), produced

---

[2]In most red algae the diploid carposporophyte is also borne on the female gametophyte.

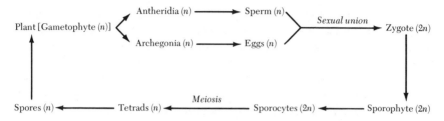

Figure 4.4   Diagrammatic summary of the life cycle of liverworts and hornworts.

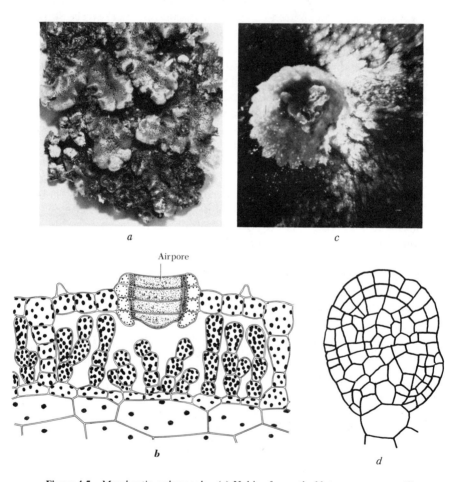

Figure 4.5   *Marchantia polymorpha.* (*a*) Habit of growth. Note gemma cups. (*b*) Transection of plant. Note air chamber and pore above, storage tissue below. (*c*) Gemma cup and gemmae, more highly magnified. (*d*) Single gemma.

within cuplike structures on the plant's surface (Figures 4.5*c* and 4.6), are the mechanisms of vegetation or asexual dissemination and subsequent development of new gametophytic plants. The **gemma cups** illustrate what has been called the splash-cup mechanism of dispersal. Drops of rain strike the cup, which becomes filled with water; the attaching stalks of the mature gemmae become loosened; and when subsequent raindrops strike the cup, the loose gemmae are splashed out of the cup for considerable distances.

Marchantia is strictly dioecious. The sex organs of *Marchantia* are borne in the plant's special branches called **antheridiophores** and **archegoniophores,** collectively termed **gametophores** (Figure 4.6*a, b*). These branches begin their development at the apices of the horizontal plant bodies and are elevated by elongation of stalks. That antheridiophores and archegoniophores are branches of the plant body is evidenced by the presence of rhizoids and scales on their stalks and on the lower surfaces of their caps. The antheridia occur in modified, pored air chambers in radiating rows on the upper surface of the antheridiophoral disc (Figure 4.6*c*). The archegonia also are in radiating rows on the lower side of the archegoniophore between the spokes (Figure 4.6*d*).

Fertilization (Figure 4.6*e*) of at least some of the archegonia occurs after the stalks of the archegoniophores have elongated and may be initiated by splashing of sperm liberated from the antheridial disc. The zygotes develop into sporophytes (Figure 4.7).

The sporophyte of *Marchantia* differs from those of *Riccia* and *Ricciocarpus* in its greater complexity and its nutrition, abundant chloroplasts being present in its diploid cells through most of the developmental period. The complexity of the sporophyte (Figure 4.7) is apparent in its differentiation in **foot, stalk** (or *seta*), and **capsule** regions, and in the presence among the spores of specialized hygroscopic cells, the **elaters,** which are involved in spore dispersal. Unlike *Ricciocarpus,* in which there is no special mechanism for spore dispersal, in *Marchantia* the setae elongate, so that the mature capsules hang down from the lower surface of the archegoniophore (Figure 4.7*b*); at this time the capsules open irregularly to shed the spores. Upon germination, the spores develop into either male or female gametophytes, their sex being genetically determined.

Leafy Liverworts

Porella.   Some species of *Porella* (Figure 4.8) grow on tree bark, others on wet stones or submerged in water. The *Porella* plant, representative of the leafy liverworts, consists of apically growing axes with three rows of leaves, the ventral row, called **underleaves,** being smaller than the two dorsal series. Midribs are absent from the leaves. The leaves of the dorsal series have infolded ventral lobes (Figure 4.8*b*), which explains the appearance of five rows of leaves suggested by superficial examination. The growth of the plants in

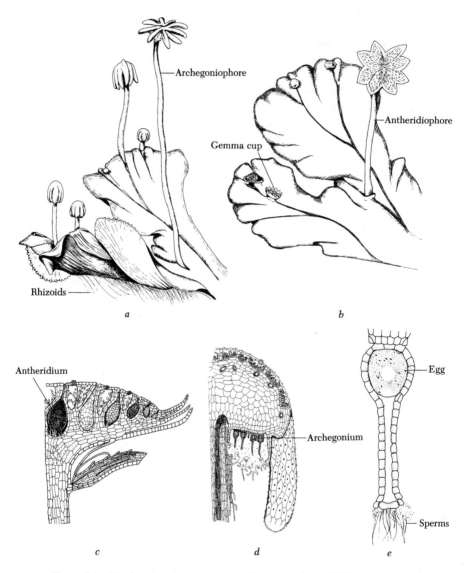

Archegoniophore

Antheridiophore

Gemma cup

Rhizoids

a

b

Antheridium

Archegonium

Egg

Sperms

c

d

e

Figure 4.6 *Marchantia polymorpha,* sexually mature plants. (*a*) Female plant with archegoniophores. (*b*) Male plant with antheridiophore and gemma cup. (*c*) Portion of antheridiophore showing antheridia. (*d*) Portion of archegoniophore showing archegonia. (*e*) Single archegonium with sperm at fertilization. [From a Kny chart.]

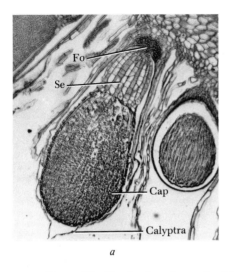

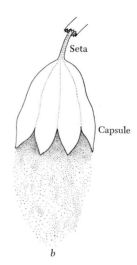

Figure 4.7 *Marchantia polymorpha.* (*a*) Median longitudinal section of an immature sporophyte. (*b*) Older sporophyte with dehiscent capsule. Cap, capsule or sporangium; Fo, foot; Se, seta.

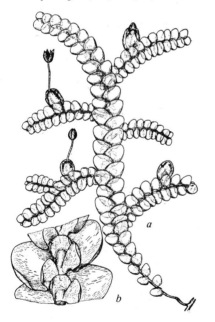

Figure 4.8 *Porella platyphylloidea,* a leafy liverwort. (*a*) Female plant with dehiscent sporophytes, dorsal aspect. (*b*) Portion of the same, ventral view. (*c*) Male plant showing antheridium with antheridial branches; portion in ventral view at left showing antheridium.

dense mats and the overlapping of the leaves and lobes are effective in holding water by capillary action. Rhizoids occur at the bases of the ventral leaves, the cells of which are isodiametric.

The plants are dioecious, the archegonia and antheridia being borne on lateral branches of limited growth (Figure 4.8*a, c*). The chlorophyllous sporophytes are like those of *Marchantia* in having foot, seta, and capsule regions, as well as elaters. The sporocytes are spherical. They differ in certain details of development and in the regular opening of the *Porella* capsules into four segments or valves (Figure 4.8a). The germinating spores give rise to a thallose structure on which a new plant arises as a bud. Although superficially similar to mosses because of their axes and leaves, the leafy liverworts are readily distinguishable by their sex organs and sporophytes.

HORNWORTS (DIVISION ANTHOCEROTOPHYTA)

The Anthocerotophyta includes about five genera—two of which, *Anthoceros* (Figure 4.9) and *Phaeoceros,* are discussed here. *Phaeoceros* differs from *Anthoceros* especially in its spores, which are yellow-brown; those of *Anthoceros* are black-walled. The gametophytes of *Anthoceros* and *Phaeoceros* are multilobed thalli that grow closely appressed to moist soil and rock. Except for ventral mucilage chambers in *Anthoceros,* they lack internal differentiation. The gametophytes usually contain nitrogen-fixing species of the blue-green alga *Nostoc* (Figure 2.8c). The cells of *Anthoceros* and *Phaeoceros* contain single, massive plastids, unlike the liverworts, in which many lenticular plastids are present in each cell.

Depending on the species of *Anthoceros,* the plants are monoecious or dioecious. The archegonia and antheridia are embedded within the dorsal tissues of the thallus (Figure 4.10); the antheridia, yellow-orange at maturity, are exposed in cavities. Fertilization of the eggs of numerous archegonia by sperm results in the production of many chlorophyllous, needlelike sporophytes (Figure 4.9), hence the name "hornworts." These are unlike those of both liverworts and mosses in their continuing development from actively dividing cells

Figure 4.9 *Anthoceros* sp., a hornwort. Gametophytes with maturing sporophytes.

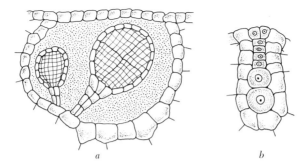

Figure 4.10 *Anthoceros* sp., sex organs. (*a*) Section of plant with antheridia. (*b*) Section of plant with archegonium.

between the foot and base of the sporophyte (Figure 4.11). The spores, accordingly, are produced over a period of several months; the mature spores are shed at the apex while newly produced sporocytes are continually undergoing meiotic division below. Some cells in the sporogenous tract remain sterile and have been called "pseudoelaters," but seemingly they do not function like the elaters of liverworts. Much of the sporophyte is composed of actively photosynthetic cells and a central strand of elongate cells, the **columella.** A cuticle and functional **stomata** with **guard cells** (see p. 114) are present on the epidermal cells of the sporophyte. The maturing apex of the latter opens into two parts, exposing the spores and columella (Figure 4.11). The spores give rise to new gametophytes, the life cycle being similar to that of liverworts.

PHYLOGENY OF HEPATOPHYTA AND ANTHOCEROTOPHYTA

Although representatives of only two orders of liverworts, the Marchantiales and Jungermanniales (which include *Porella*), have been discussed in the preceding account, one may wonder about the diversity and relationship of these thallose and leafy types. Not included in the discussion are three other orders of liverworts, two of them thallose and a third that contains a genus of erect, radially symmetrical plants without modified underleaves. The fossil record is not illuminating regarding the relationship and evolutionary sequence and, as a result, theories regarding the phylogeny of liverworts and hornworts are based on comparative morphology of the living plants. These suggested phylogenies include (1) development from a monobiontic, haploid green algal ancestor; (2) development from a dibiontic green algal ancestor; and (3) development from a vascular plant (like one of the Rhyniophyta, p. 164) by reduction. The last theory is based largely on comparision of the sporophyte of *Anthoceros* with that of the Rhyniophyta. According to the first two the-

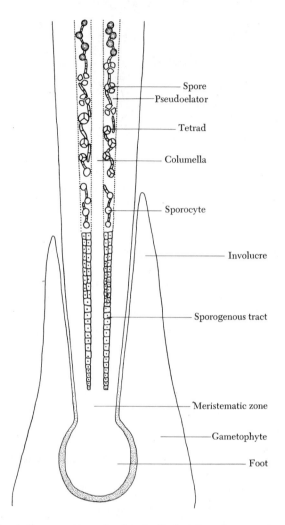

Figure 4.11 *Anthoceros* sp., median longitudinal section of a sporophyte near its base, diagrammatic. [From H. C. Bold, *Morphology of Plants,* 3rd ed. (New York: Harper and Row, Publishers, 1973).]

ories, the free-living ancestral sporophyte became phylogenetically epiphytic-parasitic on the gametophyte when the ancestral liverworts began to colonize the land. These are, of course, speculation. It seems certain, however, that the hornworts represent a distinctly different group from liverworts. The gametophytes of hornworts have single, massive chloroplasts in their cells, the sex organs are embedded within the plant body, and their sporophytes, with continuous development and spore production and a columella, are characteristics that are not present in liverworts.

MOSSES (DIVISION BRYOPHYTA)

In the Division Bryophyta, two classes of the mosses will be considered—
Mnionopsida and Sphagnopsida.

Class Mnionopsida

The Mnionopsida are often called the "true mosses" to distinguish them
from *Sphagnum,* the peat or bog moss. Mosses are widespread in rainy and
humid places, but rarer in more arid zones. Only a few species are adapted to
survive long droughts, although many can successfully withstand temporary
desiccation. The individual moss plant (Figures 4.12 and 4.13) consists of a
slender leafy axis, either erect or prostrate, that may or may not have multicellular absorptive branches called rhizoids. It is characteristic of mosses that
they rarely occur as individuals but form extensive groups or colonies on moist
soil, rocks, and wood. The largest mosses are natives of the Southern Hemisphere and may exceed a foot in length, as in the case of *Dawsonia,* but in
the Northern Hemisphere the large species of the "haircap moss," *Polytrichum,* do not usually surpass 6 to 8 inches. Mosses growing on soil are important in preventing erosion.

It is convenient to begin consideration of the moss life cycle with the
spore. Like other land plants, mosses produce airborne spores that are usually
able to withstand desiccation for long periods.[3] Most spores are widely dis-

a   b

Figure 4.12 Mosses. (*a*) *Polytrichum* sp. female plants with maturing sporophytes,
Spph. (*b*) *Funaria* sp., female branches with developing sporophytes.

[3]Certain algal spores and zygotes, as well as the spores of nonaquatic fungi, also may be
airborne.

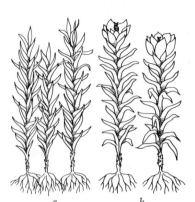

Figure 4.13 *Polytrichum* sp., (*a*) Three females, and (*b*) two male plants.

tributed in the atmosphere, and those that come to rest upon favorable, moist surfaces then absorb water and renew their growth in the process called **germination** (Figure 4.14*a*). Many moss spores require light for germination. The spores of many mosses develop into prostrate filamentous systems that branch profusely. The cells of these filaments are filled with lenslike chloroplasts. At least some cells of the filaments are separated from each other by oblique walls; some branches may be rhizoidal, penetrate the substrate, and apparently function in absorption. The system of branching filaments that develops from the germinating spore is known as the **protonema** (Figure 4.14*b, c*). After a period of development during which extensive surfaces may be covered, the protonema forms *buds* (Figure 4.14*b*), which grow into **leafy shoots** (Figure 4.14*c*). It has been shown recently that growth hormones of the cytokinin group (benzyladenine and related compounds) are active in inducing bud formation that does not occur in their absence.

At the bases of the leafy shoots, the protonema serves as a rhizoidal system; however, additional rhizoids develop from the bases of the leafy axes. Although moss leaves and stems may achieve considerable internal complexity, vascular tissues (xylem and phloem, p. 103) are absent; water is absorbed directly through the surfaces of the leaves and stems in many genera. In most populations, the densely aggregated plants tenaciously hold considerable amounts of water by capillary action.

Polytrichum (Figures 4.12*a*, 4.13) exemplifies a moss that is histologically quite complex. The centers of its stems contain water-conducting cells called **hydroids,** surrounded by food-conducting cells, the **leptoids** (Figure 4.15). Hydroids and leptoids function like xylem and phloem, respectively, although their morphological organization differs and lignin is absent.

Most mosses produce leafy shoots that persist for a number of growing seasons; such species are said to be **perennial.**

At certain times of the year, the tips of some branches of moss plants become fertile (Figure 4.13), producing sex organs. As in all land plants, re-

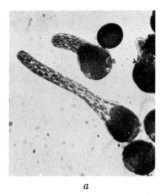

Figure 4.14 *Funaria* sp. (*a*) One unger-minated and several germinating spores. (*b*) Portion of protonema, Prne, with bud that will develop into leafy plant. (*c*) Young leafy shoots attached to proto-nema.

a

b   *c*

production is oogamous, the female gamete being a nonmotile egg cell and the male gamete, a small, motile (biflagellate) sperm. The antheridia (Figure 4.16*a*) and archegonia (Figure 4.16*b*) are multicellular as in liverworts, and the gametes are covered by a sterile cellular layer. The archegonia are borne

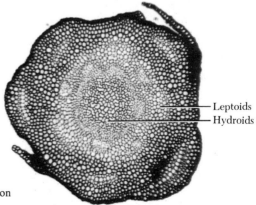

Figure 4.15 *Polytrichum* sp., transection of stem.

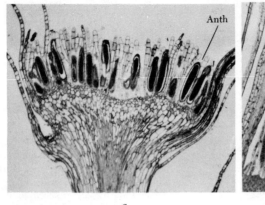

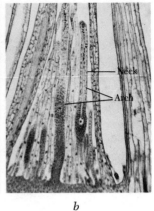

a

b

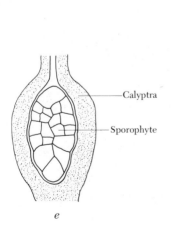

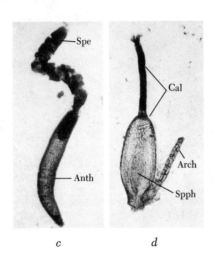

c

d

Figure 4.16 Sexual reproduction in mosses. (*a, b*) *Mnium* sp.: (*a*) median longitudinal section of apex of plant with numerous antheridia, Anth, and sterile filaments among them; (*b*) M.l.s. of apex of plant with archegonia, Arch, and interspersed sterile filaments and archegonial neck. (*c, d*) *Funaria* sp.: (*c*) antheridium, Anth, shedding sperm, Spe: (*d*) enlarging archegonium, Arch, or calyptra, Cal, containing young sporophyte, Spph. (*e, f*) Sporophyte enlarging with archegonium; note also infertile archegonium.

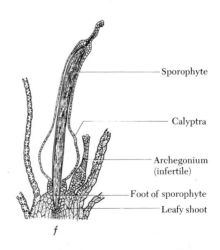

e

f

on stalks or pedicels (Figure 4.16*b*) and have long necks composed of six rows of neck cells.

Some mosses are **monoecious,** as in *Funaria,* both antheridia and archegonia being present on the same individual. Others, such as *Polytrichum* and *Mnium,* are **dioecious** (Figures 4.13 and 4.16); the individual leafy shoots are unisexual. Fertile bisexual apexes as well as male apexes of unisexual moss plants are often recognizable because the leaves form a sort of cup about the sex organs (Figure 4.13*b*). In a number of mosses, the male plants are dwarfs that grow on the leaves of the female plants in the vicinity of the archegonia. The origin of such dwarf males—that is, whether or not they arise from germinating spores and protonema—has not been satisfactorily explained.

During heavy dews or rainfall, mature antheridia discharge their sperm (Figure 4.16*c*), some of which may reach the vicinity of an archegonium; in species with unisexual leafy plants, the contact may be accomplished by splashing raindrops. The inner cells of the neck disintegrate when the archegonium is mature, leaving a liquid-filled passageway, the neck canal, to the egg. Studies of other organisms suggest that substances secreted in the moss archegonium chemically attract sperm. When a minute, biflagellate sperm, composed largely of nuclear material, swims down the canal of the archegonial neck and enters the egg cell, nuclear union (fertilization) follows, and a zygote is formed.

As in certain algae (see p. 40, Figure 3.15*c*) and liverworts, the moss zygote does not undergo meiosis, but gives rise to an alternate spore-producing phase, the **sporophyte.** Again, as in the liverworts and hornworts and unlike the algae, which have *free-living,* independent sporophytes,[4] the moss sporophyte is retained permanently on the parent gametophyte; during its early development it remains within the enlarging archegonium (Figure 4.16*d, e, f*). This circumstance, no doubt, has exerted a profound effect on the form of the moss (and liverwort and hornwort) sporophyte. Its incipient growth and nutrition certainly are based on metabolites from the archegonium (here, too, called the calyptra as it enlarges after fertilization) and the leafy axis, but very soon the cells of the developing sporophyte become chlorophyllous, an indication that the sporophyte is at least partially photoautotrophic. Still, the nitrogen and other elements that come from the soil necessarily must diffuse into the sporophyte from the gametophyte, the latter having first absorbed them from the soil.

It has been demonstrated that in the sporophytes of *Funaria,* the rate of photosynthesis exceeds that of respiration, so that the sporophyte, with respect to its carbon nutrition, is independent of the gametophyte. In *Polytrichum,* however, respiration of the sporophyte exceeds its photosynthesis, so that it is not self-sufficient with respect to carbon nutrition.

---

[4]In red algae the diploid carposporophyte is also borne on the female gametophyte.

Development of the sporophyte from the zygote is very rapid in mosses and involves the early organization of two apical cells so that the growth of the sporophyte is bipolar or biapical. The needlelike sporophyte appears above the apex of the leafy plant after the calyptra has ruptured following fertilization. Part of the calyptra is carried upward at the summit of the sporophyte (Figure 4.16*f*). When the sporophyte has reached the length characteristic of the species, its tip enlarges to form a spore-bearing region called the **capsule**, or sporangium (Figures 4.12 and 4.17*a, d*). The capsule is connected to the leafy gametophyte by a stalk, or seta, and a basal foot buried in the stem apex of the leafy shoot. Unlike the seta of the liverworts, which elongates only after the capsule has matured its spores, that of the mosses elongates throughout development of the sporophyte. The base of the capsule and the seta are developed by division of cells in an intercalary meristem.

The moss capsule is quite complex (Figure 4.17) and varies in structure among the numerous genera. It is significant that only a small fraction of the component tissues is sporogenous; the remainder are photosynthetic and vegetative in function until late in development, when the surface layers thicken and become hard and brown. The sporogenous tract is present as an urnlike (*Funaria*) or cylindrical layer (*Polytrichum*). As the capsules develop, the cells of the sporogenous tract separate to form spherical sporocytes, which undergo meiosis and cytokinesis to form four spores each.

The mechanisms of spore liberation and dissemination are fascinating aspects of mosses and well worthy of study. In most mosses, the shedding of the calyptra and capsule apex, the **operculum**, after the spores have formed reveals a structure known as the **peristome**. This is a single or double ring of toothlike segments around the mouth of the capsule (Figures 4.17*f* and 4.18). Two types of peristomial "teeth" are illustrated. The 64 short teeth of the peristome of *Polytrichum* (Figure 4.18*b*) are composed of whole cells and are fastened to the rim of the capsule and to a membrane, the **epiphragm**, at the mouth of the capsule. In *Funaria*, by contrast, an epiphragm is absent and a double circle of triangular teeth, which converge at the apex of the capsule, are composed only of the remnants of cell walls (Figure 4.18*a*).

Peristomial movements, which are triggered by slight changes in humidity, result in gradual and continuous spore dissemination under favorable (dry) conditions. The biphasic life cycle of a typical moss is summarized in Figure 4.19.

Mosses have not been studied widely in the laboratory because it seems to be difficult to grow many of them to maturity in laboratory cultures. As a result, we are inadequately informed about their physiological processes and their growth and nutritional requirements. Polyploid races of certain genera of mosses have been obtained by cutting up their setae and planting the pieces on moist substrates, as well as by wounding the base of the capsule. Since these tissues are diploid, they form diploid protonemata and, subsequently,

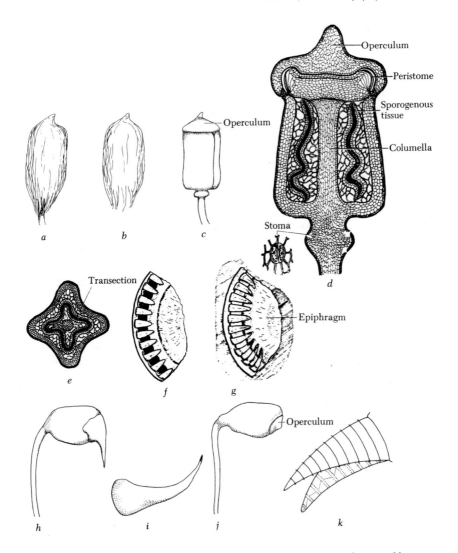

Figure 4.17   Moss, capsule structure. (*a–g*) *Polytrichum* sp.: (*a*) capsule covered by calyptra; (*b*) calyptra; (*c*) capsule with calyptra removed; (*d*) median longitudinal section of maturing capsule; (*e*) transection of preceding; (*f*) portion of capsule orifice showing peristome in open condition; (*g*) same as preceding, peristome closed. (*h-k*) *Funaria* sp.: (*h*) capsule with calyptra; (*i*) calyptra (*j*) capsule with calyptra removed; (*k*) portion of outer (above) and inner peristome.

diploid leafy shoots. This is an example of **apospory,** the development of a gametophyte from a sporophyte by an agent other than a spore. The chromosome number (*n* or *2n*) does not of itself determine whether cells are sporophytic or gametophytic. The diploid cells from the regenerating seta form

Figure 4.18 (*a*) *Funaria* sp. Portion of capsule wall and peristome, somewhat flattened (note spores); Ann, region of the annulus; IPT, inner peristome segment; OPT, outer peristome tooth; CapW, capsule or sporangium wall; Spor, spore. (*b*) Photomicrograph of some of the 64 peristome teeth of *Polytrichum* sp.

a gametophytic protonema, not a sporophyte as one might expect, even though they are diploid.

In conclusion, the gametophytic and sporophytic phases of liverworts, hornworts, mosses, and other plants should not be considered as two different, almost opposed entities, for both are manifestations of the same organism in its complete reproductive cycle. This is strikingly illustrated by the remarkable regenerative capacity of mosses: rhizoids, leaves, stems and their fragments, the various parts of the sporophyte, and even the antheridia and archegonia[5] may regenerate new protonemata, from which follow all the later stages of the complete life cycle.

Class Sphagnopsida

The class Sphagnopsida includes the single genus *Sphagnum,* of which several hundred species have been described. The genus *Sphagnum* (Figure 4.20), known as "peat" or "bog moss," is of commercial value in horticulture

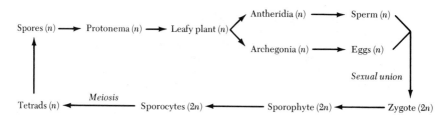

Figure 4.19 Diagrammatic summary of the life cycle of mosses.

[5]Formation of protonema from antheridia and archegonia was demonstrated in the first author's laboratory by Dr. James H. Monroe.

a   *b*

Figure 4.20 *Sphagnum* sp., a peat moss, two different species.

because of its capacity to hold water and, along with other plant remains, to increase the acidity of soils even when it is dead and pulverized.

"Milled" or chopped *Sphagnum* is often used as a germination medium or substrate for delicate seeds because its acidic property reduces the danger of the seeds rotting by discouraging the growth of molds and bacteria. *Sphagnum* often invades bodies of water and forms extensive surface mats, or "quaking bogs."

This genus differs in a number of respects from most other mosses. The mature plants lack rhizoids and are pale green because of the alternation in the leaves of small, chloroplast-containing cells with larger, nonliving, water-storage cells (Figure 4.21); the latter are also present in the weak stems. Certain branches develop downward about the stem and form a wicklike structure. The stem is composed of a central region surrounded by water storage cells. The antheridia of *Sphagnum* are long stalked and globose, and are borne in the axils of the leaves of conelike branches (Figure 4.22*a*, *b*), which may be reddish or purple; the archegonia are massive (Figure 4.22 *c*).

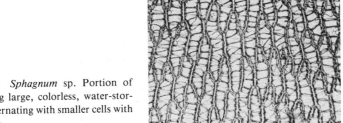

Figure 4.21 *Sphagnum* sp. Portion of leaf showing large, colorless, water-storage cells alternating with smaller cells with chloroplasts.

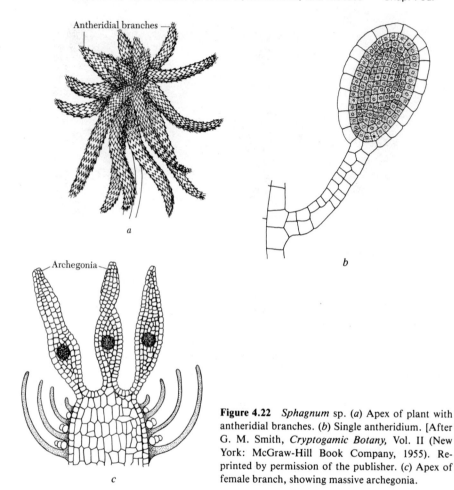

Figure 4.22 *Sphagnum* sp. (*a*) Apex of plant with antheridial branches. (*b*) Single antheridium. [After G. M. Smith, *Cryptogamic Botany*, Vol. II (New York: McGraw-Hill Book Company, 1955). Reprinted by permission of the publisher. (*c*) Apex of female branch, showing massive archegonia.

    The sporophyte of *Sphagnum* (Figure 4.23) differs from those of most mosses in lacking a peristome and in its domelike area of sporogenous tissue. Furthermore, its seta does not elongate at all, but the entire sporophyte is elevated at maturity by a gametophytic stalk, the **pseudopodium**. After elevation of the capsule, the operculum is explosively discharged from the capsule, at the annulus region, by expansion of gases within the capsule in sunshine. The shedding of the operculum is accompanied by a just-audible "pop." Spores that land upon a moist or in an aquatic substrate, if these are acidic, germinate to form protonemata. The protonema of *Sphagnum* is spatulate, and appears somewhat like that of a fern (Figure 4.24), in contrast to that of most mosses. The first leaves of the leafy shoot have all chloroplast-containing cells. Only in the fourth or fifth leaf does differentiation into photosynthetic and water-storage cells occur.

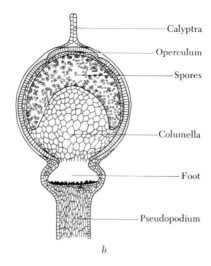

a   *b*

Figure 4.23 (*a*) *Sphagnum* sp. with sporophytes. (*b*) Section of maturing sporophyte.

Because of the extremely acid condition in bogs, which prevents the growth of most microorganisms that would cause decay, *Sphagnum* and associated plants often accumulate in the form of deep deposits called peat. The lower strata of such deposits may be of considerable age; for example, some bogs in the United States are 16,000 years old. Careful sampling and analysis of the pollen and spores preserved in successively older and deeper strata provide a history of vegetation in a given locality and, indirectly, with evidences of climatic changes (especially temperature and rainfall).

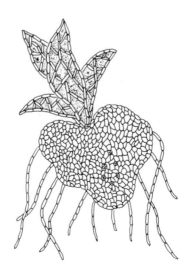

Figure 4.24 *Sphagnum* sp., Protonema with single leafy shoot.

Peat is of economic importance in improving the texture and water-holding capacity of soils, in providing nutriment to cultivated plants, and in acidifying soils. In some parts of the world where other forms of fuel are in limited supply, peat is compressed, dried, and burned. It is of interest that the flavor of Scotch whiskeys is in part due to peat smoke.

Of greater interest in relation to *Sphagnum* and peat are the bodies of human beings that have been uncovered in peat excavations in Ireland, Denmark, and adjacent parts of Germany. These include clothed bodies from the Bronze Age and, among others, the body of a man who had been hanged with a leather rope about 2000 years ago in what is now Jutland, in western Denmark.

EVOLUTION OF NONVASCULAR LAND PLANTS

The conclusion of this brief account of relatively simple, haploid, land plants—the liverworts, hornworts, and mosses—provides an opportunity for considering their origin, ancestry, and possible relationships with each other. With respect to interrelationships, once again the fossil record is not helpful. Relatively few (as compared with vascular plants) fossil liverworts and mosses are known, and these resemble our living types. Liverworts occur in Devonian strata (see Table 6.1 on p. 120), while fossilized mosses appear in Pennsylvanian strata. There is no evidence from the fossil record, however, that mosses evolved from liverworts. Comparative morphology of living mosses and liverworts reveals some radially symmetrical, erect, leafy liverworts that suggest mosses in their organization. However, the sexual reproductive organs and sporophytes of such liverworts are different from those of the mosses. Both plant groups have similar patterns of alternation of generations: the dominant phase is the haploid gametophyte, which bears the parasitic (*Ricciocarpus* and *Riccia*) or partially parasitic, albeit chlorophyllous (other liverworts, hornworts, and mosses), sporophyte upon it.

Apparently the algae were the only chlorophyllous plants on earth from Precambrian to Silurian and Devonian times (see Table 6.1), if the fossil record is at all complete. The divergence of algal progenitors into liverworts, hornworts, mosses, and the several groups of seedless vascular plants (see Chapters 6 and 7) must accordingly have been very rapid.

QUESTIONS FOR REVIEW

1. What is the origin of the name "liverwort"?
2. Where in nature should one seek *Ricciocarpus, Riccia, Marchantia, Porella,* and *Anthoceros*?
3. How do archegonia differ from algal oogonia?

4. How do the antheridia of liverworts, hornworts, and mosses differ from those of algae?

5. Define and distinguish between "thallus" and "thallose."

6. Define or explain rhizoid, dichotomous, sporocyte, calyptra, gametophore, antheridiophore, archegoniophore, gemma, "foot," seta, capsule, elater.

7. What type of nutrition supplies the sporophytes of *Ricciocarpus*?

8. What type of nutrition occurs in the sporophytes of other liverworts, hornworts, and mosses?

9. What is the role of the *Nostoc* in *Anthoceros*?

10. What are the vectors of spore dissemination in liverworts and mosses?

11. Of what does the gametophyte generation consist in mosses?

12. What explanation is there for the fact that mosses grow as groups or clumps?

13. How many flagella are present on the sperms of liverworts, hornworts, and mosses?

14. Define or explain monoecious, dioecious, fertilization, peristome, operculum, columella, apospory, polyploid.

15. Distinguish between peat and peat moss.

16. Why are *Sphagnum* plants pale green?

17. State the chromosome constitution of the following structures in terms of "*n*" or "*2n*": protonema, operculum, columella, foot, moss leaf, *Marchantia* gemma, elater, sporocyte, spore, calyptra.

18. How does the peristome of *Funaria* differ from that of *Polytrichum*?

19. Of what uses is peat?

20. How does the protonema of *Sphagnum* differ from those of *Polytrichum* and *Funaria*?

21. How do the spores of algae and those of liverworts, hornworts, and mosses differ as to the medium through which they are dispersed?

22. What is known about the fossil record of liverworts and mosses?

CHAPTER FIVE

Organization
of Vascular Plants

INTRODUCTION

In beginning our discussion of the land plants in Chapter 4, we stated that they include two major groups—those without vascular tissue[1] and those with vascular tissue. Vascular tissues are xylem and phloem (p. 103). The members of the first group, the liverworts, hornworts, and mosses, lack lignified vascular tissue and are, without exception, gametophytes with physically attached sporophytes. The second group is the larger; normally its members are diploid, spore-producing plants with well-developed vascular tissue. However, nature mocks human categories! Most liverworts, mosses, and vascular plants are terrestrial, but some of each are aquatic. Furthermore, both aquatic and terrestrial algae and fungi are known. The haploid sexual alternate (gametophyte) in the life cycle of land plants may be either free-living and photoautrophic or heterotrophic; in the latter case, the gametophyte is either saprophytic or parasitic upon the sporophyte. It has been suggested that in some of the earliest land plants the sporophytes became more complex while the gametophytes (the sexual phase), in contrast, became smaller, shorter lived, and less active in somatic or vegetative functions. In other organisms, however, such as mosses, liverworts, and hornworts, the gametophyte remained dominant, while the sporophytic phase became reduced and physically attached to it. Another theory holds that the mosses, liverworts, and hornworts are descended from gametophytic algae that "migrated" to the land; by contrast, the vascular plants are said to have derived from migrant algal sporophytes.

[1]A tissue is a group of cells united by a common function; simple tissues are composed of similar cells, while in complex tissues, several types of cells may be present.

The fossil record has not contributed materially to the resolution of these conflicting viewpoints.

Whatever their origin, vascular plants display a degree of complexity that is unmatched by nonvascular plants. Accordingly, this chapter will present a brief, general introduction to the gross and microscopic structure of the vascular plants in general. In the following chapters we shall be concerned primarily with a more specific description of the vegetative organs and the reproductive process in representative vascular plants.

A wide range of morphological form and complexity exists among vascular plants. Among the smallest is the duckweed, *Lemna* (Figure 5.1), a minute, floating, aquatic flowering plant. At the other extreme are woody vines, shrubs, and trees, climaxed by such long-lived giants as the redwood tree, *Sequoiadendron giganteum,* which may attain a height of 360 feet. Between these extremes occurs a vast assemblage of species intermediate in size. These may be **annual,** their maturity, reproduction, and death occurring in one growing season, or **perennial,** the individual plant persisting for more than one season. In spite of their tremendous variety, all individual vascular plants begin their existence as single-celled zygotes and achieve their final size by successive nuclear and cytoplasmic divisions of the zygote and its cellular descendants. Exceptions are organisms propagated vegetatively—that is, from cuttings, buds, or grafts—or those that reproduce without union of gametes, such as *Cyrtomium* (the holly fern), the common dandelion, and certain grasses.

Growth involves an increase in volume. It is accomplished most frequently by an increase in cell number and cell size and is usually accompanied

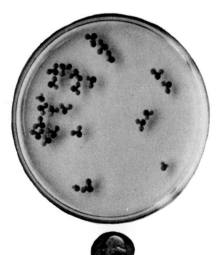

Figure 5.1 *Lemna perpusilla,* a floating, aquatic seed plant. [Courtesy of Dr. William Hillman and Dr. John H. Miller.]

by differentiation (the modification of individual cells or tissues in accordance with function). Explaining the mechanism of growth and differentiation that forms a complex organism from the cellular progeny of a single zygote is one of the most challenging problems of current biological investigations.

Growth in plants may be either generalized or localized. The axes of vascular plants, usually composed of stems and roots, develop from **apical meristems,** which are stem and root tips where cells are actively dividing. In some axes, in addition, intercalary regions of dividing cells persist, localized between base and apex like those at the joints of grass stems. Such **intercalary meristems** frequently give rise to roots when stem cuttings are placed in moist sand, soil, or water.

GROWTH AND DIFFERENTIATION IN STEMS, ROOTS, AND LEAVES

The following sections offer a more detailed discussion of the processes of growth and differentiation in the vegetative organs of vascular plants—namely, stems, roots, and leaves. The external and internal features of stems and roots will be covered separately in four sections.

External Morphology of the Stem

That portion of the axis which bears leaves is known as the **stem.** Leaves arise from the stem at **nodes;** the regions of the stem between successive nodes are the **internodes.** In most plants, stems seem to be the most obvious, dominant portion of the axis; exceptions are bulbous plants (such as onions and lilies) and ferns other than tree ferns. In these exceptional types the leaves appear to be dominant.

Growth of stems is apical; the extreme growing tip is hidden within a terminal bud (Figures 5.2 and 5.3). A **bud** is a stem with short internodes bearing early developmental stages of leaves (**leaf primordia**), or in some cases flowers, or both leaves and flowers. Lateral or **axillary buds** occur between the leaf axil and the stem. Buds may be closed (covered) or open, that is, undergoing continuous development and unfolding, as in many herbaceous plants (for example, the geranium *Pelargonium*). **Closed buds** occur on woody plants of the temperate zone and are protected by variously thickened and gummy outer leaves called **bud scales** (Figure 5.2). The bud scales are shed as spring growth is initiated, leaving behind **bud scale scars** (Figure 5.3). The age and the extent of growth of younger branches may be ascertained by examination of successive groups of bud scale scars.

Woody stems exhibit other characteristic structures during their dormant period (Figure 5.3), in addition to terminal and axillary buds and bud scale scars. **Leaf scars** and **vascular bundle scars** are often evident, as are **lenticels**

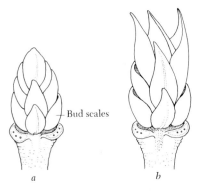

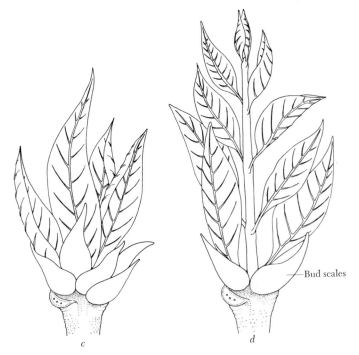

Figure 5.2 *Syringa vulgaris,* lilac. Successive stages in opening of a terminal bud.

(Figure 5.4), areas of corky tissue that develop during secondary growth, often at the sites of stomata of primary growth. Lenticels are pathways of gaseous interchange.

Stems may be self-supporting and erect, or they may require support, as in the case of various types of vines. They vary from the pendulous to horizontal.

Certain modified stem types are illustrated in Figures 5.5 and 5.6. Among these are nonerect, often horizontal, stems designated as stolons and rhizomes. **Stolons,** often called "runners," are elongate, nonfleshy, pendulous, or hor-

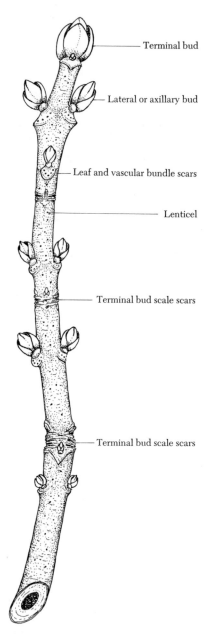

Terminal bud

Lateral or axillary bud

Leaf and vascular bundle scars

Lenticel

Terminal bud scale scars

Terminal bud scale scars

Figure 5.3 Twig of buckeye, *Aesculus* sp., dormant condition.

izontal stems that root at their nodes and give rise to leafy buds and shoots at places where they root. Strawberries (Figure 5.5*a*) regularly produce stolons, the plantlets of which are used in propagation. **Rhizomes,** which are sometimes subterranean, also are nonerect or horizontal stems, which are often fleshy because they contain large amounts of stored food. Rhizomes contin-

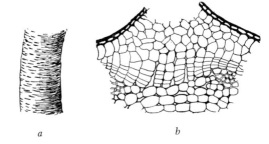

Figure 5.4 (*a*) Portion of white birch stem, showing bark with lenticels. (*b*) Section of one young lenticel. [After C. C. Curtis.]

a   *b*

ually grow at their apices and their older parts often decay so that the apically growing branches may become separate individuals. *Iris* (Figure 5.5*b*) and many ferns produce rhizomes that are used in propagation.

Tubers (Figure 5.5*c*) are the enlarged tips of subterranean stolons or rhizomes. A classic example of a tuber-producing plant is the potato, *Solanum tuberosum*. Careful examination of potato tubers that have been stored for some time will reveal the presence on their surfaces of spirally arranged buds, the "eyes." In propagating potatoes, before planting, the "seed" potatoes are cut up into segments that contain at least one eye. The eyes or buds then

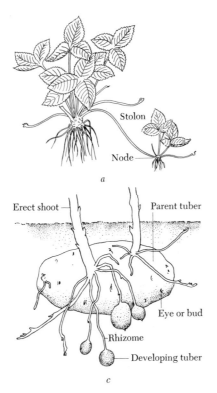

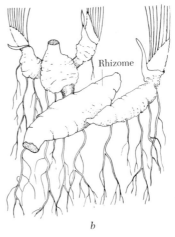

Figure 5.5 Modified stems. (*a*) Stolons of strawberry, *Fragaria* sp. Note elongate, horizontal stems that have rooted at a node, forming plantlet. (*b*) Rhizome of *Iris* sp. (*c*) Stages in development of a potato tuber (*Solanum tuberosum*).

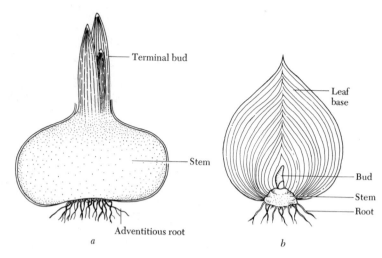

Figure 5.6   Modified stems. (*a*) Bisection of corm of *Gladiolus* sp. (*b*) Bisection of a bulb of onion (*Allium cepa*).

develop roots at their bases and begin to grow into shoots or "sprouts," which break through the soil surface. Up to this point the energy and metabolites required for growth are based on those stored in the original tuber fragment. After some weeks of photosynthesizing and growth, stolonlike branches develop at the bases of the aerial shoots and begin to enlarge at their tips (Figure 5.5*c*) to form the new crop of tubers.

Corms and bulbs differ from stolons and rhizomes in their vertical position beneath the soil. **Corms** are short, fleshy subterranean stems with buds and shoots at their apices and roots below (Figure 5.6*a*) as in *Gladiolus*. **Bulbs** are composed largely of the overlapping fleshy bases of leaves; these are full of stored food, as in the onion (Figure 5.6*b*). The stem comprises only a small basal portion of a bulb and is embedded in the fleshy leaf bases and bears a terminal bud at its apex. Bulbs and corms both are agents of vegetative propagation, meaning that a vegetative or somatic organ, rather than a reproductive one, is involved in multiplying the number of individuals.

Development of the Stem

The growth of the stem is localized in a group of actively dividing cells at its apex, called the **apical meristem.** It is usually concealed (Figures 5.2 and 5.7) by the numerous, minute leaf primordia that it bears. The cells of the apical meristem divide rapidly, thus increasing in number. Three meristematic regions, the **primary meristems,** are distinguishable just below the apical meristem: (1) the superficial **protoderm;** (2) the provascular tissue or **procambium,** in the form of a solid rod, a cylinder, or discrete strands; and (3) the **ground**

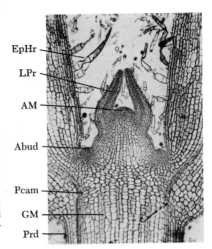

Figure 5.7 *Coleus blumei,* median longitudinal section of the stem apex. Abud, axillary bud; AM, apical meristem; GM, ground meristem; EpHr, epidermal hair; LPr, leaf primordium or percursor; Prd, protoderm (precursor of epidermis); Pcam, procambium. Apical meristem and procambium are precursors of vascular tissue and cambium.

meristem. When the apex has grown a certain distance beyond a given region of cells, cell multiplication ceases in this region, and the cells enlarge and differentiate into functional primary tissues. In many herbaceous (soft-textured, green-stemmed) plants, only these primary tissues function in the plant's normal metabolic processes throughout the existence of the organism.

As the increase in cell size and the change in form of a given region in the developing axis both decelerate, deposition of cell walls in specialized patterns completes the process of differentiation of the primary meristems into three regions of the mature stem: (1) the **vascular tissues,** collectively called the **stele,** composed of **xylem** and **phloem** (Figure 5.8) and sometimes the **cambium** layer (see p. 108), derived from the procambium; (2) the superficial **epidermal layer,** derived from the protoderm; and (3) the remainder, **cortex, endodermis,** and **pith,** if present, derived from the ground meristem. The primary vascular tissues of stems and roots are connected with each other; the veins of leaves and reproductive organs are connected to the stem by branches of vascular tissue called **traces.** Traces are established by differentiation of procambium strands into xylem and phloem.

Xylem and phloem are complex tissues and each may contain as many as four different kinds of simple tissues. The actual water-conducting cells of xylem are tracheids and vessels. A tracheid differentiates from a single procambial cell, while the ontogeny of a vessel involves a series of procambial cells each producing a vessel element, a perforated cell. Vessels occur in a few of the seedless vascular plants, but are most widespread in the flowering plants. **Tracheids** are elongate cells (Figures 5.9*b* and 5.13*d*) with somewhat pointed ends. Their walls (and those of vessels) are thickened with a mixture of cellulose and lignin, which gives them rigidity. The first tracheids to differentiate are usually lignified in an annular or helical pattern, while those that differ-

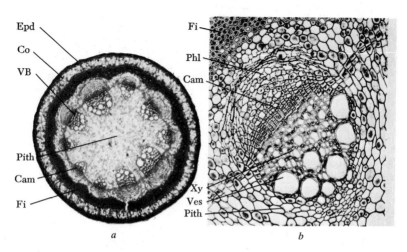

Figure 5.8 *Aristolochia* sp. (*a*) Transection of stem in region of primary permanent tissues, low magnification. (*b*) One vascular bundle and adjacent tissues. Cam, cambium; Co, cortex; Epd, epidermis; Fi, supporting fibers; Phl, phloem; VB, vascular bundle containing primary xylem within, separated by cambium from the primary phloem without; Ves, vessel of xylem; Xy, xylem. Note parenchyma and tracheids in region of xylem label line.

entiate later in the development of the stem have more lignin deposited on their walls so that only small elongated or circular thin places remain unlignified. These areas are **pits;** they are areas in the wall through which water and solutes can move more rapidly than through the lignified portions of the wall. There is evidence that **vessels** (Figure 5.9*b*) arose phylogenetically by the perforation of the end walls of tracheids to form a continuous series. Each segment of a vessel is called a **vessel member.** There may be one large or several smaller perforations between vessel members. Vessels also have a variety of patterns of lignification. In addition to the actual water-conducting tracheids and vessels, which are nonliving at maturity, living parenchyma cells and thick-walled nonliving fibers may both be present in xylem (Figure 5.13*b*). The major functions of xylem are transport of water (and solutes dissolved in it) and support.

The **sieve cells** of phloem, like tracheids, are unicellular, but they are living cells with cellulosic cell walls. The latter have certain groups of pores called **sieve areas** through which the protoplasm of adjacent sieve cells is continuous. These cells, which are very similar to sieve cells, may be connected in series, as they are in many flowering plants, to form **sieve tubes,** composed of **sieve tube members** (Figure 5.9*b*) in which the sieve areas are aggregated in the terminal walls to form **sieve plates** (Figure 5.9*c*), which facilitate conduction of large molecules. In some plants the sieve cells and tubes (which lack nuclei at maturity) are associated with smaller nucleate cells, the **com-**

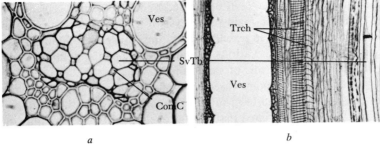

a   *b*

Sieve plate

c

Figure 5.9 Vascular tissue. (*a*) Transection of portion of vascular bundle from stem of maize (corn), *Zea mays.* Note sieve plate in one sieve tube. (*b*) Longitudinal section of vascular tissue of squash, *Cucurbita* sp. Note remains of dissolved transverse walls in xylem vessel. ComC, companion cell; SvTb, sieve tube of phloem; Trch, xylem tracheid with helical lignification; Ves, xylem vessel. (*c*) Longisection of part of sieve tube and companion cell. [After K. Esau, *Plant Anatomy.* (New York: John Wiley & Sons, Inc., (1965). Reprinted by permission of the publisher.]

panion cells (Figure 5.9*a, c*). In addition to sieve tubes, parenchyma cells and lignified fibers may be present in phloem. Phloem serves in the conduction of complex substances manufactured in the plant's metabolism.

The xylem and phloem of primary differentiation may be positioned concentrically, collaterally (opposite each other, Figure 5.8), or bicollaterally (with phloem on both sides of the xylem). In roots, by contrast, the xylem and phloem occur alternately (Figure 5.16).

In some stems the center is occupied by a pith (Figure 5.8) composed of parenchyma cells with thin, cellulose walls; these cells may function in storage. The tissue layers lying between the vascular tissues and the epidermis vary in extent and complexity. In general, the cortex is a storage region, although it is photosynthetic in young stems (and in aerial roots). The epidermis is interrupted by minute pores, the **stomata** (singular, stoma) surrounded by **guard cells** (Figure 5.20); it is also cutinized—covered by the **cuticle,** which is composed of a waxy substance (cutin) secreted by the epidermal cells as an outer covering. Stomata are the main pathways for gaseous interchange, although this also occurs to a limited extent through the cuticle. Stomata also occur on leaves and floral organs. Various glandular and nonglandular hairs (Figure 5.10) occur on the epidermis of stems and leaves.

The patterns of primary vascular organization have been summarized in the concept of the **stele,** a term often used collectively for the vascular tissue of axes and closely associated tissues. Various types of steles are illustrated in Figure 5.11 and explained in part in its caption. Some botanists refer to siphonosteles as medullated protosteles and look upon the pith either as an evolutionary invasion of cortical tissue through the leaf gaps that are associated with leaf traces (Figure 5.17b) or as parenchyma tissue that has developed instead of xylem. **Protosteles,** which in this text are considered to be central cores of xylem surrounded by phloem, may be circular, ridged, or elliptical in transection; in some cases, the phloem occurs in segments among the xylem cells. Protosteles are present in many roots and in stems of many vascular cryptogams (seedless vascular plants, see p. 122), in which they develop almost without exception in the juvenile stages. **Amphiphloic siphonosteles** that are dissected by leaf gaps into seemingly discrete strands of xylem surrounded by phloem and endodermis are known as **dictyosteles.** These occur in a number of fern rhizomes having short internodes.

Discrete vascular bundles, not all of which are separated by leaf gaps (for example, those in **eusteles** and **atactosteles** are not), characterize the stems of many angiosperms (flowering plants).

We have summarized the development and structure of primary tissue, the origin of which may be traced to the apical meristem. In some herbaceous and in all woody plants, secondary tissues (Figure 5.12) are added to the primary tissues after elongation of the axis (at a certain distance from the meristem) has ceased. The extent and the duration of this secondary growth process vary with the species. Thus, in some individuals of such long-lived trees as

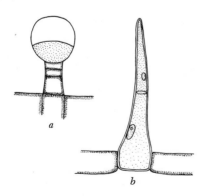

Figure 5.10 Epidermal hairs. (*a*) Multicellular glandular and (*b*) nonglandular hair of geranium (*Pelargonium*).

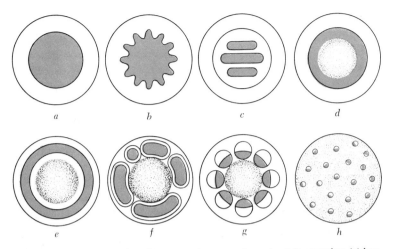

Figure 5.11   Types of steles, diagrammatic transections. (*a–c*) Protosteles: (*a*) haplostele; (*b*) actinostele; (*c*) plectostele. (*d–f*) Siphonosteles: (*d*) ectophloic siphonostele; (*e*) amphiphloic siphonostele or solenostele; (*f*) dictyostele; (*g*) eustele; (*h*) atactostele. Xylem, gray; phloem, white; pith, stippled. [From H. C. Bold, *Morphology of Plants,* 3rd ed. (New York: Harper and Row, Publishers, 1973).]

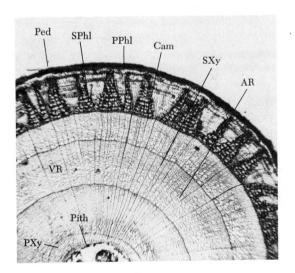

Figure 5.12   Basswood, *Tilia americana.* Sector or transection of 5-year-old stem. AR, annual ring of secondary xylem; Cam, vascular cambium; Ped, corky periderm that has replaced epidermis; PPhl, primary phloem; PXy, primary xylem covered by secondary xylem, SXy, added by cambium; SPhl, secondary phloem; VR, vascular ray; AR, annual ring.

Sequoiadendron gigantea and *Pinus aristata* (bristlecone pine), and oaks (*Quercus* species), secondary growth has been occurring for several thousand years. Were it not for this process, lumber as we know it would not exist.

Secondary growth depends on the active division of a particular layer of cells, the **vascular cambium** (Figure 5.8*a, b*), which lies between the primary xylem and the primary phloem. Most of the cells formed by the cambium differentiate into **secondary xylem** between the cambium and primary xylem (Figures 5.8*a, b,* 5.12), but some become **secondary phloem** between the cambium and primary phloem. The activity of the vascular cambium is seasonal, and in perennial woody plants this is reflected in the deposition of the secondary xylem as **annual rings**, or cylinders (Figures 5.12 and 5.13*c*). There may be parenchyma cells in radial series in the secondary xylem; these are called **rays**. The explanation for the occurrence of annual rings is that the tracheids and vessels of secondary xylem that differentiate early in the growing season have larger diameters and thinner walls than the smaller, thick-walled ones produced later in the season (Figure 5.13*c*). The annual rings vary in thickness in relation to rainfall, and it is possible by examining the rings of very old trees to infer the nature of the weather in the past.

Increased growth in the internal portion of the stem by cambial activity ruptures the epidermis and cortex, which are unable to expand. These outer layers are gradually replaced by corky layers, the **periderm**, which consists of a meristematic cylinder, or of strips of meristematic tissue, the **cork cambium** or **phellogen**, whose outer derivatives mature as cork cells and the inner as parenchyma cells, that may augment the cortex. As secondary growth continues, the cracks in the outer tissue cut more deeply, and additional layers of periderm form. Accordingly, the bark of woody plants may become quite complex, consisting of strips of periderm and other tissues such as cortex and dead secondary phloem.

Secondary xylem is known as **wood** (Figure 5.13). The hardness of wood is caused basically by the lignin that thickens the cell walls, the degree of hardness depending on the amount of lignification and the percentage of thick-walled cells present. When wood is cut, the grain and markings depend on the way in which the annual rings and rays have been exposed.

External Morphology of the Root

Roots differ from stems in lacking leaves (and hence, nodes, internodes, and axillary buds), in having an apical **root cap** (Figures 5.14 and 5.15) that covers the apical meristem, and in having an alternately radial arrangement of their primary xylem and phloem. Roots function in anchoring and absorption.

Roots are designated according to origin as primary, secondary, or adventitious. A **primary root** is the emergent root of an embryonic plant, such as that within a seed (Figure 5.14*a*); branches from it are **secondary roots**. By

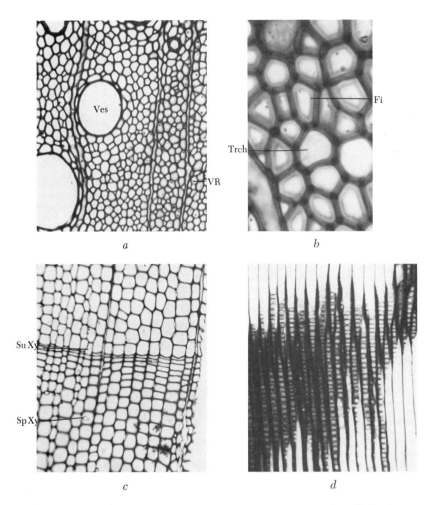

Figure 5.13 Xylem or wood. (*a*) Oak (*Quercus velutina*), transection. (*b*) Portion of oak transection enlarged. Note fibers and tracheids. (*c*) White pine (*Pinus strobus*), transection at junction of two annual rings. VR, vascular ray; Ves, vessel; Fi, fibers; Trch, tracheids; SpXy, large-celled xylem formed early in growing season; SuXy, small-celled xylem formed at end of growing season. Spring and summer xylem of one growing season constitute an annual ring. (*d*) Longisection of pine tracheids.

contrast, **adventitious roots** are not of embryonic origin but develop from superficial tissues of stems or leaves, as in rhizomes, stolons, corms, bulbs (Figures 5.5 and 5.6), and cuttings.

When the emergent primary root continues to develop in length and to function throughout the life of the plant, a **taproot system** is present. Some taproots become woody and others become fleshy (for example, beets, carrots,

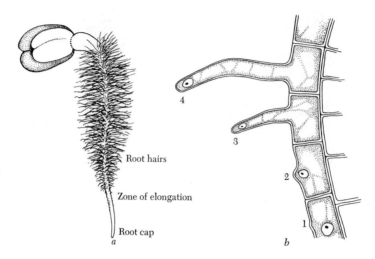

Figure 5.14 Radish, *Raphanus* sp. (*a*) Germinating seed. Note root hair zone. (*b*) Successive stages in root hair formation (numbered).

and turnips). When the primary root is not conspicuous and when adventitious or secondary roots comprise the absorbing organs, the root system is said to be **fibrous.**

Externally, roots are simpler than stems. Seedlings grown in a moist chamber illustrate (see Figure 5.14*a*) the root cap region, the zone of elongation, and the root hair zone. The root hair zone corresponds internally to the region of differentiation into the specialized primary tissues.

Development of the Root

The ontogeny of a root is illustrated in Figures 5.15 and 5.16. The apical meristem is protected by a root cap, the cells of which are slimy and thus seemingly provide lubrication and protection as the root elongates through the soil. In many roots, the provascular tissue or procambium matures into a solid core of primary xylem and phloem (Figure 5.16), a protostele, but in some a central pith is present. The vascular tissue in roots is usually surrounded by a **pericycle,** from which branch roots arise endogenously; the pericycle, in turn, is surrounded by the **endodermis,** the thickenings on the walls of which are called **casparian strips.** The walls of the endodermis are notable for their suberin (cork) thickenings of various patterns. A pericycle and endodermis are sometimes present in the stems of vascular cryptogams (seedless vascular plants) and in rhizomes.

The primary xylem and phloem of roots are alternately arranged (Figure 5.16). The cortex is an extensive layer used for storage; an extreme of this is

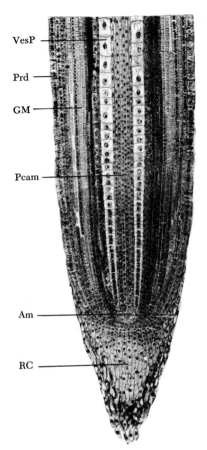

VesP

Prd

GM

Pcam

Am

RC

Figure 5.15 Maize (corn), *Zea mays;* median longitudinal section of a root tip. GM, ground meristem; Prd, protoderm; AM, apical meristem; Pcam, procambium; VesP, xylem vessel percursors; RC, root cap. [Courtesy of Dr. J. H. Leech and Dr. W. G. Whaley.]

seen in fleshy roots like sweet potatoes. The epidermal cells of roots project as **root hairs** (Figure 5.14*b*) which function in absorption; more root hairs are added constantly as increasingly distal regions of the root mature. The root epidermis, obviously, is not cutinized in the absorptive region. Like their stems, the roots of woody plants also undergo secondary thickening through the activity of both vascular and cork cambiums.

Stems and roots differ both externally and internally in a number of respects. Externally, it is obvious that stems, which bear leaves, have nodes and internodes, whereas roots lack leaves, nodes, and internodes. The apical meristem of stems is protected by the young leaves and bud scales (if present) of the terminal bud, while in roots it is covered by a root cap. Branches of stems originate superficially, usually in the axils of leaves, or by dichotomous forking of the apex. The latter occurs in some roots (for example, those of *Isoetes*, p. 139), but in most, branch roots arise endogenously from the per-

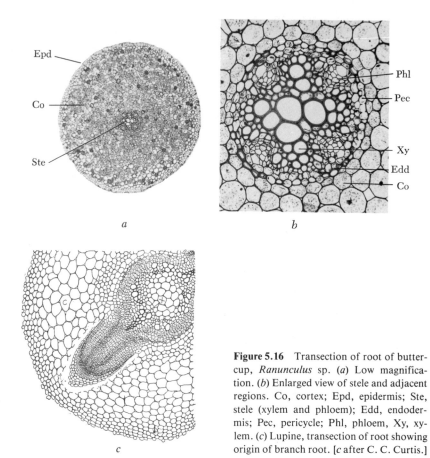

Figure 5.16 Transection of root of butter-cup, *Ranunculus* sp. (*a*) Low magnification. (*b*) Enlarged view of stele and adjacent regions. Co, cortex; Epd, epidermis; Ste, stele (xylem and phloem); Edd, endodermis; Pec, pericycle; Phl, phloem, Xy, xylem. (*c*) Lupine, transection of root showing origin of branch root. [*c* after C. C. Curtis.]

icycle and grow out through the cortex (Figure 5.16*c*). Internally, roots differ from stems in the alternating arrangement of their primary xylem and phloem, which in stems is concentric, collateral, or bicollateral.

Leaves

Leaves function as photosynthetic organs and participate in gaseous interchange. They arise from the apical meristem as localized mounds of tissue called **leaf primordia** (Figure 5.7). In contrast to axes, most leaves have a simple structure, but there is some evidence that the simplicity may be a deceptive result of secondary simplification from more complex beginnings, a phenomenon known as **reduction.** At one extreme, true leaves (those with vascular tissue) approach moss leaves in size (see Figures 6.8 and 6.13); at the other extreme are the enormous leaves of tree ferns, palms, and bananas. Large leaves (Figure 5.17*b*) with branching veins (vascular tissues) generally are

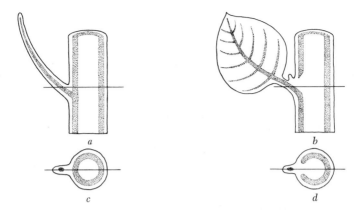

Figure 5.17   (*a,b*) Segments of longitudinal bisections of stems: (*a*) stem with microphyll; (*b*) stem with megaphyll. (*c,d*) Transections at levels of (*a*) and (*b*) indicated by lines. Steles, traces, and veins indicated by stippling. Note lack of leaf gaps in (*a*) and (*c*) and their presence in (*b*) and (*d*). [From H. C. Bold, *Morphology of Plants,* 3rd ed. (New York: Harper and Row, Publishers, 1973).]

thought to be derived from axial branches that have become flattened during the course of evolution, the cortical and epidermal tissues having extended between the branches as a sort of webbing. Certain small leaves (Figure 5.17*a*) with unbranched veins are thought to be fundamentally different: they are assumed to have developed as localized surface outgrowths that later became vascular. However, their simplicity has also been considered a manifestation of evolutionary reduction from more complex types. Some leaves, often but not always small ones (like those of Microphyllophyta, p. 126), have unbranched veins, and their traces leave no gaps in the stem steles. Such leaves are **microphylls** (Figure 5.17*a, c*). By contrast, **megaphylls** (Figure 5.17*b, d*) have branching veins, and their traces do leave gaps in the stem stele, which is usually a siphonostele.

In external form, leaves may have whole or divided blades (Figures 5.18*a–c*); the former are **simple** and the latter **compound leaves.** The **petiole** (leaf stalk) of compound leaves thus bears a number of **leaflets,** which are shed as a unit with the petiole. Buds occur only at the base of the petiole in both simple and compound leaves, not at the bases of the leaflet stalks. Various types of compound leaves occur, the commonest ones being either **palmately** or **pinnately compound.** In palmately compound leaves (Figure 5.18*b*), the leaflets emerge from the apex of the petiole, whereas in pinnately compound leaves, the leaflets are attached along a prolongation of the petiole known as the **rachis** (Figure 5.18*c*).

Leaf blades are traversed by an extensive system of veins, which are the ultimate branches of the vascular traces. Microphylls, as noted above, have single unbranched veins. Megaphylls may have dichotomous, striate, or netted

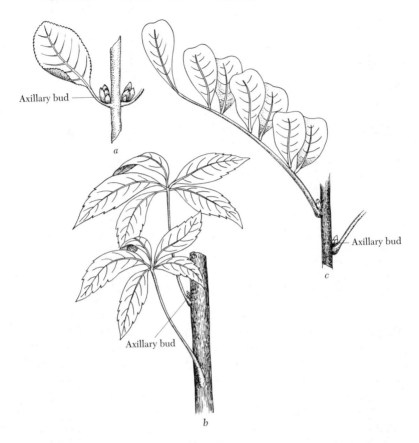

Figure 5.18 Leaf structure. (*a*) Simple leaf, *Euonymus* sp. (*b*) Palmately compound leaves, *Schefflera* sp. (*c*) Pinnately compound leaf, *Sophora* sp.

venation (Figure 5.19). Two patterns of netted venation—namely, **pinnate** and **palmate**—are widespread.

As compared with axes, most leaves are relatively simple internally. Secondary growth is limited, if it occurs, and affects only the vascular tissues. The leaf surfaces are covered by a cutinized, more or less waxy, and impervious **epidermis** that is interspersed with stomata and guard cells (Figures 5.20 and 5.21). The intervening tissues (Figure 5.21), known as **mesophyll**, the major site of photosynthesis and gaseous exchange, are frequently differentiated into an upper series of columnar cells, the **palisade mesophyll**, and a lower series of loosely contiguous cells, the **spongy mesophyll;** however, in some leaves the mesophyll is essentially a homogeneous region. The mesophyll cells are rich in chloroplasts and thus active in photosynthesis. None of these cells is far from a vein; hence, transfer of substances to and away from the photosynthesizing mesophyll cells is possible.

a

Figure 5.19   Venation patterns. (*a*) Dichotomous venation in *Ginkgo biloba,* maidenhair tree. [Courtesy of Professor H. J. Arnott.] (*b*) Parallel or striate venation in *Cyperus* sp. (*c*) Netted venation in *Sophora* sp. [*b* and *c* courtesy of Professor H. W. Bischoff and Professor D. A. Larson.]

b

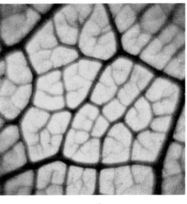

c

Leaves differ in texture, in degree of cutinization, and in the amount of supporting tissue present; they vary also in their pattern of attachment to the stem and in their arrangement in the bud, known as **phyllotaxy.** Leaves may be attached to the stem in opposite, alternate (spiral), or whorled patterns. The general pattern of arrangement is genetically determined; it is already evident in the bud phyllotaxy, but it may change somewhat during development. Inasmuch as buds, which may give rise to branches, are present in the leaf axils, the arrangement of stem branches is related to that of leaves; thus, leaf arrangement has a profound effect on overall shoot morphology. Whorled phyllotaxy is rarer than the other types. Phyllotaxy of alternate leaves may be expressed by fractions such as ½, ⅓, and ⅖, the denominator indicating the number of vertical rows of leaves between two vertically aligned leaves, the numerator the number of turns about the stem between two such leaves.

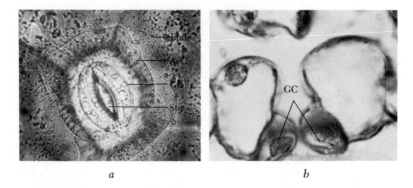

a

b

Figure 5.20   Stomata. (*a*) Surface view of stoma and associated cells of leaf of
Rhoeo discolor. (*b*) Transection of stoma and guard cells of privet leaf, *Ligustrum*
sp. (see Figure 5.21). AcC, accessory cell; EpdC, epidermal cell; GC, guard cell;
Sto, stoma.

With respect to leaves, plants may be **evergreen** (never completely without leaves) or **deciduous** (all the leaves are shed periodically). Leaf fall is accomplished usually by the formation of a special separating layer, the
abscission layer, which severs the leaf at its base or at the base of the petiole
(Figure 5.22). In certain geographical regions, especially northeastern America

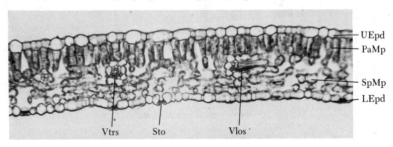

a

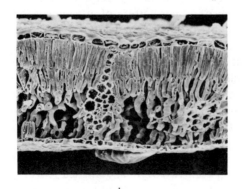

b

Figure 5.21   Privet, *Ligustrum* sp., sector of transection of a leaf. LEpd, lower
epidermis; Vlos, longisection of a vein;
PaMp, palsiade mesophyll; Sto, stoma in
section; SpMp, spongy mesophyll; UEpd,
upper epidermis; Vtrs, transection of a
vein. (*b*) Pecan, *Carya* sp. Scanning-elec-
tron micrograph of a leaflet; note vein and
cuticle, etc. [*b* courtesy of Professor H. J.
Arnott.]

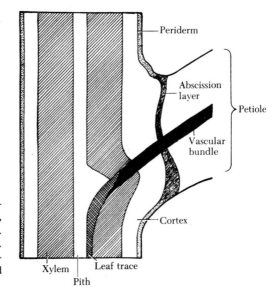

Figure 5.22 Longisection of branchlet and leaf base (petiole) of walnut, showing abscission layer. [After J. B. Hill, L. O. Overholts, and H. W. Popp, *Botany* (New York: McGraw-Hill Book Company, 1936). Reprinted by permission of the publisher.]

and in Scandinavia, the leaf fall of deciduous trees is preceded by the phenomenon of autumnal coloration. The chlorophyll of the leaves disintegrates, leaving the yellow-orange pigments (carotenes and xanthophylls), which then increase in amount. Scarlet coloration often reflects development of the pigment anthocyanin in cell vacuoles.

ADAPTATIONS OF VASCULAR PLANTS

Although some nonvascular chlorophyllous plants (certain algae and most liverworts, hornworts, and mosses) are terrestrial in habitat and grow even in environments unfavorable for vascular plants, the latter comprise the major vegetation of the land wherever conditions are favorable for their growth. The explanation for this resides in the capacity of vascular plants, through morphological and physiological adaptations, to live under more rigorous and inhospitable conditions, especially with respect to availability of water. Of great adaptive significance in this connection are the cuticle, stomata, and vascular tissue described earlier. These make possible efficient conservation and translocation of water and its solutes, at the same time providing a pathway for gaseous interchange. There is little doubt that the greater size of most vascular green plants, as compared with nonvascular ones, is correlated with these adaptations as well as with the presence of a root system, which is rarely absent among living vascular plants.

The development of the extensive, vascularized, subterranean system that we call roots, for anchorage and absorption, must have been of tremendous significance in the evolution of land plants. The origin and course of evolution of the root are unknown. It is probable that certain branches of rhizomes became modified with respect to the functions of anchorage and absorption. Organs of anchorage and absorption are, of course, present in certain algae, liverworts, and mosses, but these lack vascular tissue. It has been suggested that the alternate arrangement of xylem and phloem in roots (in contrast to their commonly collateral arrangement in stems, including rhizomes) facilitates the absorption and conduction of water; if the arrangement were collateral, water would have to pass through the phloem before reaching the xylem. It has also been suggested that the root cap is an adaptation that protects the root's apical meristem, which penetrates the soil more rapidly than does the tip of a rhizome.

QUESTIONS FOR REVIEW

1. To what does the term "land plants" usually refer? Why is this somewhat inaccurate?
2. What range of plant size, macroscopically, can you cite from members of the plant kingdom?
3. Define or explain node, internode, bud, abscission layer, axillary bud, terminal bud, leaf primordium, bud scale, bud scale scars, lenticel, apical meristem, primary meristems, procambium, protoderm, ground meristem, primary tissues, herbaceous, xylem, phloem, vascular cambium, cork cambium trace, endodermis, cortex, pericycle, secondary tissues, secondary growth, suberin, and leaf primordium.
4. Define and make labeled drawings to illustrate stolons, rhizomes, corms, bulbs, and tubers.
5. In what respects do stems and roots differ?
6. With the aid of labeled drawings, distinguish between tracheids and vessels, sieve cells, sieve tube members, sieve area, sieve tubes, sieve plates, and companion cells.
7. With the aid of labeled drawings, define and explain stele, protostele, siphonostele, dictyostele, eustele, and atactostele.
8. Distinguish among primary, secondary, and adventitious roots.
9. What is a "root hair"?
10. Distinguish between tap and fibrous root systems.
11. Are all leaves fundamentally similar or homologous? Explain.
12. Define or explain simple and compound leaf, pinnately and palmately compound, dichotomous, striate, pinnate and palmate venation, rachis, mesophyll, stoma and guard cells, abscission layer, deciduous, evergreen.
13. What types of phyllotaxy or leaf arrangement occur in the plant kingdom? Give examples.

CHAPTER SIX

Seedless Vascular Plants I: Divisions Psilotophyta, Microphyllophyta, and Arthrophyta

INTRODUCTION

Vascular plants include two major types, seedless and seed-bearing. The seedless types are sometimes spoken of as **vascular cryptogams,**[1] while those with seeds are called **phanerogams.** The fossil remains of seedless vascular plants have been identified with certainty in rock strata as ancient as early Silurian (Table 6.1). Both seedless and seed-bearing types have persisted to the present day.

The presence of vascular tissue in the diploid sporophytic phase of all of the vascular plants has often been interpreted as evidence of kinship through descent from a common precursor. Accordingly, these plants are sometimes classified in a single division, the Tracheophyta (see Table 1.1), a name that emphasizes the presence of vascular tissue. The significance thus attached to vascular tissue has not been universally accepted, however; some students of evolutionary relationships, **phylogeny,** consider the widespread occurrence of vascular tissue to be a manifestation of parallel evolution, or **homoplasy.** Proponents of this interpretation classify the vascular plants in a number of separate groups, the ranks of which vary with the classifier (see Table 1.1).

Whatever rank may be assigned them, there is almost unanimous agreement that the living, seedless vascular plants include four major groups, in this book accorded divisional rank: Division Psilotophyta, the psilotophytes; Division Microphyllophyta, the club and spike "mosses"; Division Arthro-

---

[1]The name originated long ago because in the absence of seeds, their method of reproduction was unknown, or "concealed." Nonvascular cryptogams are algae, liverworts, hornworts, and mosses; the fungi are included in this designation by some botanists.

TABLE 6.1   Geologic Time as Related to Occurrence of Major Plant Groups and Fungi

Era	Period	Epoch	Estimated time, in 10^6 years, from beginning of epoch	Probable time of origin of plant groups
Cenozoic	Quaternary	Recent		
		Pleistocene	1.5–2	
	Tertiary	Pliocene	7	
		Miocene	26	
		Oligocene	37–38	
		Eocene	53–54	
		Paleocene	65	
Mesozoic	Cretaceous	Upper (Late)		
		Lower (Early)		—— Angiosperms
			140	
	Jurassic	Upper (Late)		
		Middle (Middle)		
		Lower (Early)		
			200	
	Triassic	Upper (Late)		
		Middle (Middle)		
		Lower (Early)		
			240	
Paleozoic	Permian			
			280	
	Carboniferous			
	Pennsylvanian	Upper (Late)		
		Middle (Middle)		
		Lower (Early)		—— Mosses
			320	
	Mississippian	Upper (Late)		
		Lower (Early)		—— Gymnosperms
	Devonian	Upper (Late)	360	<—— Liverworts
		Middle (Middle)		—— Pteridophytes
				—— Trimerophytophytes
		Lower (Early)		—— Zosterophyllophytes
			395	—— Microphyllophytes
	Silurian	Upper (Late)		
			430–440	—— Rhyniophytes
	Ordovician	Upper (Late)		
		Middle (Middle)		
		Lower (Early)	500	
	Cambrian	Upper (Late)		
		Middle (Middle)		
		Lower (Early)		
			570	
Precambrian			2000	—— Algae
			3100	—— Blue-green algae,
			4500	bacteria, and fungi

phyta, the arthrophytes; and Division Pteridophyta, the ferns. The first three groups are discussed in this chapter and the fourth in Chapter 7.

DIVISION PSILOTOPHYTA

In the extinct Devonian (Table 6.1) floras, there were several kinds of vascular plants without leaves and roots. These are known through such examples as well-preserved specimens of *Rhynia,* a member of a group of extinct plants classified in the Division Rhyniophyta (p. 164). Among extant plants, *Psilotum* (the whisk fern, Figure 6.1*a*) is one of the very few that display somewhat similar organization. The superficially leafy genus *Tmesipteris* is fundamentally similar in organization to *Psilotum.* Both are psilotophytes.

Psilotum

Psilotum nudum (Figure 6.1) is a herbaceous, dichotomously branching plant approximately 2 feet in height. Its axes (both the erect ones and the rhizomes) contain vascular tissue (Figure 6.2). The plant is tropical and subtropical in habitat. Sometimes it is **epiphytic,** that is, it grows upon other plants, presumably using them only for support. In the United States *Psilotum* occurs in Hawaii, Florida, Louisiana, Arizona, South Carolina, and Texas.

Psilotum plants consist of dichotomously branching rhizomes and erect stems as tall as 18 to 24 inches. The stems arise by upgrowth of some of the rhizome tips. This can be stimulated by exposing them to light. The erect axes are ridged in various patterns and the number of ridges varies with the level above the point of origin from the rhizome, being fewer distally. The erect axes bear small leaflike appendages, called **bracts** or **prophylls** (Figure 6.1*b*).

a   *b*

Figure 6.1 *Psilotum nudum.* (*a*) Habit of growth. (*b*) Portion of axis with bracts or prophylls.

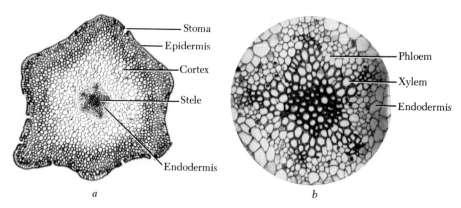

Figure 6.2 *Psilotum nudum.* (*a*) Transection of stem. (*b*) Stele, more highly magnified.

Because these usually lack vascular tissue, they are not recognized as leaves by most botanists, although they may be leaf precursors or reduced structures. The evidence for this is the presence in some instances of traces that depart from the stem stele toward the prophyll base, albeit they do not enter it.

Branching of the erect stems and rhizomes is dichotomous and initiated at the apices, and growth may be traced to a single apical cell. The stele in *Psilotum* has been interpreted as a protostele or as a siphonostele. This is because the center of the stele consists of thick-walled, nonliving **sclerenchyma cells,** which conceivably could represent either a sclerotic pith or part of the primary xylem. The latter is surrounded by primary phloem. The stele in both the erect branches and rhizomes is bounded externally by an endodermis, the innermost layer of the cortex. The latter consists of three different tissues: (1) an outer, photosynthetic layer adjacent to the epidermis; (2) a zone of sclerenchyma cells; and (3) an inner zone of parenchyma cells, which probably function in storage. Externally, the erect axes are bounded by a heavily cutinized epidermis with stomata and guard cells (Figure 6.2). Some of the surface cells of the rhizome produce one- to several-celled rhizoids. Its cortical cells may contain fungi, whose role is obscure at present. Such an association of fungi with rhizomes (and roots, if present) of vascular plants is called a **mycorrhiza.** Roots and vascularized leaves are absent in *Psilotum.*

In mature plants many of the axes become fertile, producing trilobed **synangia** on very short lateral branches, which also bear two bracts (Figure 6.3*a,b*). The synangia are thus **cauline,** or borne on stems. A synangium consists of several fused or united sporangia. In *Psilotum* each synangial lobe undergoes dehiscence when the spores are mature. Meiosis in *Psilotum,* as in mosses, liverworts, hornworts, and all vascular plants, is sporic; it occurs when the spores (meiospores) arise in groups of four from the diploid sporocytes or spore mother cells in the synangia. When the spores have matured, the syn-

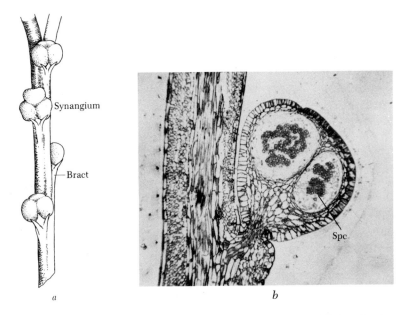

Figure 6.3 *Psilotum nudum.* (*a*) Portion of axis with synangia. (*b*) Longisection of stem and synangium. Dark cells in synangium are sporocytes, Spc.

angia crack open and the smooth-walled spores are disseminated. As in all plants with sporic meiosis and morphological alternation of generations, the spores in further development produce the sexual gametophytic phase. *Psilotum* and all the vascular cryptogams are dibiontic, that is, both the gametophyte and sporophyte are free-living, individual entities.

The spores of *Psilotum* germinate very slowly, about six months after they have been planted or fall on a suitable substrate, and then only in darkness. In nature or in the greenhouse, the gametophyte of *Psilotum* is a minute (about 2 millimeters in diameter), subterranean, branched cylindrical structure (Figure 6.4a) devoid of chlorophyll and, therefore, saprophytic. In some instances, only the antheridia and archegonia (Figure 6.4a,b) enable one to distinguish the gametophyte with certainty from the young sporophytic axis. The gametophyte, like the rhizome, contains mycorrhizal fungi and is covered by rhizoids.

After fertilization is effected by a multiflagellate sperm, the zygote undergoes nuclear and cell division to form a young sporophyte, which at first is attached to the gametophyte (Figure 6.5) by a foot, which probably absorbs food for the sporophyte. Development of the gametophyte from the spore and of the sporophyte from the zygote are both rather slow processes in *Psilotum*.

Psilotum and certain extinct fossil psilotophytes that are similar in organization are unique among vascular plants in lacking both roots and leaves.

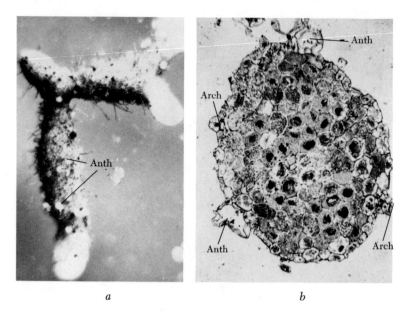

a   b

Figure 6.4 *Psilotum nudum.* (*a*) Enlarged view of cylindrical gametophyte. (*b*) Transection of gametophyte. Anth, antheridia; Arch, archegonia. [Courtesy of Professor David Bierhorst.]

Until recently, most botanists have interpreted them as primitive plants, not greatly modified from their hypothetical, sporophytic, algal progenitors (see, however, p. 125 for a different viewpoint).

It is of interest that two races of *Psilotum nudum* occur, one diploid with haploid gametophytes ($n = 52$ to 54 chromosomes) and one tetraploid with diploid gametophytes. In some of the latter, a vascular strand surrounded by an endodermis is present; the strand may be discontinuous. The presence of vascular tissue in both gametophyte and sporophyte suggests the fundamental similarity between the alternating generations. Furthermore, it is again clear that the chromosome number itself does not determine whether sporophytic or gametophytic characters prevail. The mechanism that controls this is still obscure.

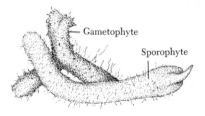

Figure 6.5 *Psilotum nudum,* young sporophyte still attached to gametophyte (foot not visible).

Tmesipteris

The superficially leafy genus *Tmesipteris*[2] (Figure 6.6), fundamentally similar in organization to *Psilotum,* occurs natively in New Caledonia, Australia, and New Zealand. Depending on the species, the plants may be either erect or pendulous epiphytes. The flattened, leaflike appendages, each with a single vein, are usually interpreted as stem branches. Associated with some of these appendages are bilobed synangia, the spores of which develop into cylindrical subterranean gametophytes much like those of *Psilotum.* However, one of the leading students of the group regards *Tmesipteris* as a primitive fern and the axes with their bladelike appendages as pinnately compound leaves. The cylindrical, subterranean, saprophytic, mycorrhizal gametophytes of *Tmesipteris* and *Psilotum* were considered to be almost unique, but Dr. D. W. Bierhorst has found similar ones in certain ferns, namely, *Schizaea melanesica* and *Stromatopteris moniliformis.* Furthermore, the embryogeny and the subterranean and erect axes of these ferns are similar to those of *Psilotum* and *Tmesipteris,* at the same time showing such fernlike attributes as circinate vernation (see page 151) and frondlike organization. In light of these and other similarities, Bierhorst has recommended that *Psilotum* and *Tmesipteris* be classified as primitive members of the Pteridophyta (ferns) rather than as the Psilotophyta; the latter category would then contain only extinct plants.

On the other hand, the ferns in question do have roots and their sporangia differ considerably in organization from those of *Tmesipteris* and *Psilotum. Psilotum* is in some respects (absence of roots and leaves, dichotomous erect branches and rhizomes) similar to the extinct *Rhynia* (see Figure 7.16) and *Sawdonia* (see Figure 7.18*b*), which flourished in Devonian times. How-

Figure 6.6 *Tmesipteris* sp., living plant from the Philippines [Courtesy of Dr. Don Reynolds.]

[2]The first "t" is silent.

ever, 400 million years intervene between these extinct fossils and the extant *Psilotum,* so that one must be cautious in suggesting relationships.

DIVISION MICROPHYLLOPHYTA

A second group of vascular plants with Devonian (Table 6.1) precursors comprises the club and spike "mosses." Two series of these are distinguishable among both the living and fossil members of the group on the basis of whether or not their leaves bear ligules. A **ligule** is a minute tonguelike appendage borne within the tissue at the base of the microphyllous leaves in certain genera, such as *Selaginella* and *Isoetes. Lycopodium,* which lacks ligules, will be discussed first. All the members of this group have vascularized leaves and roots.

Lycopodium and *Selaginella* have been called "mosses" because living species are for the most part small-leaved, herbaceous plants. The "club" and "spike" portions of their names refer to the localization of spore-bearing leaves, called **sporophylls,** at the tips of certain branches with short internodes; such branches are known as **strobili** (Figure 6.8*a*) or **cones.** A **strobilus** is a stem with short internodes and spore-bearing appendages at its nodes.

Three of the living genera, *Lycopodium, Selaginella,* and *Isoetes,* which belong to this division, are rather widely distributed in both temperate and tropical habitats. A fourth, *Stylites* (similar to *Isoetes*), grows in the Andes mountains of Peru, and a fifth, *Phylloglossum* (Figure 6.7), is native to New Zealand and Australia.

Lycopodium

Species of *Lycopodium,* commonly known as "ground pine" and "trailing evergreen," are abundant on the floor of coniferous forests of the temperate zone, although some tropical species are epiphytes.

A comparison of the plant body of *Lycopodium* (Figure 6.8) and other club mosses with that of *Psilotum* at once reveals two striking differences: unlike *Psilotum,* the club mosses have both vascularized leaves with stomata, and roots. The axes elongate by growth of the apices and produce a profusion of small, mosslike leaves, each with a single unbranched vein. Leaves with single, unbranched veins, the traces of which do not leave marked gaps (see Figures 5.17*a, c* and 6.9) as they leave the vascular system of the stem, are called **microphylls.** The stem in most species of *Lycopodium* contains some type of protostele (Figure 6.9), as do the roots, which branch dichotomously. Because of the dense arrangement of the leaves and shortness of the internodes, leaf traces are always visible in transections of the stem.

The sporangia of *Lycopodium* are borne at or near the bases of certain leaves and on their upper (adaxial) surfaces (Figure 6.10*a*). Such fertile leaves

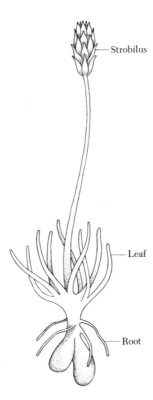

Figure 6.7 *Phylloglossum drummondii.*

are known as **sporophylls.** In some species of *Lycopodium,* there is evidence that every leaf potentially is a sporophyll (Figure 6.8*b*). In *L. lucidulum,* for example, zones of sporophylls alternate with zones of sterile leaves (Figure 6.8*b, c*). In many others, only the apical leaves of certain branches are fertile; they are associated in strobili. Each sporangium produces a number of sporogenous cells; these enlarge, often separate from one another, become spherical, and function as sporocytes. They then undergo meiosis and give rise to tetrads of haploid spores (meiospores). When the spores have matured, each sporangium develops a fissure through which the spores are disseminated.

When the spores separate from the tetrad, they may be seen to have markings on their walls (Figure 6.10*b*) where the members of the tetrad formerly cohered. These markings are known as **triradiate ridges.** Any spores, living or fossil, which have triradiate ridges are assumed to have arisen from sporocytes that underwent meiosis.

The spores of some species of *Lycopodium* (*L. obscurum, L. complanatum*) germinate very slowly in nature, and the resultant gametophytes (Figure 6.11) are subterranean fleshy structures several millimeters long and devoid of chlorophyll. They contain mycorrhizal fungi and lead a saprophytic existence.

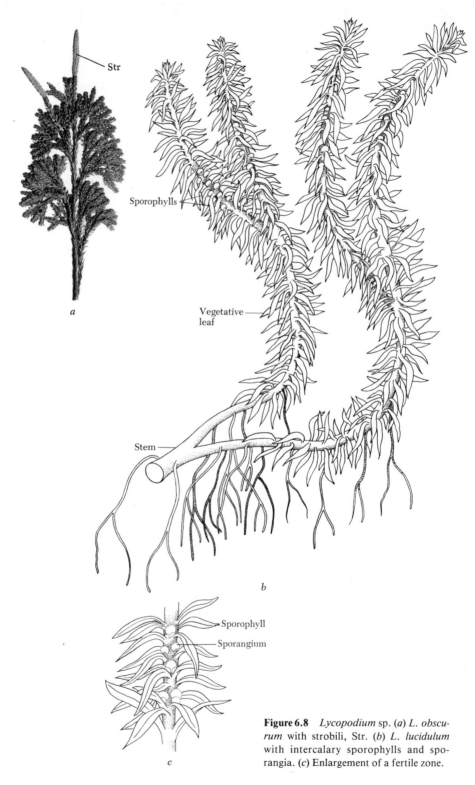

Str

Sporophylls

Vegetative
leaf

Stem

a

b

Sporophyll

Sporangium

c

Figure 6.8 *Lycopodium* sp. (*a*) *L. obscurum* with strobili, Str. (*b*) *L. lucidulum* with intercalary sporophylls and sporangia. (*c*) Enlargement of a fertile zone.

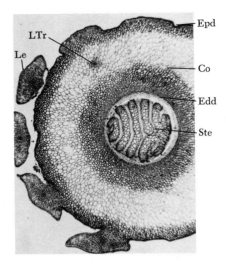

Figure 6.9 *Lycopodium clavatum,* transection of stem. Co, cortex; Epd, epidermis; Edd, endodermis; Le, leaf; LTr, leaf trace; Ste, stele (plectostele; see Figure 5.11).

Their slow germination has been speeded in laboratory culture by subjecting them to sulfuric acid, which softens the spore wall. The spores of other species (*L. cernuum*) germinate more rapidly and form epiterranean gametophytes with fleshy bases and green, photosynthetic lobes. The bases contain mycorrhizal fungi. Gametophytes without mycorrhizal fungi have been grown in culture for some species, the gametophytes of which contain fungi in nature.

After fertilization of an egg by a biflagellate sperm, the zygote develops into an embryonic sporophyte (Figure 6.11*b, c*). The early leaves of this sporophyte lack vascular tissue, although typical microphylls develop later. The gametophytes of a number of species are quite persistent, and are recognizable long after the embryonic sporophytes have become established. The life cycle of *Lycopodium* is summarized in Figure 6.12.

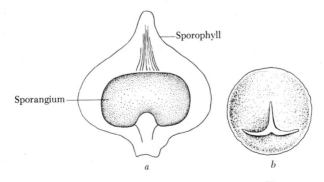

Figure 6.10 (*a*) *Lycopodium obscurum,* adaxial view of sporophyll and sporangium. (*b*) Spore showing triradiate ridge.

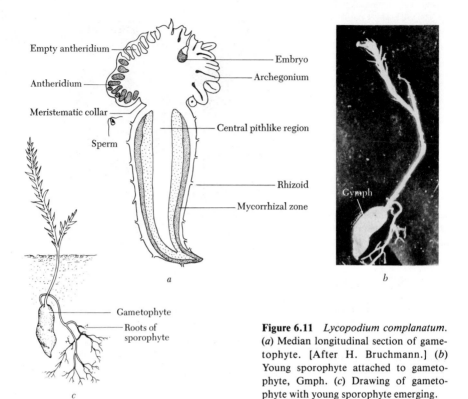

Figure 6.11 *Lycopodium complanatum.*
(*a*) Median longitudinal section of gametophyte. [After H. Bruchmann.] (*b*)
Young sporophyte attached to gametophyte, Gmph. (*c*) Drawing of gametophyte with young sporophyte emerging.

Selaginella

Selaginella, the spike "moss," belongs to that series of Microphyllophyta in which the leaves have basal ligules. It is a large genus containing
several hundred species, many of them tropical and hydrophytic. *Selaginella
apoda* is a creeping hydrophytic species similar to the African *S. kraussiana*
(Figure 6.13*a*). Some species of *Selaginella,* by repeated branching in one plane,
produce frondose branches as in *S. pallescens* (Figure 6.14*a, c*).

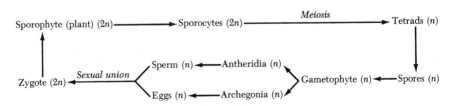

Figure 6.12   Diagrammatic summary of the life cycle of *Lycopodium.*

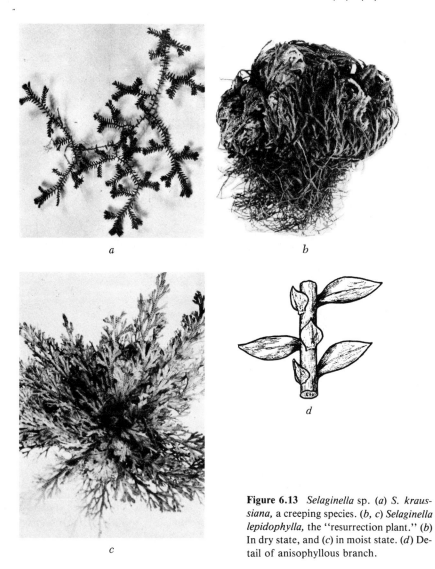

a

b

c

d

Figure 6.13 *Selaginella* sp. (*a*) *S. kraussiana,* a creeping species. (*b, c*) *Selaginella lepidophylla,* the "resurrection plant." (*b*) In dry state, and (*c*) in moist state. (*d*) Detail of anisophyllous branch.

Several species of *Selaginella,* by contrast, live a xerophytic existence in arid habitats or those subject to periodic desiccation. Among these are *S. lepidophylla* (Figure 6.13*b, c*), the resurrection plant of the southwestern United States, and *S. arenicola,* which grows largely on exposed rocky situations in the southern United States.

In some species (*S. riddellii*) the microphylls are equal in size and borne spirally on the stems (Figure 6.14*b*). In many others (*S. kraussiana, S. lepidophylla,* Figure 6.13*a, c*), a dimorphism in leaves accompanies dorsiventrality

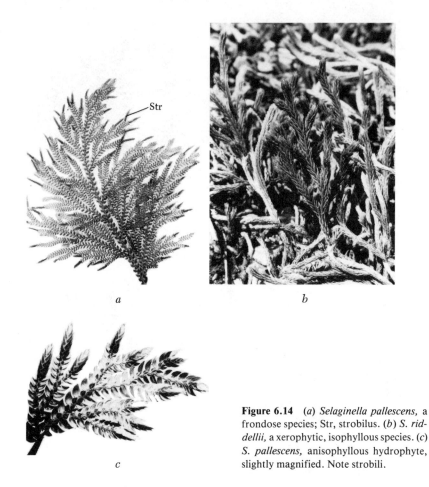

a

b

c

Figure 6.14   (*a*) *Selaginella pallescens,* a frondose species; Str, strobilus. (*b*) *S. riddellii,* a xerophytic, isophyllous species. (*c*) *S. pallescens,* anisophyllous hydrophyte, slightly magnified. Note strobili.

of the axes. Here the leaves are borne in four rows on the stems, two dorsal and two ventral, the dorsal leaves being markedly smaller. In this case the plants are said to be **anisophyllous** (Figure 6.13*d*), in contrast to the species with uniform leaves, which are **isophyllous.**

The leaves themselves have single unbranched veins and stomata borne along the midrib on their lower (abaxial) surface. Growth of the stems is apical. In the mature region of the stem a transection (Figure 6.15) reveals the presence of a cutinized epidermis without stomata, a broad cortex and, depending on the species, one or more protosteles. These may be present in the center of a cavity and connected to its walls by elongate endodermal cells. Each leaf receives a single trace from the stem stele.

Long, naked axes, the **rhizophores,** extend from the stems to the soil, where they branch dichotomously to form a mass of small roots. The nature of the rhizophore has been a subject of dispute, some botanists considering it

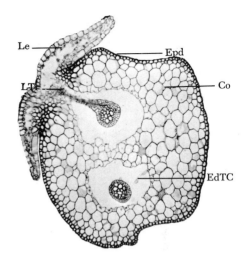

Figure 6.15 *Selaginella caulescens,* transection of stem at a node. Co, cortex; Epd, epidermis; EdTC, endodermal trabecular cell; Le, leaf; Ltr, leaf trace.

to be a stem because it may, under certain circumstances, produce leaves, and others interpreting rhizophores and roots together as a root system.

The sporophylls in all species of *Selaginella* occur in more or less compact strobili, are equal in size, and arranged in four vertical rows (Figure 6.16*a*).

Sporogenesis in *Selaginella* is especially significant and instructive. The sporophylls of a particular strobilus produce some sporangia that develop essentially like those of *Psilotum* and *Lycopodium,* resulting in the production of a large number of spores (Figures 6.16*b* and 6.17 left) by the meiotic division of the sporocytes. In other sporangia in the strobili of *Selaginella,* however, development of most of the sporocytes is arrested before meiosis; in most cases, only one sporocyte in such a sporangium completes the meiotic process, while the remainder degenerate. As the single spore tetrad forms, there is available a vast amount of nutritive material originally incorporated within the aborted sporocytes. The members of the single tetrad apparently absorb this and other material, enlarging enormously until they actually distend the sporangial wall (Figures 6.16*c* and 6.17 right). These large spores are called **megaspores** (Figure 6.18); the cells from which they arise are **megasporocytes.** In contrast, the ordinary-sized spores have come to be called **microspores** (Figure 6.18), although they are about the same size as the spores of many other plants that lack this spore dimorphism or **heterospory.** The sporangia that bear megaspores are **megasporangia** (on **megasporophylls**), while the microspores arise in **microsporangia** (on **microsporophylls**). *Selaginella,* with its two kinds of spores, is **heterosporous,** whereas *Phylloglossum, Lycopodium, Psilotum,* mosses, liverworts, and hornworts are **homosporous.**

In all heterosporous plants, microspores develop into male gametophytes

a

Figure 6.16 *Selaginella pallescens.* (*a*) Strobilus, enlarged. (*b*) Adaxial view of microsporophyll. (*c*) Adaxial view of megasporophyll.

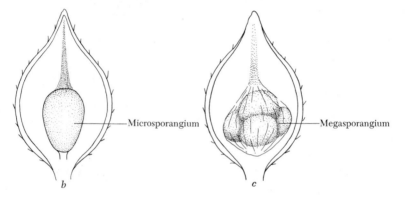

Microsporangium

Megasporangium

b   *c*

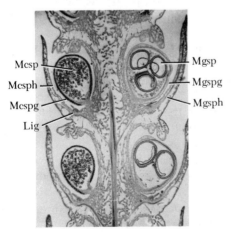

Mcsp

Mcsph

Mcspg

Lig

Mgsp

Mgspg

Mgsph

Figure 6.17 *Selaginella* sp., portion of a longitudinal section of the strobilus. Lig, ligule; Mgspg, megasporangium; Mgsp, megaspore; Mgsph, megasporophyll; Mcspg, microsporangium; Mcsp, microspore; Mcsph, microsporophyll.

Figure 6.18 *Selaginella pallescens,* megaspores and microspores. Note triradiate ridge on megaspore. [Courtesy of Dr. William Ruf and Dr. Michael Hoban.]

and megaspores into female gametophytes. Early or complete development may occur within the spore wall and is, accordingly, termed **endosporic.**

The microspore forms the male gametophyte internally (Figure 6.19*a–c*) by nuclear and cell divisions. The male gametophyte consists largely of an antheridium composed of spermatogenous tissue surrounded by a jacket of sterile cells and of one additional cell (the smaller of the first two formed), often called the **prothallial cell** or **sterile cell.** About 128 to 256 biflagellate sperms are produced. The male gametophytes may protrude from the microspore wall before the sperms are mature. Ultimately, mature sperms are freed from the gametophytes (Figure 6.20*c*).

The female gametophytes, which develop largely within the megaspore walls in early development, arise by a process called **free-nuclear division.** This is initiated by the megaspore nucleus, which undergoes division not followed immediately by cytokinesis, so two nuclei lie free in the same cytoplasm (Figure 6.19*d*). These continue to divide until numerous nuclei are formed just below the triradiate ridge. Ultimately, cytokineses occur, so the multinucleate cytoplasm is divided into gametophytic cells just under the triradiate ridge. Expansion of these cells ruptures the megaspore coat. Several archegonia are then organized on the surface of the female gametophyte (Figure 6.19*e*). These have short necks composed of two tiers of four cells (Figure 6.20*b*). Three tufts of rhizoids develop from lobes of the protuberant female gametophyte (Figures 6.19*e, f* and 6.20*a*).

Both the male and female gametophytes lack chlorophyll and are saprophytic. Their development to maturity is dependent entirely on metabolites stored in the microspores and megaspores.

In some species of *Selaginella (S. riddellii, S. peruviana)* the spores remain uninucleate, and germination does not occur until after the spores have been shed. In most others, however, germination is precocious, the spores

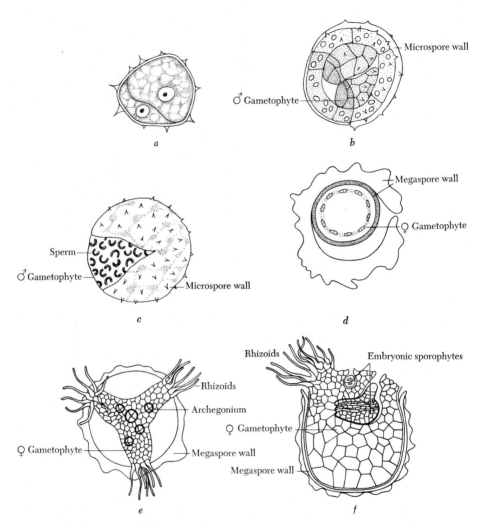

Figure 6.19 *Selaginella* sp. (*a–c*) Development of the male and (*d*), (*f*) female gametophytes. (*e*) Development of female gametophyte, in apical view. (*f*) Megaspore, female gametophyte, and embryos.

undergoing nuclear and cell division before they have been shed from their sporangia. The male gametophytes may mature, that is, contain ripe sperm, and the female gametophytes may have young archegonia before the microspores and megaspores have been shed. Fertilization occasionally occurs while the megaspores and their contained gametophytes are still in the megasporangia (Dr. E. W. Ruf, Jr., personal communication).

   Although more than one egg may be fertilized by a biflagellate sperm, usually only one zygote develops into an embryonic sporophyte (Figure 6.19*f*).

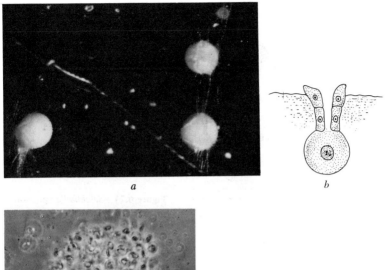

a *b*

c

Figure 6.20   (*a*) *Selaginella lepidophylla,* photomicrograph of living megaspores and female gametophytes. (*b*) Archegonium in longisection. (*c*) *S. pallescens.* Microspore with male gametophyte liberating sperm. [*a* and *c* courtesy of Dr. William Ruf.]

As the latter grows, it emerges from the female gametophyte and megaspore (Figure 6.21), its foot remaining in contact with the former. In *Selaginella,* as in other plants, the embryonic or primary root may be called the **radicle** and the two (in *Selaginella*) primary leaves are often called **cotyledons.**

A number of phenomena that occur in the reproduction of *Selaginella* just summarized also characterize the reproductive process in seed plants. These include (1) localization of sporangium-bearing appendages in strobili, (2) heterospory, (3) endosporic and intrasporangial development of the gametophytes (in some species) and dioecious gametophytes. The life cycle of *Selaginella* is summarized in Figure 6.22.

Isoetes

Although the leaves of the quillwort, *Isoetes* (Figure 6.23), are much larger than those of *Lycopodium* or *Selaginella,* these leaves are considered to be microphylls because they have single, unbranched veins, and their traces

Figure 6.21 *Selaginella* sp., young sporophyte, Spph, attached to gametophyte within megaspore, Mgsp; Rt, root.

do not leave gaps as they pass out from the stem stele. The various species of *Isoetes* are either submerged aquatics or terrestrial, living in marshy areas. The quill-like leaves arise spirally from an extremely short, fleshy, cormlike structure (Figure 6.23). The leaves are traversed longitudinally by four air chambers.

A sectional view of the "corm" (Figure 6.24) reveals that it is composed of two regions, an upper portion from which the leaves arise and a lower from which the roots arise. The lower surface contains a furrow or groove from the flanks of which the dichotomously branching roots emerge. Internally, the stele consists of a central mass of xylem surrounded by phloem, sometimes called the "prismatic layer." There are few actual conducting cells or tracheids in the xylem, apparently a reflection of the aquatic habitat of the plant. Out-

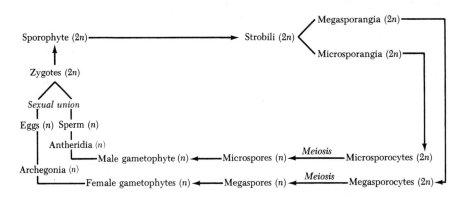

Figure 6.22 Diagrammatic summary of the life cycle of *Selaginella*.

Figure 6.23 *Isoetes lithophila,* single plant washed free of soil.

side the stele is a cylinder of meristematic cells called the cambium or lateral meristem. This adds mostly parenchyma cells to the cortex, the outer surface of which is eroded each season as older leaf bases disintegrate. The apical meristem is sunken in a depression at the top of the corm (Figure 6.24) and growth in the length of the latter is very slow.

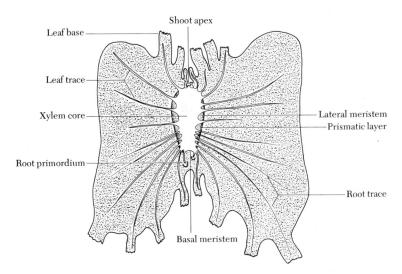

Figure 6.24 *Isoetes* sp., diagrammatic longisection of "corm." [After D. J. Paolillo.]

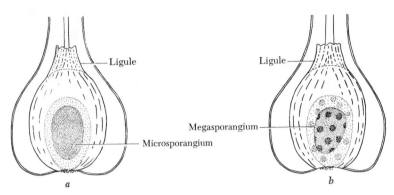

Figure 6.25 *Isoetes* sp. (*a*) Adaxial view of microsporophyll and microsporangium. (*b*) Adaxial view of megasporophyll and megasporangium.

Every leaf of an *Isoetes* plant is potentially a fertile sporophyll; like *Selaginella, Isoetes* is heterosporous (Figure 6.25). The massive sporangia are partially partitioned by septa covered by a **tapetum,** a nutritive tissue. Unlike those of *Selaginella,* each megasporangium produces several hundred megaspores, while the microsporangium produces up to a million microspores. The leaves and sporophylls of both *Selaginella* and *Isoetes* have at their bases the small appendages known as the ligules (Figure 6.25).

The spores of *Isoetes* do not germinate until after they have been set free by decay of their sporangia, differing in this respect from the spores of *Selaginella.* The endosporic gametophytes (Figure 6.26*a, b*) are much like those of *Selaginella* (Figure 6.19), but the sperms of *Isoetes* are multiflagellate and only four are produced by each male gametophyte. An embryonic sporophyte, emergent from the female gametophyte and megaspore, is illustrated in Figure 6.26*d.*

It is sometimes maintained that *Isoetes,* with multiflagellate sperms, persistent leaf bases, and secondary growth in the stem, is too different from *Lycopodium* and *Selaginella* to be included in the Microphyllophyta and that it should be classified in a group of its own, but this view has not gained wide acceptance.

DIVISION ARTHROPHYTA

Both woody and herbaceous arthrophytes inhabited the earth in Pennsylvanian times (Table 6.1). Their fossil remains are at once recognizable by the whorled arrangement of their branches and fertile appendages, and in many cases by their ridged stems. The clearly defined nodes and internodes give the plant a jointed appearance, and have suggested the name arthrophytes.

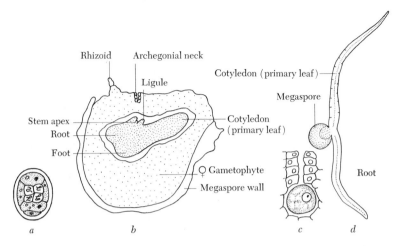

Figure 6.26 (a) *Isoetes lacustris*. Section of microspore containing mature gametophyte. Note prothallial cell (bottom cell), jacket cells, and four spermatogenous cells. [After J. Leibig.] (b) *Isoetes lithophila*. Sectional view of megaspore with mature gametophyte and young embryo. (c) Single archegonium, median longitudinal section. [b and c after C. Lamotte.] (d) Juvenile sporophyte attached to gametophyte within megaspore.

This third group of seedless vascular plants, far more widespread and abundant in Pennsylvanian times (see Table 6.1) than at present, is represented in our living flora only by *Equisetum* (Figure 6.27). Species of this genus are known as "horsetails," "pipes," and "scouring rushes," the last name being inspired by the siliceous texture of some of the species.

Equisetum

The whorled habit of growth of arthrophytes is well illustrated by branching species of *Equisetum,* such as *E. arvense* and *E. telmateia* (Figure 6.27a). In these, a circle of branches originates at each node. Other species, such as *E. hyemale* (Figure 6.27b), are unbranched during most of the growing season. If their stem apices are cut off, lateral branches may develop at the nodes; this is an example of apical dominance in which auxins from the apical meristem inhibit the expansion of lateral buds. After the stem apex has differentiated into a strobilus, branches may develop at some of the nodes below.

The nodes are marked by a leaf sheath composed of a number of minute, toothlike leaves joined at their bases (Figure 6.28). The photosynthetic activity of the leaves is negligible; the bulk of photosynthesis occurs in the vertical, ribbed stems, as in *Psilotum*. These erect stems arise from deeply subterranean rhizomes that bear whorls of wiry roots and may produce tu-

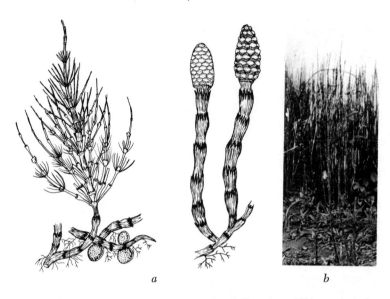

Figure 6.27 (*a*) *Equisetum arvense,* vegetative (left) and strobiliferous branches arising from rhizome. (*b*) *Equisetum hyemale,* growth habit.

berlike structures (Figure 6.27*a*). The roots and stems of *Equisetum* develop from apical meristems in which single, prominent apical cells are present.

Intercalary meristematic tissue persists at each node and may give rise to adventitious roots as well as add to the length of a given internode. It has been shown that branches of *E. hyemale* detached from a colony of plants

Figure 6.28 *Equisetum hyemale,* portion of axis magnified to show ridges and leaves at nodal region. [Courtesy of Dr. William Ruf.]

may be carried downstream and develop roots en route, a probable means of vegetative propagation.

Figure 6.29*a* illustrates the transection of an internode of an *Equisetum* stem. The vascular tissue forms a circle of discrete strands, a eustele. At maturity the vascular tissue of each strand is associated with a canal (Figure 6.29*b*) that lies on the same radius as a surface ridge. The central part of the pith is absent. A prominent endodermis is present outside the circle of vascular bundles and, in some species, inside this circle as well. The cortex also has canals; these correspond in position to the valleys of the ridged stem surface. The epidermal cells are silicified, and numerous stomata and guard cells occur on the flanks of the ridges. The stomata are sunken below the surface cells.

As in the spike mosses and most club mosses, the sporangia of *Equisetum* are localized in strobili (Figures 6.30 and 6.31). In the common *Equisetum arvense,* the strobiliferous branches, which appear early in the spring, lack chorophyll. As they shed their homosporous spores, green vegetative shoots develop from other buds on the same rhizome. In such evergreen species as *Equisetum hyemale,* by contrast, the strobili arise at the tips of the vegetative shoots as these shoots mature (Figure 6.30*b*). The appendages that bear the sporangia in *Equisetum* are known as **sporangiophores,** rather than sporophylls, inasmuch as good evidence from the study of fossils indicates that these appendages are not leaves. Each sporangiophore bears from 5 to 10 cylindrical sporangia on its adaxial surface (Figure 6.30*c*). These sporangia contain sporogenous tissues that give rise successively during the stages of maturation to sporocytes, tetrads, and mature spores (meiospores) as the meiotic process takes place.

The spores of the homosporous arthrophyte *Equisetum* are remarkable because of their appendages, the **elaters,** which arise by the cracking of the outermost layer of the spore wall (Figure 6.31*b*). The elaters are exceedingly sensitive to moisture, contracting and expanding with slight variations in rel-

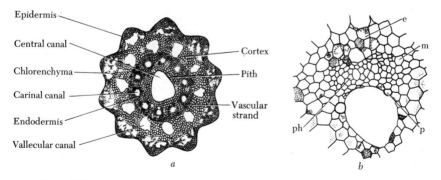

Figure 6.29 *Equisetum arvense. (a)* Transection of erect stem. (*b*) Single vascular strand, more highly magnified: e, endodermis; m and p, cells of xylem; ph, phloem.

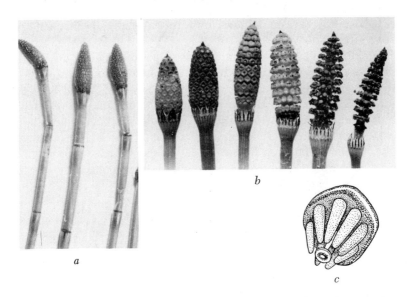

Figure 6.30 Strobili of *Equisetum*. (*a*) *E. arvense.* (*b*) *E. hyemale,* vegetative branches with terminal strobili, increasingly mature, left to right. (*c*) *E. arvense,* sporangiophore and sporangia. [Courtesy of Dr. William Ruf.]

ative humidity. These elaters differ, of course, from liverwort elaters, which are cellular. The thin-walled green spores are liberated from the strobili by elongation of the internodes, curvature of the sporangiophore stalks, and bursting of the sporangia; they germinate rapidly (Figure 6.31*c*).

The richly chlorophyllous spores of *Equisetum* develop on moist soil into minute, moundlike green gametophytes (Figure 6.32*a*). These grow at their margins and their rhizoids penetrate the substratum.

The gametophytes consist of solid tissue near the substrate and bear green lamellate branches that rise above the substrate (Figure 6.32*a*). There is good evidence that the gametophytes are of two kinds with respect to the production of sex organs. Some produce only antheridia, while others produce archegonia first and antheridia later. This arrangement, which occurs also in certain ferns, is a mechanism that favors out-crossing or cross-fertilization, but one which also makes possible self-fertilization. The antheridia are borne near the apices of the photosynthetic lamellae and, accordingly, above the surface of the substrate. The sperms are multiflagellated. The archegonia are borne on the solid tissue at the base of the lamellae. Their necks have four rows of neck cells, the most distal tier flaring and divergent at maturity.

In *Equisetum,* after fertilization, a number of zygotes develop into sporophytes (Figure 6.32*b*). These consist in the juvenile stage of an absorptive foot, an erect shoot composed of nodes and internodes, and a radicle, which penetrates the soil. Apical growth of both the root and shoot soon establish

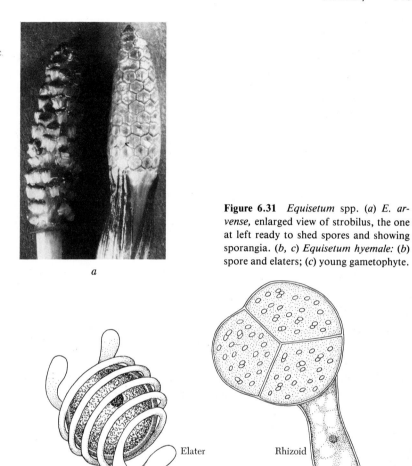

Figure 6.31 *Equisetum* spp. (*a*) *E. arvense,* enlarged view of strobilus, the one at left ready to shed spores and showing sporangia. (*b, c*) *Equisetum hyemale:* (*b*) spore and elaters; (*c*) young gametophyte.

a

Elater   Rhizoid

b   *c*

the young sporophyte as an independent plant, although the gametophyte is long-persistent in laboratory cultures.

SUMMARY

The Microphyllophyta and Arthrophyta, and probably the Psilotophyta, represent ancient lines of plant life with few present survivors. These groups can be traced back in the fossil record through the Devonian (see Table 6.1). Although living members of these groups are herbaceous, relatively small, in-

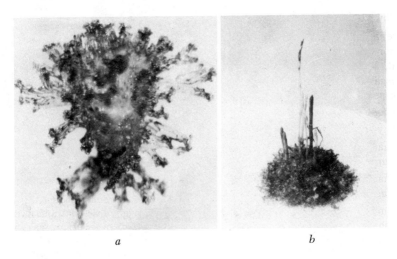

a   *b*

Figure 6.32 *Equisetum hyemale.* (*a*) Living gametophyte. (*b*) Gametophyte with young sporophytes attached.

conspicuous plants, woody treelike members were abundant during the Carboniferous (see Table 6.1 on p. 120).

Generally, the living representatives are either leafless (Psilotophyta) or microphyllous (Microphyllophyta), although the leaves of *Equisetum* may be much-reduced megaphylls. The sporangia of these plants are borne either at the tips of stem branches (as in Psilotophyta and *Equisetum*) or in association with leaves (as in Microphyllophyta). The sporangium-bearing appendages of *Equisetum, Selaginella,* and most species of *Lycopodium* are grouped in strobili.

All the living genera alternate a dominant, free-living sporophytic phase with a less conspicuous gametophytic phase. *Selaginella,* however, exhibits extreme reduction of the gametophytic phase along with a tendency to retain the gametophytes upon the sporophyte, both of which are characteristic of seed plants (see Chapters 8 and 9). The affinities of *Psilotum* in relation to the fossil record are not clear.

QUESTIONS FOR REVIEW

1. Name the divisions of vascular cryptogams and give their vernacular names.
2. In what respects does *Psilotum* differ from other vascular cryptogams?
3. Define or explain cryptogam, vascular and nonvascular cryptogam, phanerogam, prophyll, cauline, mycorrhiza, synangium, meiospore.
4. Of what significance do you consider the fact that diploid gametophytes of *Psilotum* may contain vascular tissue?

5. Why are *Psilotum* and *Tmesipteris* sometimes classified with ferns?

6. Define or explain microphyll, strobilus, sporophyll, sporangiophore, ligule, homospory, heterospory, triradiate ridge, rhizophore, isophyllous, anisophyllous, adaxial, abaxial, megasporocyte, microsporocyte, megasporophyll, microsporophyll; megasporangium, microsporangium; megaspore and microspore; prothallial cell, suspensor, foot, cotyledon, free-nuclear division.

7. Where may spore germination occur in the genus *Selaginella*?

8. Why are some species of *Equisetum* called "scouring rushes"?

9. What is the distribution of archegonia and antheridia in the gametophytes of *Equisetum*?

10. What type of nutrition characterizes the gametophytes of *Psilotum, Lycopodium, Selaginella, Isoetes,* and *Equisetum*?

11. Compare and contrast the vegetative and reproductive characteristics of the sporophytes of the vascular cryptogams discussed in this chapter.

12. Compare and contrast the vegetative and reproductive characteristics of the gametophytes of the vascular cryptogams discussed in this chapter.

CHAPTER SEVEN

Seedless Vascular Plants II: Division Pteridophyta and Fossil Seedless Vascular Plants

DIVISION PTERIDOPHYTA

Of the seedless vascular plants, the Psilotophyta, Microphyllophyta, and Arthrophyta have few representatives in our present flora. By contrast the Pteridophyta[1] (ferns), although probably equally ancient in origin (see Table 6.1), apparently have been more successful in competing for survival. This chapter includes both an account of the Pteridophyta and a comparative summary of the seedless vascular plants and some of their fossil precursors.

Because of the aesthetic appeal of their foliage, ferns are widely cultivated and appreciated. They are often used as ornamental plants in temperate and tropical gardens as well as in conservatories. The species with large, finely divided leaves are highly prized by connoisseurs of foliage plants. Some ferns, however, have simple leaves, that is, leaves without divided blades. The wiry root mass of certain ferns (e.g., *Osmunda*) is sometimes used as a substrate for growing epiphytic orchids.

The representatives of the three groups of vascular cryptogams discussed in Chapter 6 were leafless (psilotophytes), microphyllous (club and spike mosses), or characterized by much-reduced leaves (arthrophytes). In striking contrast to these are the ferns (Figures 7.1 and 7.2), which, like the seed plants, have **megaphylls.** The latter, it will be recalled, have branching veins, and the emergence of their traces leaves gaps in the vascular tissue of the stem (see Figure 5.17*b, d*), except in a few genera where there is a protostele in the stems of the mature plant. Even in the mind of the layperson, the leaf is the dom-

---

[1]The Division Pteridophyta in this book is conceived more narrowly than in the older classification of Eichler (1883), (Table 1.1), where it included all the vascular cryptogams.

Figure 7.1 *Thelypteris dentata,* a "shield fern." Note rhizome covered by leaf bases, circinate young leaves, mature leaf, and roots.

Rhizome

Rhizome

Figure 7.2 *Adiantum capillus-veneris,* "Venus maidenhair fern."

inant organ of the fern plant, and this impression has a sound scientific foundation.

The ferns exhibit considerable diversity of habitat and growth habit. At one extreme are the erect-stemmed, large-leaved tree ferns that grow in tropical rain forests (Figure 7.3a) and even on exposed hillsides as they do near Auckland, New Zealand; tree ferns may exceed 75 feet in height. At the other extreme are small aquatic organisms such as *Salvinia* and *Azolla* (Figure 7.13). A large group of ferns that are intermediate in size includes the familiar cultivated varieties and the natives of shady ravines and woodlands in both the temperate zones and the tropics. As a group, ferns thrive best in moist, shady environments, although a few inhabit rock fissures in bright sunlight (the latter are subject to periodic desiccation, however). Ferns are, with the rarest exceptions, perennials. In the temperate zone, they survive from year to year by means of fleshy, often subterranean rhizomes. The portions of the leaves above

Fertile portion

Vegetative portion

a　　　*b*

Figure 7.3　(*a*) *Cyathea* sp., a tree fern, from the West Indies. [Courtesy of Dr. W. H. Hodge.] (*b*) Portion of a leaf of *Lygodium* sp., a "climbing" fern.

the soil die at the end of each growing season; a new set of leaves, already developed near the rhizome apex during this growth season, is elevated the following spring.

Vegetative Organization

The fern leaf is the dominant organ of the plant, except perhaps in the tree ferns, in which the leaf is challenged by the trunklike stem. In most ferns, the leaves have a unique arrangement in the bud known as **circinate vernation.** By vernation is meant the arrangement of leaves in the bud. In circinate vernation the lower or abaxial surface of the leaf during early development consistently grows more rapidly than the upper surface, this resulting in the coiling of the leaf. The large, circinate leaves of certain ferns have suggested the name "fiddle head." This comparison is the more apt, because in a number of ferns the fiddle heads are covered by brown scales.

Fern leaves may be either simple, with undivided blades, or compound in various forms, with the divided blades (leaflets) attached to a **rachis,** a prolongation of the petiole. Stomata and guard cells occur predominantly in the lower epidermal layer; the upper and lower epidermal layers are cutinized, and enclose a mesophyll region rich in chloroplasts. The mesophyll is traversed by strands of xylem and phloem, which form the veins.

The stems of most ferns other than tree ferns are prostrate and fleshy, at the surface of or under the soil. Their apical meristems in many instances contain tetrahedral apical cells from which cellular derivatives arise in three ranks. In such a fern as the climbing fern, *Lygodium* (Figure 7.3*b*) the stems are small, while the rachises of the compound leaf undergo long-persistent apical growth and "climb." The wiry roots of ferns originate among the leaf bases. The addition of secondary tissues by cambial activity does not occur in most ferns, and even the stems of tree ferns are entirely primary in origin. The stems of a few ferns contain protosteles, but in most they are siphonosteles or dictyosteles.

With few exceptions, conduction in the xylem of most fern stems is via single-celled tracheids; vessels (multicellular, perforated tubes) do occur, however, in the xylem of the bracken fern, *Pteridium,* and in *Marsilea,* as they do sparingly in *Selaginella* and *Equisetum,* discussed in Chapter 6.

Reproduction

As in all vascular plants, the commonly seen plant itself is the sporophyte, and, accordingly, at maturity it develops sporogenous tissue. In the common ferns, here under consideration, this tissue is borne on modified segments of leaves, or on abaxial (lower) surfaces of the vegetative leaves themselves (Figure 7.4). The fertile regions on fern leaves that bear sporangia are known as **receptacles,** and the group of sporangia upon a single receptacle is called a **sorus.** In many species, but by no means in all, the sorus of sporangia is covered during development by a flap of epidermal tissue (a **true indusium,** Figure 7.4*a, b*) or by the inrolled margin of the leaf (a **false indusium,** Figure 7.4*c, d*). The sporangia of some (mostly tropical) ferns are rather massive and thick-walled, and produce numerous spores, as do those of the club mosses, spike mosses, and *Equisetum.* Although a few genera are heterosporous, most are homosporous. In the more familiar ferns, such as *Adiantum,* the maidenhair fern, and *Thelypteris,* the lady fern, the numerous sporangia, grouped in sori on the backs or margins of the leaves, are comparatively small, thin-walled, and long-stalked (Figure 7.5*a*); these sporangia produce only from 32 to 64

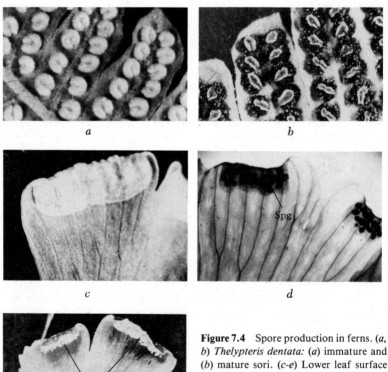

Figure 7.4   Spore production in ferns. (*a, b*) *Thelypteris dentata:* (*a*) immature and (*b*) mature sori. (*c-e*) Lower leaf surface of *Adiantum* sp.: (*c*) immature and (*d*) mature stages. The leaf margin covers the sporangia in (*c*) and (*d*) (cleared preparation), while the sporangia, Spg, are exposed in (*e*); Indusium shriveled, exposing sporangia.

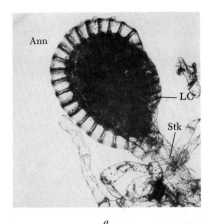

a

Figure 7.5 *Thelypteris dentata.* (*a*) Mature, intact sporangium. (*b*) Sporangium after contraction of annulus. (*c*) Empty sporangium. Ann, annulus; LC, lip cells; Spo, spore; Stk, stalk; WC, wall cells.

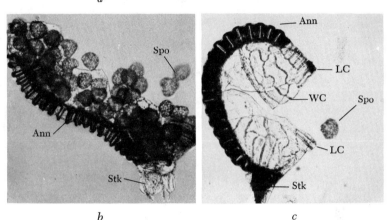

b   c

spores. Such spores (meiospores) arise by meiosis from sporocytes, and at maturity their walls thicken with a dark brown, impervious substance, resulting in the brown color of the mature sori.

The sporangia differ from those of other vascular cryptogams and seed plants in origin and in a number of other respects, and are said to be **leptosporangiate,** in contrast to **eusporangiate** sporangia. In the origin of the latter, a single superficial meristematic cell, or more often a group of them, undergoes periclinal division to form two layers of cells. By further divisions, the outer layer forms the sporangial wall and the inner the sporogenous tissue. The method of sporangial ontogeny differs from that in common ferns, the leptosporangiate pattern, in which each sporangium arises from a single superficial meristematic cell that undergoes approximately periclinal division (Figure 7.6). Here the major portion of the sporangium, both wall and spo-

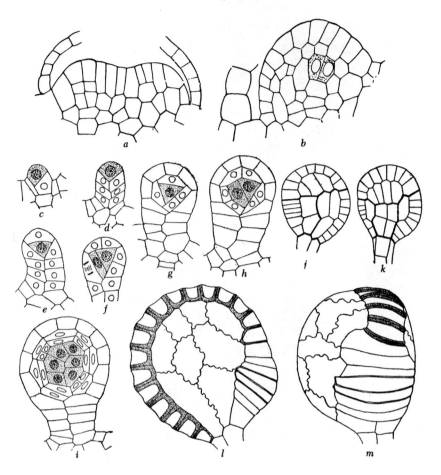

Figure 7.6 Comparison of eusporangiate and leptosporangiate sporangium development. (*a, b*) Two stages in eusporangiate development [After D. H. Campbell.] (*c–m*) Eleven stages in leptosporangiate development. [After G. M. Smith, *Cryptogamic Botany*, Vol. II (New York: McGraw-Hill Book Company, 1955). Reprinted by permission of the publisher.]

rogenous tissue, develops from the outer product of the periclinal division. There are other differences between eusporangiate and leptosporangiate sporangia, which may be summarized as follows:

Eusporangiate sporangia	Leptosporangiate sporangia
1. Massive, potentially producing an indefinitely large number of spores	1. Small, potentially producing 32–64 spores
2. Sporangial wall more than one layer of cells thick	2. Sporangial wall one layer of cells thick

A few ferns produce sporangia somewhat intermediate between the eusporangiate and leptosporangiate types.

The sporangia of common ferns are attached to the receptacles by stalks. Several types of cells comprise the sporangial wall. In addition to the ordinary sporangial wall cells, which have transparent cell walls, a specialized layer of thick-walled cells, the **annulus,** runs vertically around the sporangium. It is interrupted at one point by several thin-walled **lip cells** (Figure 7.5).

The indusia, if present, ultimately shrivel when the spores have matured, exposing the sporangia (Figure 7.4*b, e*). The spores are ejected from the sporangia, which crack open (Figure 7.5*b*) in the region of the delicate lip cells as the thickened cells of the hygroscopic annulus, a ringlike layer of cells, contract and then expand suddenly. This serves to catapult the spores into the air. Tremendous numbers of spores are produced by ferns, but the special requirements of most species for moisture and shade effectively reduce the number of gametophytes that develop from these spores.

Spores that are deposited by air currents upon sufficiently moist soil and rocks germinate within 5 to 6 days (Figure 7.7*a*) and initiate development of the gametophyte. Early in germination, a colorless rhizoidal cell arises at the base of the filament of green cells (Figure 7.7*a*). Most fern spores require light for germination, those of the bracken fern, *Pteridium aquilinum,* being an exception. The early cell divisions are all in the same plane or direction, but, in the presence of light of blue wavelength, an apical cell is formed in the terminal cell of the filament, which begins to cut off cellular derivatives in two directions. As a result, a flat spatulate structure (Figure 7.7*b*) develops with the apical cell in a slight depression.

It has been demonstrated in one *Thelypteris*-like fern that extracts of the sporophytic roots inhibit the development of gametophytes from spores of the same species. This may explain the usual absence of gametophytes from the *immediate* vicinity of fern sporophytes.

The central portion of the developing gametophyte is several cell layers thick, but the wings have only one layer. Additional rhizoids emerge from the cells of the ventral surface and penetrate the substrate. When the germinating spores are well separated, the resulting gametophytes are heart-shaped and may in some species approach 0.5 inch (1.2 centimeters) in diameter. The fern gametophyte was long ago designated the **prothallus** or **prothallium**, as it was known to be the precursor of the fern plant even before its sexual function was clearly understood.

As well-nourished, monoecious gametophytes mature—about 40 to 60, days after the spores have been planted in laboratory culture—they develop antheridia and archegonia normally on their ventral surfaces (Figure 7.7*c*).

The archegonia have their basal portions (venters) sunken in the central cushion of the gametophyte. They have four rows of neck cells in their rather short necks. The antheridia (Figure 7.7*c*) are globose structures consisting of spermatogenous cells surrounded by three jacket cells. Two of these are ring-

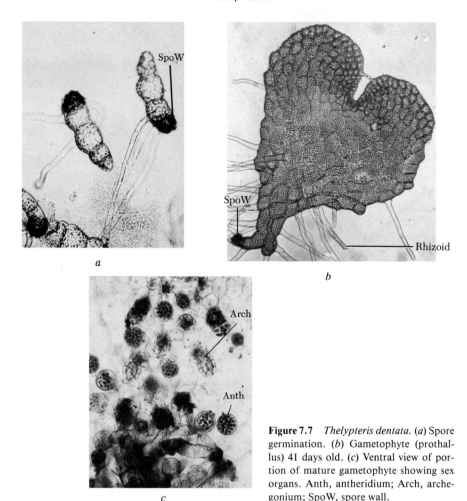

Figure 7.7 *Thelypteris dentata.* (*a*) Spore germination. (*b*) Gametophyte (prothallus) 41 days old. (*c*) Ventral view of portion of mature gametophyte showing sex organs. Anth, antheridium; Arch, archegonium; SpoW, spore wall.

like, while the most distal serves as a cover cell. The sperms are multiflagellated, like those of *Psilotum, Isoetes,* and *Equisetum.*

It has been demonstrated that development of antheridia in the gametophytes of certain ferns is enhanced by the addition of antheridiogen to immature gametophytes. **Antheridiogen** is a substance produced by somewhat precocious gametophytes, which themselves produce archegonia. This is a mechanism that favors cross-fertilization. Later, the gametophytes, which formed antheridia under the stimulus of antheridiogen, also develop archegonia, so that provision for self-fertilization also is present. A somewhat similar situation was described in the preceding chapter in relation to cross- and self-fertilization in *Equisetum.* It is of interest that antheridiogen may also bring about germination of fern spores in darkness.

Slight accumulations of moisture between the substrate and the ventral surface of the gametophyte suffice to open both the antheridia, which discharge the multiflagellate sperm, and the necks of mature archegonia. The cells inside the necks of the mature archegonia dissolve and are extruded; thus, a moist passageway develops through which the sperms swim to the mature eggs. The eggs of several archegonia may be fertilized, but usually only one of the zygotes develops into a juvenile sporophyte (Figure 7.9).

The sporophyte development, which is very rapid in the common garden and woodland ferns, is initiated by three successive nuclear and cell divisions of the zygote within the archegonium, forming what is called an octant (Figure 7.8). By further cell divisions, an embryonic root, leaf, stem, and foot are organized. The foot seemingly functions in nutrient absorption from the gametophyte. In many ferns, the primary or embryonic leaf (Figure 7.9) emerges through the apical notch. The stem develops slowly, but ultimately it produces additional leaves. The first few leaves of juvenile ferns differ from those of the mature sporophyte. As growth continues, the later-produced leaves finally come to resemble those typical of the adult species. When the minute sporophyte has become established, the membranous gametophyte dies. The gametophyte generation, then, in the ferns, as in other seedless vascular plants, is relatively short-lived and simple in structure. The sporophytic phase is dominant in the life cycle. The fern life cycle is summarized in Figure 7.10.

The time required for ferns to complete their life cycles from spore to spore varies with the species. The longest segment of the cycle is taken up with the maturation of the young sporophyte to the stage where it can produce spores. The shortest complete cycle recorded is that of the annual fern, *Ceratopteris thalictroides,* a floating aquatic of warm waters, often cultivated in aquaria; its life cycle can be completed in 3½ months from spore to spore. *Thelypteris dentata,* by contrast, requires about 18 months under greenhouse conditions.

In a number of species of ferns, the gametophyte stage either fails to develop any sex organs at all, or lacks archegonia or antheridia. In such cases, the vegetative tissue of the gametophyte, below its apical notch, develops without fertilization into a juvenile sporophyte that then matures. This is the phenomenon of **apogamy,** the development of an embryo without union of

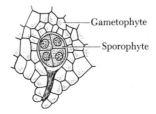

Figure 7.8 Section of postfertilization fern gametophyte, sporophyte within archegonium (calyptra) in octant stage.

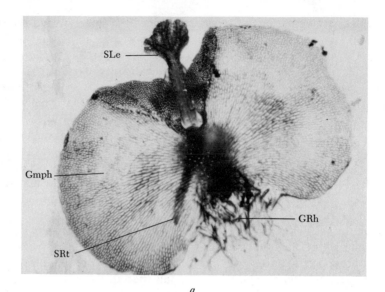

a

b

Figure 7.9 *Thelypteris dentata.* (*a, b*) Successively older stages. Leaf and root of sporophyte emergent from gametophyte. Gmph and p, gametophyte; Sle and 1, sporophyte of leaf; Srt and R, root of sporophyte; GRh and Rh, rhizoids of gametophyte.

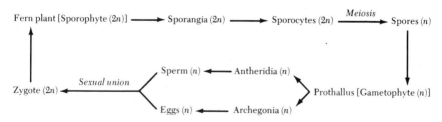

Figure 7.10   Diagrammatic summary of the life cycle of ferns.

gametes. In such ferns, sporophyte and gametophyte have the same chromosomal constitution (2*n*), further evidence that, as we noted in the mosses, sporophytes and gametophytes are not merely the expression of diploid and haploid chromosome complements.

An additional phenomenon that occurs in ferns is **apospory,** already cited in Chapter 4 on mosses. If the leaves of young sporophytes are incised at their margins, aposporic regeneration to form 2*n* gametophytes occurs.

The preceding paragraphs have emphasized the organization and reproduction of ferns such as *Adiantum* and *Thelypteris,* which are abundant and conspicuous representatives of the fern flora of the temperate zone.

Other Ferns

The Psilotophyta, Microphyllophyta, and Arthrophyta are relatively small groups, together probably not numbering more than 1,200 to 1,500 species, but the Pteridophyta, the ferns, comprise about 10,000 species. Accordingly, considerable diversity is apparent among them. In illustration, a brief account follows of certain aquatic ferns and certain primitive, eusporangiate ferns.

The Heterosporous Water Ferns.   These include the amphibious genera *Marsilea, Regnellidium,* and *Pilularia* (Figures 7.11, 7.12), and the strictly aquatic genera *Salvinia* and *Azolla* (Figure 7.13).

Marsilea may be mistaken for wood sorrel (sour grass) or for four-leaved clover by the layperson. This genus grows in or at the margins of shallow bodies of water or in marshy meadows, the cloverlike leaves arising alternately from prostrate stolons (Figure 7.11*a*) that are rooted at the nodes. The young leaves are circinately vernate, and the two pairs of leaflets are dichotomously veined. The stomata of the floating leaflets occur only on the upper surfaces.

The sporangia, which are small like those of *Adiantum* and *Thelypteris,* lack annuli and lip cells. They develop within **sporocarps** (Figure 7.11*a*) that are probably modified leaflets, brown, hard, and nutlike at maturity. *Marsilea* is heterosporous. Two kinds of sporangia—megasporangia and microsporangia—are present within the sporocarp, each megasporangium containing only one ovoid megaspore at maturity.

Unlike those of *Selaginella,* the megaspores and microspores of *Marsilea* do not germinate until they have been shed into the water by disintegration of the sporocarp wall. Germination can be hastened by cutting or filing away a segment of this wall. When such has been done, the gelatinous contents of the sporocarp become hydrated and swell; in expanding, they carry the sori of microsporangia and megasporangia out into the water (Figure 7.12*a*). The megaspores and microspores (Figure 7.12*b*) then germinate rapidly to form small ephemeral male and female gametophytes. After fertilization by a large,

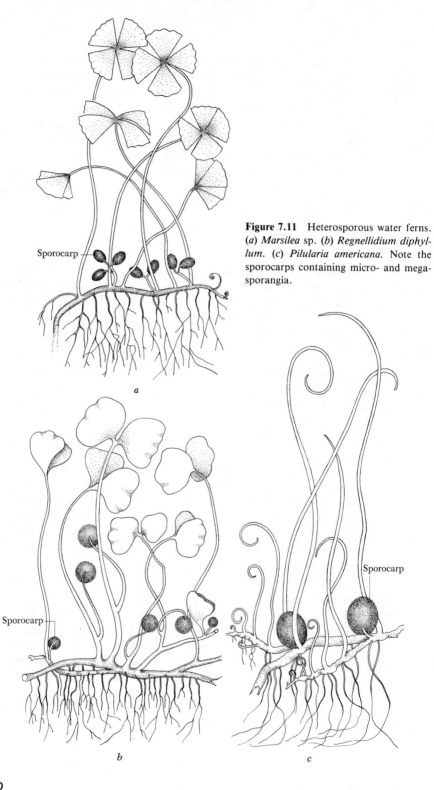

Figure 7.11 Heterosporous water ferns. (*a*) *Marsilea* sp. (*b*) *Regnellidium diphyllum*. (*c*) *Pilularia americana*. Note the sporocarps containing micro- and megasporangia.

Sporocarp

a

Sporocarp

b

Sporocarp

c

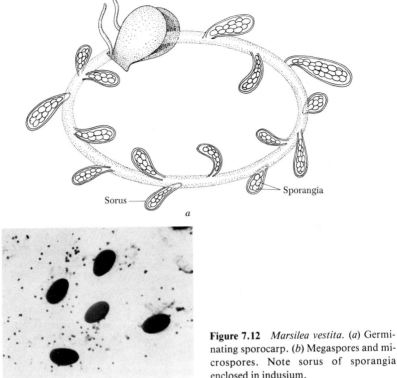

Sorus

Sporangia

a

b

Figure 7.12 *Marsilea vestita.* (*a*) Germinating sporocarp. (*b*) Megaspores and microspores. Note sorus of sporangia enclosed in indusium.

multiflagellated sperm, the single zygote of each female gametophyte develops into an embryonic sporophyte.

The male gametophyte is colorless and saprophytic, as is the female during early development; however, the latter develops photosynthetic tissue and rhizoids after fertilization.

Marsilea and the related *Regnellidium* and *Pilularia* provide evidence that heterospory apparently evolved more than once in different vascular plants (recall *Selaginella* and *Isoetes,* pp. 130 to 140, and see *Salvinia* and *Azolla,* following).

Salvinia and *Azolla* (Figure 7.13) are minute, floating aquatics that, although heterosporous, are not closely related to *Marsilea, Regnellidium,* or *Pilularia.* Like those three genera, *Salvinia* and *Azolla* bear their sporangia in sporocarps; however, their sporocarps are enclosed in a hardened indusium. Their heterospores also produce minute, colorless gametophytes after being shed from the sporocarps.

Eusporangiate Ferns.   In the ferns so far described, the leptosporangiate sporangia are small, delicate, thin-walled structures containing few spores (up

Figure 7.13   Heterosporous ferns. (*a, b*) *Salvinia natans.* (c, d) *Azolla caroliniana* (*b* and *d* are considerably enlarged).

to 64). About six genera of mostly tropical ferns differ in having massive, thick-walled sporangia each of which produces a large number of spores (up to 15,000); they are thus eusporangiate.

Two genera of eusporangiate ferns occur in the temperate zone. These are *Ophioglossum,* the "adder's tongue fern" (Figure 7.14), and *Botrychium,* the "grape fern" or "moonwort" (Figure 7.15). In both, the large sporangia occur on axes that arise at the junction of blade and petiole. These axes are called **fertile spikes** and are thought to represent modified leaflets. The sporangia open transversely in shedding the spores.

Unlike those of almost all other ferns, the gametophytes of *Ophioglossum* and *Botrychium* are subterranean, fleshy, achlorophyllous structures con-

Figure 7.14 *Ophioglossum engelmannii,*
the adder's tongue fern. [Courtesy of Dr.
William Ruf.]

Figure 7.15 *Botrychium virginianum,* the
grape fern or rattlesnake fern.

taining fungi in some of their cells. The gametophytes are slow-growing and monoecious. The gametophytes of *Botrychium* and *Ophioglossum* (free of fungi) have been grown in laboratory culture. The nutrition of these gametophytes is saprobic, like that of *Psilotum*.

SOME FOSSIL SEEDLESS VASCULAR PLANTS

The evidence of the fossil record indicates that land plants—that is, liverworts, hornworts, mosses, and seedless vascular plants—were not prominent on the earth before Silurian and Devonian times, approximately 400 million years ago. The remainder of this chapter will describe some representative plants from the past, which, like the living Psilotophyta, Microphyllophyta, Arthrophyta, and Pteridophyta, had vascular tissues but lacked seeds. Some of these extinct fossil plants display characteristics similar to those of members of the four extant groups of seedless vascular plants. Others are less clearly related. Seedless vascular plants or vascular cryptogams are currently classified in seven groups, representatives of which will be briefly cited.

Division Rhyniophyta

The members of the Rhyniophyta had plant bodies not differentiated into roots, stems, and leaves (Figure 7.16). They consisted entirely of stemlike axes, which in some cases are known to have branched from prostrate or sub-

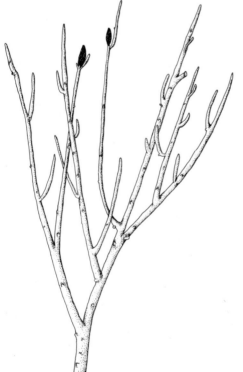

Figure 7.16 *Rhynia gwynne-vaughanii,* a Middle Devonian (see Table 6.1) fossil vascular plant. [After D. S. Edwards. Reprinted with permission of the Palaeontological Association from the original figure in *Palaeontology,* Vol. 13, pp. 451–461.]

terranean rhizomes. *Rhynia gwynne-vaughanii,* a Lower Devonian (see Table 6.1) fossil, was such a plant, about 8 inches tall. The rhizomes bore absorptive rhizoids. Sections of the axes show that the vascular tissues were entirely primary in origin and protostelic. Stomata occurred on the epidermis of the stem. Certain branches of *Rhynia* were fertile and enlarged at their apices to form terminal sporangia (Figure 7.16). The occurrence of tetrads of spores within some of these indicates that the plants were sporophytes.

Even more ancient members of the Rhyniophyta have been described from Silurian and Lower Devonian strata as species of *Cooksonia* (Figure 7.17), about 3 to 6 inches (7.5 to 15 centimeters) tall. Branching in *Cooksonia* was dichotomous, as in *Rhynia,* and some of the branches enlarged as globose sporangia.

The gametophytes of *Cooksonia* are unknown. It has been suggested that the gametophytes of *Rhynia gwynne-vaughanii* were very similar to the sporophytic rhizomes, as in *Psilotum.*

Division Zosterophyllophyta

Members of the Zosterophyllophyta have also been described from Lower and Middle Devonian (see Table 6.1) strata. Like the Rhyniophyta, these plants consisted of aerial branches and rhizomes, which contained protosteles. The sporangia were lateral and not terminal as in Rhyniophyta, and were produced along the flanks of terminal branches. *Zosterophyllum,* about 6 inches tall, is illustrated in Figure 7.18*a*. Another member of the Zosterophyllophyta, *Sawdonia ornata* (Figure 7.18*b*), was a slightly taller plant, had spinelike emergences over the axes, and bore lateral sporangia near the tips of the branches.

Division Trimerophytophyta

Sometimes included in Rhyniophyta, these plants differ in having spiny appendages on their axes and pseudomonopodial branching resulting from

Figure 7.17 *Cooksonia caledonica.* [After D. S. Edwards. Reprinted with the permission of the Palaeontological Association from the original figure in *Palaeontology,* Vol. 13, pp. 451–461.]

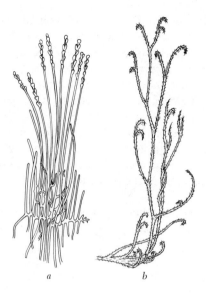

Figure 7.18 (*a*) *Zosterophyllum myretonianum.* [After J. Walton.] (*b*) *Sawdonia ornata.* [After H. N. Andrews and A. Kasper.]

a   *b*

dominance of one branch of successive dichotomies, as in *Psilophyton princeps* (Figure 7.19). The terminal branches were truly dichotomous and ended as elongate, pendulous sporangia. The axes contained protosteles.

The preceding three series of plants were formerly classified within a single division, the Psilotophyta, along with the living genera *Psilotum* and *Tmesipteris*. The latter certainly differs from the fossils described above in having vascularized appendages of the axes, which are lacking in the fossils.

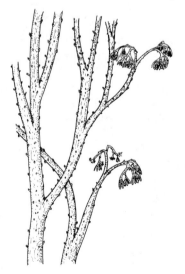

Figure 7.19 *Psilophyton princeps.* [From H. N. Andrews, after F. M. Hueber.]

Psilotum (see Figure 6.1), which has gametophytes and synangia similar to those of *Tmesipteris,* lacks vascularized appendages on its axes. Its sporangia are lateral and borne somewhat like those of *Sawdonia ornata,* but approximately 400 million years separate these plants, so *Psilotum* and *Tmesipteris,* are in this book assigned to a separate division, the Psilotophyta.

Division Microphyllophyta

Unlike the Divisions Rhyniophyta, Zosterophyllophyta, and Trimerophytophyta, which have no clearly related living representatives, a number of both extinct and extant plants have been classified in the Division Microphyllophyta. The latter include *Lycopodium, Selaginella,* and *Isoetes,* discussed in Chapter 6, as well as both herbaceous and woody fossils.

Among the former have been described the genera *Lycopodites* (Figure 7.20*a*), from Upper Carboniferous (see Table 6.1) rocks. These plants were

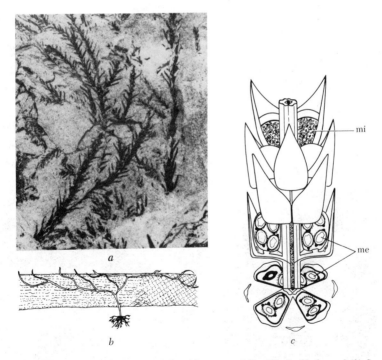

Figure 7.20   (*a*) *Lycopodites pendulus.* [Courtesy of Dr. W. G. Chaloner.] (*b*) *Selaginella fraipontii,* habit of growth on fallen *Lepidodendron* log. (*c*) *S. fraipontii,* reconstruction of strobilus. Note microspores, mi, and megaspores, me. [After Schlanker and Leisman. Reprinted from "The Herbaceous Carboniferous Lycopod *Selaginella fraipontii* Comb. Nov.," *Bot. Gaz.,* Vol. 130, pp 35–41, by permission of the University of Chicago Press.]

relatively delicate in texture and, like *Lycopodium,* were lacking in ligules and homosporous. Originally described from the Carboniferous (see Table 6.1) as *Selaginellites*—"ites" having the connotation of fossil or extinction—*S. fraipontii* (Figure 7.20*b*) is now considered to be entirely similar to *Selaginella* and is assigned to that genus. This plant was isophyllous like some extant species of *Selaginella* and the leaves were ligulate. The creeping axes grew from a basal root-bearing axis or rhizophore (Figure 7.20*b*). The well-preserved strobili contain basal megasporangia with megaspores and distal microsporangia with microspores (Figure 7.20*c*). Fossilized plants designated *Isoetites* or *Isoetes,* from Cretaceous (see Table 6.1) rocks, also have been described.

In addition to this herbaceous series of fossil Microphyllophyta, a number of large, woody fossils are well known. For example, *Sigillaria* (Figure 7.21) grew in Carboniferous (see Table 6.1) swamps and probably exceeded a height of 100 feet (about 33 meters). The main stems were unbranched and borne on dichotomously branching rhizophores from which emerged rootlike structures. The branches at the top of the trunk were dichotomously forked

Figure 7.21   Reconstruction of a coal-age (Pennsylvanian) forest. C, *Calamites* sp., a giant arthrophytan plant; Le, *Lepidodendron,* a treelike form reminiscent of *Lycopodium* and *Selaginella;* S, *Sphenophyllum* sp., a herbaceous genus; SF, an unidentified seed fern; Si, *Sigillaria,* a treelike form also reminiscent of *Lycopodium* and *Selaginella* and related to *Lepidodendron.* [Courtesy of Illinois State Museum.]

and densely clothed with microphylls, which in some species attained a meter in length. These leaves, after abscission, left prominent scars on the trunk. The primary xylem in older parts of the stem was clothed with additional layers of secondary xylem through cambial activity. However, most of the diameter of the stem was the result of increase in the thickness of the cortex. Strobili occurred on the apical branches, and there is good evidence that most of the plants were heterosporous.

The woody members of the Microphyllophyta all have become extinct.

Division Arthrophyta

Although the extant *Equisetum* alone survives, the Arthrophyta contained a larger assemblage of plants in earlier geologic history. These extinct plants were both herbaceous and woody.

Among the herbaceous types may be cited the genus *Sphenophyllum* (Figure 7.21), which grew from Upper Devonian through the early Triassic (see Table 6.1). Nodes and internodes were prominent in *Sphenophyllum* as they are in *Equisetum,* and the internodes of the young stems were ribbed. The wedge-shaped leaves were dichotomously branched and borne in whorls. The primary protostele of *Sphenophyllum* was augmented by cambial activity, which added secondary xylem and phloem, although the plants remained herbaceous. Some of the distal whorls of leaves bore branching sporangiophores (Figure 7.22*b*), which produced sporangia with homosporous spores.

Equisetites (Figure 7.22*a*), known from Mesozoic and Cenozoic strata (see Table 6.1), also was herbaceous and is thought by some paleobotanists to be indistinguishable from *Equisetum.*

a

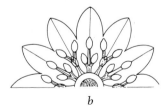

b

Figure 7.22 (*a*) Equisetites platyodon. [After M. Hirmer.] (*b*) *Sphenophyllum* sp., half of one whorl of bracts with sporangiosphores.

By contrast *Calamites* is representative of the giant, treelike Arthrophyta, which were present on earth from the Upper Devonian through the Permian. The trunklike stem of *Calamites,* which became up to 90 feet tall and was 1 foot in diameter, arose from a large horizontal, subterranean, root-bearing rhizome. Secondary growth occurred in the stems, which contained canals in association with the primary xylem, as in *Equisetum.* The elongate, slender leaves were borne in whorls. The sporangia were borne on sporangiophores in the axils of whorls of bracts and in strobili. Some species of *Calamites* were homosporous and some heterosporous.

Many fossil Arthrophyta, like the living *Equisetum,* are readily recognizable by the whorled arrangement of their leaves and branches, by the ribbing of their stems, and by their sporangiophores. The nature of the gametophytes of fossil Arthrophyta is unknown.

Division Pteridophyta

Megaphyllous vascular cryptogams, ferns or fernlike precursors, also are known from the fossil record. In the supposed fernlike precursors, distinction between leaves and stems was not always as clear as in most modern ferns. It has been suggested that the large, complex megaphylls of the latter are not strictly homologous with microphylls, but rather that they represent stem branch systems that gradually become flattened, with tissues filling the spaces between the branches. Although there are a relatively large number of fossil ferns and fernlike precursors, space permits discussion here of only a few.

Calamophyton (Figure 7.23*a*) from the Middle Devonian (see Table 6.1) had main stem branches more than 2 feet in height. These were branched in various patterns and had appendages, some of which recurved and bore elongate sporangia.

Psaronius (Figure 7.23*b*) from Pennsylvanian and Permian strata (see Table 6.1) was tree-fern-like in habit, with trunks up to 2 feet in diameter. The large fronds were borne in a terminal crown and were several times pinnately compound. The trunks contained concentric siphonosteles dissected by leaf gaps to form dictyosteles.

More recent rocks contain species of ferns related to the extant leptosporangiate ferns. A segment of a frond of such a fern, *Woodwardia,* from Eocene rocks in Oregon, is illustrated in Figure 7.24.

Division Aneurophyta

Members of this division are of great interest to students of plant evolution because, while they lack seeds, they have certain morphological characteristics suggestive of gymnospermous seed plants.

The representative here chosen, *Archaeopteris* (Figure 7.25*a*), has been found in Upper Devonian (see Table 6.1) rocks. It was a huge tree of which

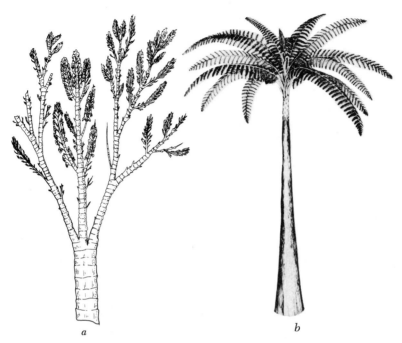

Figure 7.23 (a) *Calamophyton primaevum.* [After R. Krausel and H. Weyland.]
(b) *Psaronius* sp. [After L. Morgan, from H. N. Andrews. Reprinted from *Studies in Paleobotany* (New York: John Wiley & Sons, Inc., 1961), by permission of the publisher.]

Figure 7.24 *Woodwardia* sp., from the Oligocene of Oregon. [Courtesy of Professor T. Delevoryas.]

171

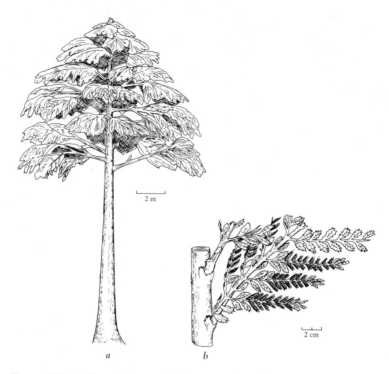

Figure 7.25 *Archaeopteris* sp. (*a*) Reconstruction. (*b*) Portion of axes with branches, leaves, and elongate sporangia. [After C. B. Beck.]

trunks have been found as large as 5 feet in diameter. These trunks were long known to paleobotanists, and on the basis of the structure of their xylem tracheids, which has bordered pits like gymnosperms (p. 174), they had been thought to be gymnospermous seed plants. Recently, however, branches with leaves and attached sporangia (Figure 7.25*b*) were found. It is probable that some species of *Archaeopteris* were heterosporous.

SUMMARY

The preceding paragraphs have briefly discussed representatives of seven groups of fossil, seedless vascular plants. In the first three (Rhyniophyta, Zosterophyllophyta, and Trimerophytophyta), the plants seemingly lacked roots and vascularized leaves. Although the living *Psilotum* similarly lacks roots and vascularized leaves, it is separated by approximately 400 million years from these groups, so some caution is indicated in postulating relationships.

By contrast, the divisions Microphyllophyta, Arthrophyta, and Pteridophyta evidently have extinct fossil members that are similar to living plants classified in the same groups. Finally, the Aneurophyta have no living representatives.

It should also be clear from the discussion that the fossil record, as far as it has become known, indicates that the presently living seedless vascular plants represent separate lines of evolutionary development, and the ultimate relationships between them remain obscure.

QUESTIONS FOR REVIEW

1. Which is the largest group of vascular cryptogams insofar as number of genera and species is concerned?
2. Why are tree ferns not used for lumber?
3. Define or explain circinate vernation, rachis, indusium, false indusium, receptacle, sorus, lip cells, annulus, prothallus, antheridiogen, apogamy, apospory, sporocarp, fertile spike.
4. Distinguish between eusporangiate and leptosporangiate sporangia.
5. What length of time is involved in the life cycle of various ferns from spore to spore?
6. With the aid of labeled drawings, review the structure and reproduction of a fern such as *Thelypteris*.
7. What genera of ferns grow in your locality? In what habitats?
8. What types of vascular cryptogams were growing on earth during Devonian times?
9. How did some of the ancient Microphyllophyta differ from our extant genera?
10. Describe some extinct fossil relatives of *Equisetum*. How do some of them differ from the latter?
11. Of what significance are the Aneurophyta?
12. Name the vascular cryptogams with photosynthetic gametophytes.
13. Name the vascular cryptogams with saprobic gametophytes.
14. Compare and contrast, in tabular form, the sporophytes and gametophytes of all the genera of vascular cryptogams discussed in this and in the preceding chapter.

CHAPTER EIGHT

Seed Plants I:
Gymnosperms

INTRODUCTION

Plants may be divided into two great groups on the basis of whether or not they produce seeds; those that do not are, as we know, called cryptogams and those that do are known as phanerogams.[1] The two preceding chapters have discussed the **vascular cryptogams,** seedless vascular plants with xylem and phloem. This chapter and the one that follows will be devoted to a discussion of the **phanerogams,** vascular plants that produce seeds.

Among the seed plants themselves, two types are clearly distinguishable; the distinctions relate primarily to the location of the seeds, but are also based on other attributes. In one type, the seeds are commonly borne *within* structures known as fruits (Figure 8.1*a, b, c*); these may open at maturity, exposing and shedding seeds, but at least in the early stages of development the seeds are enclosed. Plants that bear their seeds in this manner are known as **angiosperms,** or "flowering plants" (see Table 1.1). In the other group, the **gymnosperms,**[2] the seeds develop on the surface or at the tip (Figure 8.13) of an appendage (which has various names, for example, ovuliferous scale or peduncle), and are not enclosed in it (Figure 8.1*d, e*). Although the seed-bearing structures of gymnosperms may occur in cones or strobili (Figure 8.1*d*) that hide the seeds from view, the seeds are not enclosed within the structures that bear them, but are merely concealed by the grouping and overlapping of those structures.

Gymnospermous plants may be woody trees, shrubs, or vines. Familiar

[1]From the Greek *phainein* (to show) plus *gamia* (reproduction).

[2]Although "Gymnospermae" has been abandoned by many as a formal taxon (see Table 1.1), "gymnosperm" remains a useful descriptive term.

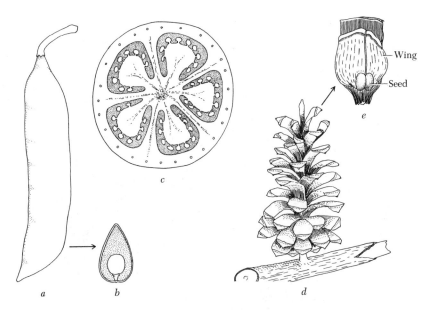

Figure 8.1 Methods of bearing seeds. (*a–c*) Angiospermy: (*a*) pod (fruit) of garden pea; (*b*) the same in transection showing enclosed seed; (*c*) transection of tomato fruit with enclosed seeds. (*d, e*) Gymnospermy: (*d*) seed cone, or strobilus, of pine; (*e*) portion of one of segments of (*d*) showing unenclosed, winged seeds.

examples include the pine, hemlock, spruce, fir, juniper, cypress, and maidenhair tree, *Ginkgo biloba;* other gymnosperms are the perhaps less familiar fernlike and palmlike cycads (Figures 8.2, 8.3). Among the flowering plants, in contrast, both woody and herbaceous types are abundant, but the herbaceous outnumber the woody in genera, species, and individuals. Stems of herbaceous plants are green and soft in texture because very little (if any) secondary xylem is added by the vascular cambium, if, indeed, this cambium is present at all (see Chapter 5). In woody plants, of course, the vascular cambium adds annual increments of secondary xylem or wood (see p. 108). Oaks,

Figure 8.2 *Zamia floridana,* plant with ovulate strobilus (arrow).

a   b

Figure 8.3   Cycads. (*a*) *Cycas revoluta.* [Courtesy of Professor Elsie Quarterman.] (*b*) *Dioon edule.*

elms, maples, lilacs, roses, and grapes are woody angiosperms that are familiar to most people; iris, grasses, daisies, tomatoes, and morning glories are common examples of herbaceous angiosperms.

The classification of seed-bearing plants, like that of other organisms, varies with the classifer (see Table 1.1). The discovery in Carboniferous rocks of fossil fernlike leaves with attached seeds, representative of a group of extinct plants known as "seed ferns" (p. 199), suggested that seed-bearing plants and ferns evolved from a common ancestor. This discovery, and the fact that seed ferns and other seed plants are megaphyllous, inspired some to classify both ferns and seed plants in a single taxon, the Pteropsida. Other classifiers, including the authors, look upon the ferns, seed plants, and even the gymnosperms and angiosperms, as separate lines of evolutionary development, and, accordingly, classify them in several separate divisions of the plant kingdom.

The remainder of this chapter discusses reproduction in gymnosperms and considers certain representative types. In Chapter 9 we shall discuss the angiosperms in detail.

REPRODUCTION IN GYMNOSPERMS

Before we examine the several groups of gymnosperms and their reproduction, let us consider in general terms the reproductive process that results in the production of seeds. In all seed plants, as in all seedless vascular plants, the dominant phase is the sporophyte. Accordingly, at maturity certain portions of the vegetative organism become fertile—that is, reproductive—and produce spores. In most gymnosperms, as in the club mosses, spike mosses, and *Equisetum,* the spore-bearing appendages are aggregated in localized regions of the axes to form cones or strobili (Figure 8.1*d*). As noted earlier, the spores (meiospores) produced by the sporophytes of all land plants arise by meiosis in sporocytes, eventually developing into the sexual, gametophytic phase of the plant's life cycle.

In connection with the present discussion, several phenomena that occur in *Selaginella* (see p. 137) are especially noteworthy. The spores of *Selaginella* are of two sizes, and they differ both in origin and in subsequent development. The smaller spores, the microspores, produced in large numbers in their sporangia, develop into male gametophytes. Other spores, the megaspores, of which only four are typically produced in a given sporangium, become filled with stored foods, enlarge tremendously, and upon germination produce female gametophytes. The production of two types of spores, it will be recalled, is known as **heterospory.** A further significant feature of *Selaginella* is that the early stages of both the male and female gametophytes of some species develop within the microspores and megaspores, respectively; this is called **endospory.** The gametophytes are dependent for nutrition on materials stored in the spores. In some species the spores may be retained within their sporangia until they have developed into mature, or almost mature, gametophytes. Sometimes the spores are retained until the gametophytes have matured and fertilization has occurred. In summary, we observe in *Selaginella* the presence of (1) heterospory (involving tremendous size differences between the microspores and megaspores); (2) the inevitable corollary of heterospory, dioecious gametophytes; (3) dependence of the developing gametophytes on nutrients from the sporophyte; (4) endosporic development of the gametophytes; and (5) prolonged retention of the spores and their contained gametophytes within the sporangia in some species. With certain modifications and innovations, these same phenomena occur in reproduction leading to the formation of seeds.

All seed plants produce two kinds of spores in different sporangia: those spores that grow into male gametophytes are usually called microspores; those that grow into female gametophytes are usually called megaspores (although they do not differ markedly in size).[3] These spores of seed plants and the sporangia that produce them differ from those of *Selaginella* in several important aspects, briefly summarized as follows:

[3]The megaspores of seed plants are not very different in terms of size from the microspores. Can we say, then, that the seed plants are heterosporous in the sense that seedless vascular plants are? The terms "microspore" and "megaspore" have been applied to the male-gametophyte-producing and female-gametophyte-producing spores of seed plants, respectively, in spite of their similarity in size, because their developmental role is different. A suggested explanation of the similarity is that permanent retention of the megaspores during evolution within the megasporangium has reduced the size of the megaspore.

1. The megasporangia in seed plants are surrounded by cells that form a covering, or **integument;** these covered megasporangia are called **ovules.**

2. Of the four potential spores formed in the megasporangium at meiosis, only one, the **functional megaspore,** usually survives.

3. The functional megaspore is never freed from the megasporangium.

4. The surviving megaspore at maturity approximates the size of the microspore, and in most cases lacks a markedly thickened wall and stored foods, although it enlarges considerably during the development of the female gametophyte.

5. The microspores are shed ultimately as **pollen grains,** which contain the male gametophyte; these grains are transferred, by various mechanisms, from the microsporangium to a point more or less closely proximate to the ovule containing the megaspore (and later containing the female gametophyte). This transfer is called **pollination.**

6. The megaspore completes its development in the megasporangium into a mature female gametophyte, using metabolites transferred to it from the surrounding tissues of the megasporangium and parental sporophyte; the functional megaspore may thicken its wall during this process.

7. The sperms or sperm nuclei are brought into the vicinity of the egg directly or indirectly by means of an outgrowth of the male gametophyte, called the **pollen tube.**

8. Fertilization and development of an embryonic sporophyte regularly take place within the female gametophyte, still within the megaspore, and in turn, within the megasporangium (thus within the ovule). When the embryo within the female gametophyte has developed, the ovule is called a **seed,** the end product of these correlated phenomena.

The structures and activities summarized in 1 to 8 above represent, of course, only an outline of a rather complicated process resulting in the production of seeds, but this summary will be useful for repeated reference as the details of the reproductive process in the several types of seed plants are described.

One further point is noteworthy: In gymnosperms, the ovule does not increase much in size after fertilization. In angiosperms, by contrast, fertilization stimulates rapid growth of the ovule as it matures into the seed.

CLASSIFICATION OF GYMNOSPERMS

Gymnospermous seed plants comprise three or four different evolutionary lines, depending on the classifier. These include the Divisions Cycadophyta, Ginkgophyta, Coniferophyta, and Gnetophyta. Some authors include the single extant member of the Ginkgophyta, *Ginkgo,* in the Division Coniferophyta. Representatives of these four groups are discussed in the following paragraphs.

Division Cycadophyta

Members of this small group of ten tropical, strobilate genera (Cycadophyta, see Table 1.1) are reminiscent of the tree ferns because of their fleshy, trunklike stems and pinnately compound leaves; the leaflets of some—for example *Cycas*—have circinate vernation, as in ferns. The leaves also suggest palms, which are, however, angiosperms. Cycads are limited to the tropics and subtropics of both hemispheres. In the United States, only *Zamia* (Figure 8.2) occurs natively, in Florida. In addition, the genera *Cycas* (Figure 8.3*a*) and *Dioon* (Figure 8.3*b*) are widely cultivated for their stately, palmlike foliage. The stems of cycads are mostly unbranched, slow-growing (both in height and in girth), and covered by the leaf bases of preceding seasons. Although a cambium layer is present in the stems, additions of secondary tissues are composed in large part of thin-walled parenchyma cells; thus, the stems are not very woody. Abundant mucilage canals occur in cycads.

In *Zamia,* the microstrobili and megastrobili appear among the leaf bases (Figures 8.2 and 8.4). The microsporophylls produce a number of shiny, white, eusporangiate microsporangia on their abaxial surface (Figure 8.4*d*). The microsporocytes undergo meiosis, produce microspores, and these, like those of many species of *Selaginella* and all seed plants, begin their development into male gametophytes while they are still enclosed in the microsporangia. Two successive nuclear and cell divisions give rise within the microspore of a three-celled, immature male gametophyte consisting of a **prothallial** or **sterile cell,** a **generative cell,** and a **tube cell** (Figure 8.5*a*). The microspores with their

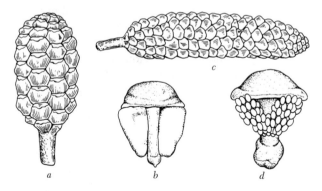

Figure 8.4 Strobili and sporophylls of *Zamia* sp. (*a*) Megastrobilus. (*b*) Megasporophyll and ovules. (*c*) Microstrobilus. (*d*) Microsporophyll and microsporangia, lower surface.

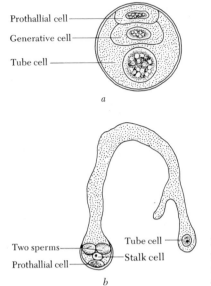

Prothallial cell
Generative cell
Tube cell

a

Two sperms
Prothallial cell
Tube cell
Stalk cell

b

Figure 8.5 *Zamia* sp., development of the male gametophyte. (*a*) Pollen grain at shedding. (*b*) Mature male gametophyte dissected from megasporangium.

contained immature three-celled male gametophytes are shed at this stage and are called **pollen** or **pollen grains.**[4]

The ovulate strobili, **megastrobili,** or seed cones (Figures 8.2 and 8.4*a*), which occur on other individuals than those that produce microstrobili, are stems with short internodes and megasporophylls. Each of the latter bears two ovules (Figure 8.4*b*), which, it should be remembered, are megasporangia covered with an integument except for the **micropyle.** Each ovule develops a single megasporocyte that undergoes meiosis and cell division, forming a row or **linear tetrad,** of megaspores. Three of these (usually those nearest the micropyle) degenerate, leaving one **functional megaspore** (Figure 8.6*b*). The latter, as in *Selaginella* and all seed plants, undergoes a period of free-nuclear division, ultimately followed by cell divisions, and forms the female gametophyte. The metabolites and energy required for development of the female gametophyte are supplied by the vegetative or sterile cells of the megasporangium; most of the latter is thus digested by the parasitizing female gametophyte, the cells of which lack chloroplasts. At maturity several very large archegonia are organized at the micropylar end of the gametophyte (Figure 8.7); each of the archegonia has one tier of four neck cells.

After they have been shed from the microsporangia, some of the pollen grains are transferred by air currents to the megastrobili, which have devel-

---

[4]The term "microspore" is usually restricted to the spore before it has undergone nuclear division to form the male gametophyte; after the nucleus has divided, the microspore is called a pollen grain.

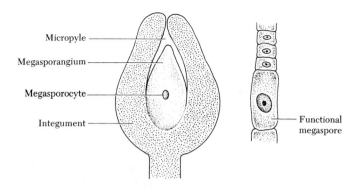

Figure 8.6 *Zamia* sp., longisection of ovule containing a megasporocyte; linear tetrad at the right.

oped fissures between adjacent megasporophylls. Some pollen grains reach the micropyles of the ovules where **pollination droplets** are present. As these dry and contract, the pollen grains are drawn into a small depression, the **pollen chamber** (Figure 8.7), at the apex of the megasporangium. The transfer of the pollen grain from the microsporangium to the micropyle of the ovule in the cycads and other gymnosperms is known as **pollination.**

Once within the pollen chamber, the pollen grains germinate, that is, renew their development, each forming a tube that digests its way through the apex of the megasporangium, thus parasitizing it (Figures 8.5*b* and 8.7). Meanwhile, the functional megaspore will have produced the female gametophyte (Figure 8.7).

The female gametophytes and archegonia, and especially the egg cells,

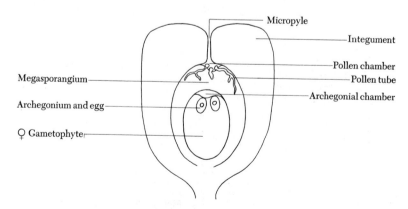

Figure 8.7 *Zamia* sp., median longitudinal section of ovule (diagrammatic) made near the time of fertilization. Note pollen grains attached to megasporangium in pollen chamber.

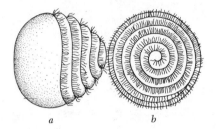

Figure 8.8 *Cycas* sp., sperm in (*a*) lateral, and (*b*) apical aspects. Note many cilia.

a   *b*

are readily visible to the naked eye; they are the largest among those of the seed plants. The generative cell (Figure 8.5*a*) of the male gametophyte divides to form two cells, the "stalk" and "body" cells; subsequently the latter divides to form two sperm cells (Figure 8.5*b*). The sperms of cycads are the largest in the plant kingdom, often more than 300 micrometers[5] in diameter, and are motile through the beating of numerous **cilia** (Figure 8.8).

The interval between pollination and fertilization is about 5 months in *Zamia,* and it is during this period that the male and female gametophytes mature.

Although the eggs of all the archegonia may be fertilized and initiate development of embryos, usually only one embryo is present in the mature seed (Figure 8.9). Embryogeny in the cycads and in all gymnosperms is begun with a period of free-nuclear division on the part of the zygote nucleus. This is followed by partition of the multinucleate embryonic protoplasm into cells that become organized as an embryonic sporophyte attached to a coiled **suspensor.** The embryo itself consists of primary root or **radicle,** two **cotyledons,** and a terminal bud or **plumule.** During maturation of the seed, the integument becomes differentiated into an outer, scarlet-yellow, fleshy layer and an inner stony layer. A **gymnospermous seed,** like that of cycads, therefore, consists of an embryonic sporophyte embedded in the remains of the female gametophyte

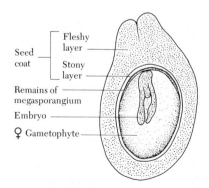

Seed coat { Fleshy layer — Stony layer —
Remains of megasporangium —
Embryo —
♀ Gametophyte —

Figure 8.9 *Zamia* sp., longisection of a seed.

[5]One micrometer (formerly called a micron) equals 0.001 millimeter.

within the megaspore and megasporangium, all surrounded by the modified integuments, now called seed coats. The seeds of *Zamia* and *Cycas* germinate readily at maturity. Germination is more rapid if the fleshy and stony layers of the seed coat are removed before planting.

Division Ginkgophyta

The Ginkgophyta contain only the single living species *Ginkgo biloba* (Figure 8.10), the maidenhair tree, native to eastern China but cultivated all over the world. The common name of the tree is occasioned by the resemblance of its fan-shaped leaves and their venation (Figure 5.19*a* on p. 115) to those of the pinnules of the maidenhair fern *Adiantum* (p. 149).

Ginkgo is widely cultivated in temple precincts in Japan, where specimens with a diameter at breast height of 10 to 12 feet are not uncommon. The trees are richly branched and consist of two kinds of shoots—long shoots and

Figure 8.10 *Ginkgo biloba,* the maidenhair tree. [Courtesy of New York Botanical Garden.]

spur shoots (Figure 8.11). Growth in length of the spur shoots is very slow, and the closeness of the nodes gives the spirally arranged leaves a clustered appearance.

Like the conifers, to be discussed later, *Ginkgo* is extremely woody because of the activity of a cambium layer that adds cylinders of secondary xylem each growing season. The epidermis of the young, green long shoot is replaced in older portions of the stem by a corky layer. The roots, too, become woody through secondary thickening by cambial activity. Mucilage canals, like those of cycads, are present throughout the plant.

Ginkgo, like the cycads, is strictly dioecious. The reproductive structures are produced by mature individuals among the leaves in spur shoots as the leaves emerge each spring. The microspores are produced in lax, pendulous strobili (Figure 8.11*a*), whereas the ovules occur on different individuals in pairs at the tips of delicate stalks or **peduncles** (Figure 8.11*b*).

As in all seed plants, the microspores begin their development into male gametophytes before they are shed from the microsporangia. At shedding they contain (Figure 8.12) four cells of the immature male gametophyte, namely, two prothallial or sterile cells, a generative cell, and tube cell. Pollination occurs in the spring through the agency of air currents. Here, too, some pollen grains are carried to pollination droplets at the micropyles of the ovules and ultimately come to rest in the pollen chamber where they form tubes in which two multiciliate sperm, much like those of the cycads, are produced. Megasporogenesis and development of the female gametophyte occur while the pollen tube is digesting its way through the megasporangium. At this time, the generative cell forms stalk and body cells and sperms, as in the cycads.

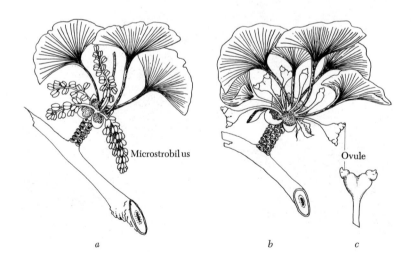

Figure 8.11 *Ginkgo biloba. (a)* Spur shoot with microstrobili. (*b*) Spur shoot with ovules. (*c*) One pair of ovules, enlarged.

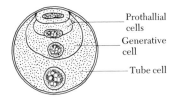

Figure 8.12   *Ginkgo biloba,* pollen grain at shedding.

In *Ginkgo,* as in the cycads, several months elapse between pollination and fertilization, and during this period the ovules enlarge greatly. They are abscised and fall to the ground in late August and September in the United States; hence, fertilization and embryogeny may occur after the ovules have been shed. The motile, ciliate sperms of *Ginkgo* are not quite as large as those of the cycads. As *Ginkgo* seeds ripen, the outer layer of the integument gets fleshy, the seeds having the appearance of mottled plums (Figure 8.13). The fleshy layers of the mature seed may cause nausea if smelled, and superficial skin lesions in some individuals if the seeds are touched. Although *Ginkgo* grows rapidly and is cultivated widely in the temperate zone, and especially in oriental temple grounds, it seems almost to have disappeared in nature, although it is reported to be native to eastern China. The reasons for its near extinction are unknown. In the United States, *Ginkgo* flourishes as an ornamental tree in the parks and on the streets of many cities, such as New York City and Washington, D. C. The graceful trees take on a brilliant golden yellow hue in the autumn.

Division Coniferophyta

Pines and associated conifers form extensive forests in various parts of the world. They are highly important commercially as sources of lumber, wood pulp for the manufacture of paper, and naval stores (a general term for the products of coniferous gums or resins). Like many woody plants, the apical growth of *Pinus* is seasonal. During dormant periods, the delicate tips of the

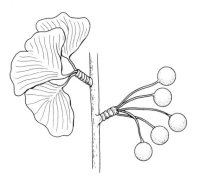

Figure 8.13   *Ginkgo biloba,* maturing seeds.

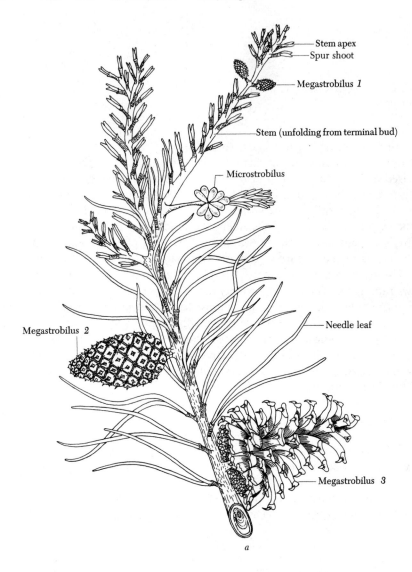

Stem apex
Spur shoot

Megastrobilus *1*

Stem (unfolding from terminal bud)

Microstrobilus

Needle leaf

Megastrobilus *2*

Megastrobilus *3*

a

branches are covered by relatively impervious scales, forming covered buds. During the growing season, these buds unfold by division and elongation of the stem cells within the bud (Figure 8.14). Pine leaves, familiarly known as needles, have little surface area. Within the leaves and throughout the plant are numerous canals filled with a secretion known as resin. In most species the needles are borne in clusters on minute lateral branches of the main axes, called **spur shoots** (Figure 8.15). These occur in the axils of minute scale leaves (Figure 8.15*b*). In *Juniperus,* "red cedar," by contrast, while juvenile indi-

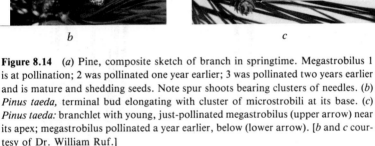

b   c

Figure 8.14 (*a*) Pine, composite sketch of branch in springtime. Megastrobilus 1 is at pollination; 2 was pollinated one year earlier; 3 was pollinated two years earlier and is mature and shedding seeds. Note spur shoots bearing clusters of needles. (*b*) *Pinus taeda,* terminal bud elongating with cluster of microstrobili at its base. (*c*) *Pinus taeda:* branchlet with young, just-pollinated megastrobilus (upper arrow) near its apex; megastrobilus pollinated a year earlier, below (lower arrow). [*b* and *c* courtesy of Dr. William Ruf.]

viduals produce needle leaves, the leaves of adults are scale leaves. The stems and roots of pine contain active, vascular cambial layers that add secondary xylem and phloem, thus increasing the woodiness and diameter of the axes. The wood of pine is homogeneous, consisting largely of conducting cells (called tracheids) and associated living parenchyma cells. Canals, which are lined with secretory cells, are present in the wood and elsewhere in the plant; these contain resin.

The needle leaves are much reduced in surface. In transection (Figure 8.16), it is seen that they are covered by a heavily cutinized epidermis with sunken stomata and a hypodermis. Resin canals occur in the mesophyll. A prominent endodermis surrounds the vascular tissue, which, depending on the species, may be in one or two groups.

Reproduction.   After a number of years of purely vegetative development from the seed and seedling stages, young trees begin to produce strobili and spores. Unlike the cycads and *Ginkgo,* pine is monoecious, microstrobili and megastrobili occurring on the same individual.

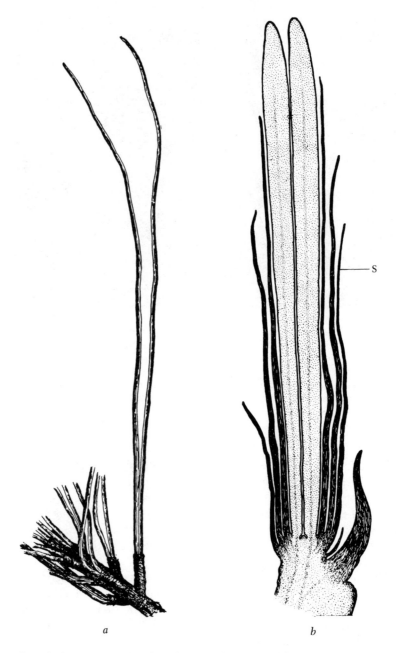

S

a   *b*

Figure 8.15   *Pinus* s. (*a*) Portion of branch with two-needled spur shoots. (*b*) Median longitudinal section of a young, single spur shoot; note scale leaves, S. [After C. J. Chamberlain, *Gymnosperms* (Chicago: The University of Chicago Press, 1935.]

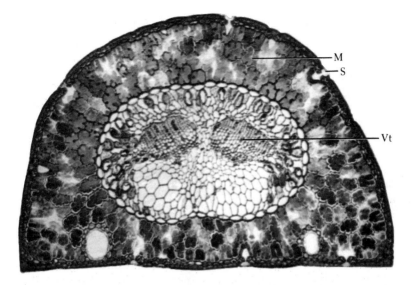

Figure 8.16 *Pinus nigra,* transection of needle leaf; M, mesophyll; S, stomatal region; Vt, vascular tissue.

The microstrobili occur in subterminal clusters (Figure 8.14) as the buds unfold at the beginning of the growing season, while the minute, light green (or red in some species) megastrobili are borne on short lateral branches of the expanding axes of terminal buds. Thus, they become visible only as the latter expand in the spring. Megastrobili occur most abundantly on higher branches of the trees. The microstrobilus is composed of an axis bearing microsporophylls, each with two elongate microsporangia on its abaxial surface (Figure 8.17a). Early in the spring, the microsporocytes produce tetrads of haploid microspores as a result of meiosis; these separate into individual microspores with inflated (''winged'') cell walls (Figure 8.17b) called ''air bladders.'' The exact time at which microsporogenesis and meiosis occur varies

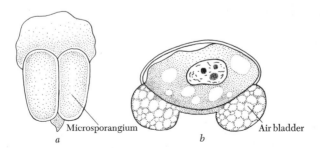

Figure 8.17 *Pinus* sp. (*a*) Microsporophyll with two microsporangia, undersurface. (*b*) Maturing microspore.

with the season and with latitude. For example, in 1975, during several warm periods around February 15, these processes occurred in *P. taeda* (yellow pine) near Bastrop in central Texas. In another species of *Pinus, P. virginiana,* growing near Ashland City, Tennessee, microsporogenesis occurs between March 15 and April 1 each year.

The megastrobili are more complex in organization. The axes of the strobili bear bracts from which ovule-bearing appendages, the **ovuliferous scales** (Figure 8.18*a*), emerge. These seemingly represent evolutionarily modified fertile spur shoots. Each bears two ovules (Figure 8.18*b*). An ovule, as we saw, is a megasporangium covered with an integument (Figure 8.19*a*); the passageway through the integument is known as the micropyle. A single megasporocyte in each ovule forms a row of four megaspores by meiosis; of these, the three nearest the micropyle degenerate, leaving one functional megaspore (Figure 8.19*b*). This is approximately the same size as the microspore and lacks a thickened wall; it is intimately associated with the surrounding cells of the megasporangium, from which it no doubt draws nutriment, instead of being free from the sporangial wall as are the megaspores of *Selaginella.* With the formation of microspores and megaspores by meiosis, sporogenesis is complete, and the development of the sexual phase, the gametophytes, follows.

The microspores of *Pinus,* as in all seed plants and some species of *Selaginella,* begin their endosporic development into male gametophytes before they are shed from the microsporangia. They are freed as pollen at the time they become four-celled, containing two sterile or prothallial cells, a generative cell, and a tube cell (Figure 8.20).

The opening of the microsporangia releases large clouds of these sulfur-

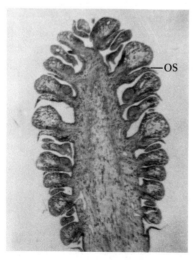

a

Figure 8.18 *Pinus* sp. (*a*) Longisection of young megastrobilus. (*b*) Ovuliferous scale (OS) with two ovules, upper surface.

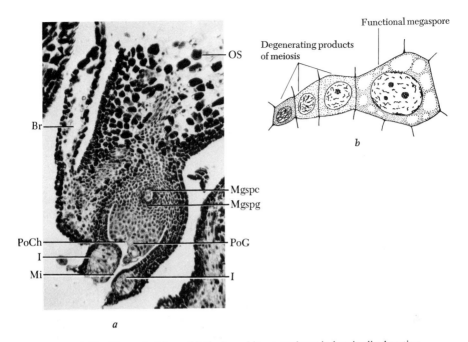

a

Figure 8.19 *Pinus virginiana.* (*a*) Ovule and its appendages in longitudinal section soon after pollination. (*b*) Functional megaspore with degenerating products of meiosis. Br, bract; I, integument; Mgspc, megasporocyte; Mgspg, megasporangium; Mi, micropyle; OS, ovuliferous scale; PoCh, pollen chamber; PoG, pollen grain.

colored, dustlike pollen grains (with their contained male gametophytes), which are transported great distances by air currents. At the same time in the spring that the pollen is being shed, the internodes of the axes of the current season's megastrobili elongate slightly, causing fissures to form between successive ovuliferous scales. Some of the airborne pollen grains sift into these fissures and come into contact with the tips of the ovules, which at this time have secreted a pollination droplet through the micropyle. Upon contact with this droplet, the pollen grains float through it, or are drawn by its contraction, into the pollen chamber (Figure 8.19*a*), a slight depression in the apex of the mega-

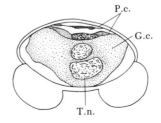

Figure 8.20 *Pinus virginiana.* Development of the male gametophyte. Microspore containing immature male gametophyte. G.c., generative cell; P.c., prothallial cell; T.n., tube nucleus.

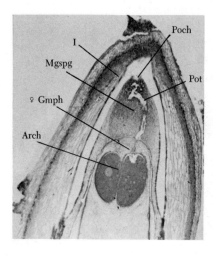

Figure 8.21 *Pinus virginiana,* longitudinal section of upper half of ovule at fertilization. Arch, archegonium; Gmph, female gametophyte; I, integument; Mgspg, megasporangium; Poch, pollen chamber; Pot, pollen tube.

sporangium. The transfer of pollen from the microsporangium to the micropyle of the ovule here again is called pollination.

After pollination, the functional megaspore (Figure 8.19*b*) in each ovule initiates the development of a female gametophyte by a series of nuclear divisions followed by synthesis of cytoplasm, which proceeds at first without wall formation, that is, by free-nuclear division. The female gametophyte parasitizes and digests the megasporangium; later, wall formation does occur in the female gametophyte. The ovules and all the tissues of the megastrobilus enlarge during this process. The mature female gametophyte finally differentiates two or three archegonia at its micropylar pole (Figure 8.21). The interval between pollination and maturation of the male and female gametophytes of pine is about 13 to 14 months.

Meanwhile, the pollen grains, stranded on the surface of the pollen chamber (megasporangial apex) when the pollination droplet disappears, will have germinated to form pollen tubes (Figures 8.21 and 8.22). These parasitically digest the tissues of the megasporangium and convey the sperm to the mature archegonia.

During its invasion of the megasporangium, the male gametophyte completes its maturation, the generative cell dividing into two cells, the stalk cell and the body cell, the latter dividing later into two sperms. The sperm cells

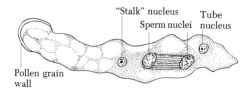

"Stalk" nucleus   Tube
Sperm nuclei   nucleus

Pollen grain
wall

Figure 8.22 *Pinus virginiana,* mature male gametophyte (within the ovule at maturity). Note pollen tube and two sperm nuclei, just after division.

of pine, consisting largely of nuclei, lack cilia, unlike those of the cycads and *Ginkgo.*

The pollen grain and tube with their component cells represent the mature male gametophyte. Union of one of the sperm nuclei with the egg nucleus at fertilization transforms the egg nucleus into a zygote nucleus. The second sperm nucleus degenerates.

The eggs of all the archegonia of a single female gametophyte may be fertilized (Figure 8.23), but only one embryo normally is present in the mature seed; however, **simple polyembryony** occurs, that is, several zygotes initiate embryogeny. As in the cycads and *Ginkgo,* embryogeny includes free-nuclear division stages, but only four free nuclei are produced in pine. These migrate to the base of the archegonium where, by three additional nuclear and cell divisions, they organize a 16-celled proembryo consisting of four tiers of 4 cells each (Figure 8.24*a*). The four most basal cells function as embryo-forming cells, while the cells of the adjacent tier elongate to thrust the embryo-forming cells into the tissues of the female gametophyte. The cells that function in this way are called **suspensor cells** (Figure 8.24*b*). In pine (and some other conifers) the four tiers of cells may separate along their longitudinal axes, so that four embryo-forming cells with their suspensors begin development of embryos. This phenomenon is known as **cleavage polyembryony,** in contrast to simple polyembryony already mentioned. Simple polyembryony is analogous to multiple fertilizations in some animals, whereas cleavage polyembryony is like the division into two or four units of the early cellular progeny of an animal zygote to form identical twins or quadruplets.

As the embryo develops, it grows out of the base of the archegonium (Figure 8.24*b*) into the vegetative tissues of the female gametophyte, a good deal of which it absorbs before it becomes dormant, several months after fertilization. During embryogeny, the cells of the integument harden by thickening their cell walls.

Similarly, soon after pollination the appendages that bear the ovules begin to enlarge (Figure 8.14) and harden, so by the time the embryos have become dormant, the megastrobilus is extremely hard. The ovules themselves

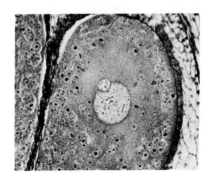

Figure 8.23 *Pinus virginiana.* Fertilization: union of small male nucleus with egg nucleus.

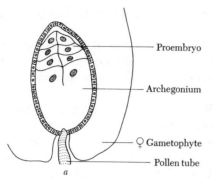

Proembryo

Archegonium

♀ Gametophyte

Pollen tube

a

Figure 8.24 *Pinus* sp., development of embryo and seed, and germination. (*a*) Section of archegonium with proembryo soon after fertilization. (*b*) Elongation of suspensor, which pushes embryo-forming cells out of archegonium into female gametophyte. (*c*) Median longitudinal section of seed.

Embryo initial

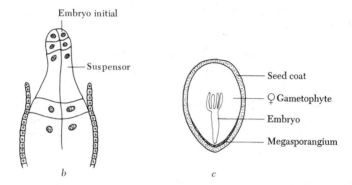

Suspensor

Seed coat

♀ Gametophyte

Embryo

Megasporangium

b

c

enlarge considerably. The ovule with its embryo comprises the seed. Once again, a gymnospermous seed (Figure 8.24*c*) is an embryonic sporophyte, surrounded, in turn, by the female gametophyte, the megaspore wall, and remains of the megasporangium, all of which are surrounded by the hardened integument, now called the seed coat.

As the seeds mature, the appendages of the megastrobilus that bear them spread apart (Figure 8.14*a*) and the winged[6] seeds (Figure 8.25*a*) are shed. The embryos of those seeds that fall in suitable environments renew growth through seed germination (Figure 8.25*b*). The embryonic leaves of seed plants are called **cotyledons.** There are 3 to 18 cotyledons among various species of pine. Unlike those of the cycads and *Ginkgo,* the cotyledons of pine are raised above the soil during germination of the seeds.

The seed, then, is in a sense a prefabricated miniature of the mature seed plant, in this case, the pine; the "germ" of a seed is its embryo. The seed develops as the result of the series of correlated morphological and physiological processes just summarized.

The reproductive process described for pine occupies about 18 to 20

[6]Some species of pine lack winged seeds.

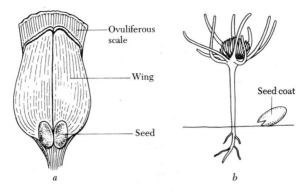

Figure 8.25   (*a*) *Pinus taeda,* ovuliferous scale with mature, winged seeds. (*b*) Seedling.

months, depending on the latitude and season. Every year a new crop of microstrobili develops on the trees. These shed their pollen, some of which is blown to the delicate megastrobili that same year, at the tips of certain branches. The male and female gametophytes, both now within the ovules of the megastrobilus, require many months from the time of pollination to mature, so fertilization occurs about 13 to 14 months after pollination. About four additional months are required for embryogeny and seed development, so the mature seeds are not shed until about 17 to 18 months after pollination. By this time the megastrobili have enlarged greatly and have developed into the familiar brown, woody pine-cone state.

Pinus is but one of some 40 to 50 genera of conifers, including more than 500 species, distributed in both hemispheres except in the tropics. This group includes cedars, larches, cypresses, spruce, and yew, among others. The reproductive process in all these plants is similar, in general, to that of the pine, except for certain variations in detail.

Although the term ''conifer'' is sometimes considered synonymous with evergreen, several genera, such as cypress (*Taxodium*), larch (*Larix*), and dawn redwood (*Metasequoia*), are deciduous. The true cedar (*Cedrus*) is widely cultivated as an ornamental in the United States, where the native species of juniper (*Juniperus*), from the wood of which pencils and cedar chests are made, is often called ''red cedar.'' Its seeds are used in the manufacture of an alcoholic drink, gin. *Juniperus* (Figure 8.26*a*) is dioecious and matures its seeds during a single growing season, as *Tsuga* (hemlock) and many other conifers do.

The conifers include some of the largest and longest-lived trees. Among them is the California redwood (*Sequoiadendron giganteum*), certain individuals of which may exceed 300 feet in height. Some living individuals of the California bristlecone pine, *Pinus aristata,* are more than 4000 years old.

Among conifers native to the Southern Hemisphere, two, *Podocarpus*

Figure 8.26 (*a*) *Juniperus virginiana,* ovulate branch. (*b*) *Araucaria imbricata* in cultivation at Seattle, Washington. (*c*) *Podocarpus* sp. [Courtesy of Professor Richard Norris.]

a

b

c

(Figure 8.26*c*) and *Araucaria* (Figure 8.26*b*), are widely cultivated as ornamentals in the United States and Europe. In the southern United States *Podocarpus* is called "yew," a vernacular name used for *Taxus* in some other parts of the world. Two species of *Araucaria*—*A. araucana,* the "monkey puzzle tree," and *A. heterophylla,* the "Norfolk Island Pine"—are widespread in cultivation.

Division Gnetophyta

This division includes three genera, *Ephedra, Gnetum,* and *Welwitschia,* often classified in the same order, but seemingly not very closely related, certainly insofar as their vegetative organization is concerned. They are restricted in distribution and not widely cultivated; accordingly, they are probably less familiar than other gymnosperms.

Only *Ephedra* (Figure 8.27*a*) is native to the United States, where it grows as a shrub or vine in Texas, New Mexico, Arizona, California, and Nevada, although it can survive in cultivation outdoors in such northern latitudes as in Boston, Massachusetts; Marburg, Germany; and Cambridge, England. In vegetative appearance, *Ephedra* suggests *Equisetum,* as both have green stems with minute leaves. Most species of *Ephedra* are dioecious, and some are called "joint fir." Among *Ephedra, Gnetum,* and *Welwitschia, Ephedra* is considered to be primitive because its female gametophytes produce archegonia. In *Gnetum* and *Welwitschia,* archegonia are not developed, the free egg cells being fertilized as in angiosperms (see Chapter 9).

Gnetum (Figure 8.27*b*), a vine or small tree, is pantropical and has broad, deciduous leaves, like a dicotyledonous angiosperm.

The third genus, *Welwitschia* (Figure 8.28), grows natively in Angola (Portuguese West Africa) under extremely arid conditions. *Welwitschia* is unique, its slow-growing toplike, concave stem ending in a deeply growing taproot. The first pair of true (postcotyledonary) leaves persists as the only leaves, although they split longitudinally, in their basal growth throughout the life of this gymnospermous plant.

In contrast to other gymnosperms, these three genera have some multicellular vessels in their xylem, in addition to the unicellular tracheids. All are dioecious, with relatively reduced gametophytes. The female gametophytes of *Gnetum* and *Welwitschia* are angiospermlike in producing eggs not contained in archegonia. The sperms of all three genera lack cilia. In discussions of the evolutionary origin of the angiosperms, these gymnosperms have often been suggested as possible precursors.

We should emphasize that the extant gymnosperms are vegetatively quite diverse, although all have a generally similar pattern of reproduction in which the manner of seed production especially differentiates them from angio-

a   *b*

Figure 8.27   (*a*) *Ephedra antisyphilitica.* (*b*) *Gnetum gnemon,* greenhouse-grown seedling.

Figure 8.28   *Welwitschia mirabilis.*

sperms. As compared with angiosperms, gymnosperms are decidedly a minority group in our present flora.

FOSSIL GYMNOSPERMS

Other than the Division Gnetophyta, the fossil record of which is sparse, gymnosperms were seemingly well represented in extinct floras, their history extending back into the Mississippian and Pennsylvanian (see Table 6.1) and possibly into the Upper Devonian. This statement is based on the report of the occurrence of a fossil seedlike structure called *Archaeosperma arnoldii* (Figure 8.29). This fossil consists of cupules surrounding structures called "seeds," but the absence of a megasporangium around the megaspores makes this questionable.

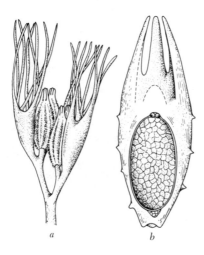

a   *b*

Figure 8.29   *Archaeosperma arnoldii,* an Upper Devonian seed. (*a*) Cupules containing two seeds in each. (*b*) A single seed. Note the large functional megaspore with three degenerate megaspores and the integumentary lobes. [After J. M. Pettitt and Beck.]

A few representatives of these extinct plants, both similar to and different from some of those in the Divisions Cycadophyta, Ginkgophyta, and Coniferophyta, will be discussed in the following account.

The Pteridosperms, or Seed Ferns

Many fernlike leaves and/or their impressions occur in Carboniferous strata, the period in which they lived often being referred to as "The Age of Ferns." However, it is now clear that seeds were attached to some of these leaves, which are representatives of a completely extinct line of plants, the seed ferns. *Lyginopteris* of the seed ferns, which occurs in Pennsylvanian (see Table 6.1) strata, is a well-known representative of this group. Its reconstruction (Figure 8.30) is based on knowledge about the leaves, stems, roots, and reproductive structures. In habit of growth, *Lyginopteris* had an erect slender stem in which some secondary growth occurred. The leaves were large and several times pinnately compound. Like those of modern tree ferns, some of the roots of *Lyginopteris* arose from the erect stem and penetrated the soil. The supposed microsporangia of *Lyginopteris* were borne on certain of the pinnules, and the ovules were borne in cuplike bracts within which they matured as seeds. *Medullosa* (Figure 8.31) is another quite well-known genus of seed ferns found in rocks from the Mississippian through the Permian (see Table 6.1).

Cycadeoids

A second line of fossil gymnosperms has been designated the cycadeoids because, although they differ from modern cycads, their growth habit was cycadlike. One of these plants, *Cycadeoidea,* is illustrated in Figure 8.32. Here the pinnately compound leaves arose from a large bulbous stem. The reproductive organs of *Cycadeoidea* differed greatly from those of modern cycads, which are dioecious. In *Cycadeoidea* the complex reproductive structure consisted of a conical receptacle on which stalked ovules were borne between ster-

Figure 8.30 *Lyginopteris oldhamnia,* a seed fern. [Courtesy of Chicago Field Museum of Natural History.]

Figure 8.31 Fossil gymnosperm. *Medullosa noei,* a fossil Carboniferous seed fern, reconstruction. [Courtesy of T. Delevoryas.]

ile appendages. These were surrounded by a hoodlike complex on which the microsporangia occurred in rows. Cycadeoids flourished during the Mesozoic (see Table 6.1), which is sometimes called "The Age of Cycads."

Fossil Cycads

Leptocycas (Figure 8.33) is an example of a true cycad, that is, one with strobili, like living cycads, which lived in Upper Triassic (see Table 6.1) times. One of the specimens bore a leaf and attached microstrobilus. The fossil record of cycads is not abundant, and the nature of the precursors of extant cycads has not been elucidated by the fossil record.

Figure 8.32 *Cyadeoidea* sp., reconstruction. [After T. Delevoryas.]

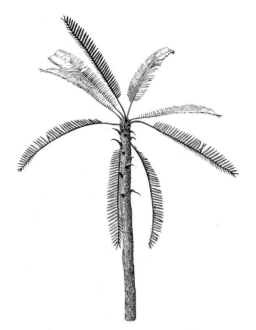

Figure 8.33 *Leptocycas gracilis,* from the Triassic, much reduced. [After T. Delevoryas and R. C. Hope.]

Fossil Ginkgophytes and Conifers

Two probable relatives of *Ginkgo* described from the fossil record are illustrated in Figure 8.34. *Baiera* is known through its palmately branched leaves. The leaves of *Ginkgoites* (Figure 8.34) are much like those of the extant *Ginkgo.* Many *Ginkgo*-like fossils have been described extending through Permian, Mesozoic, and Tertiary rocks (see Table 6.1).

The fossil record of conifers is better known—the fossil history of mod-

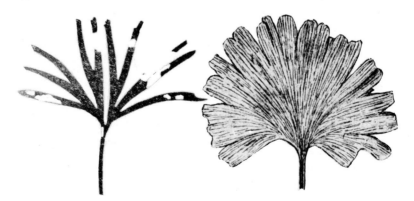

Figure 8.34 Fossil Ginkgophyta leaves. (Left, *Baiera* sp.; right, *Ginkgoites* sp.) [After A. C. Seward.]

a   *b*

Figure 8.35 (*a*) *Cordaites borasifolius,* reconstruction. (*b*) *Lebachia piniformis* var. *solmsii,* a fossil conifer from the Upper Carboniferous, reconstruction. [After R. Florin, from T. Delevoryas.]

ern conifers extends back to the Triassic period—and two representatives will be discussed. *Cordaites,* reconstructed in Figure 8.35*a* from Paleozoic remains, was a tall tree with many branches near the top, and it seemingly grew in groves or forests. The stems increased in diameter by secondary growth. The leaves were elongate and straplike, while the roots contained protosteles. Microsporangia were borne on the apical appendages of conelike structures; the ovules developed at the tips of other conelike lateral branches.

In *Lebachia* (Figure 8.35*b*), from both Pennsylvanian and Permian (see Table 6.1) rocks, the stems were clothed with densely, helically arranged small leaves. The long-stalked ovules occurred associated with sterile, helically arranged bracts in strobili (Figure 8.35*b*). The microsporangia were borne on the abaxial faces of scalelike microsporophylls arranged in strobili.

QUESTIONS FOR REVIEW

1. Distinguish between angiospermy and gymnospermy.
2. Name the divisions of gymnospermous seed plants.
3. What accounts for the woodiness of many gymnosperms?
4. Define or explain wood, endospory, ovule, pollen chamber, pollination in gymnosperms, seed of gymnosperms, linear tetrad, functional megaspore, free-nuclear division, pollen tube, suspensor, seed coat, cotyledon, plumule, hypocotyl, pollen.
5. Are the spores of gymnosperms homosporous? Explain.
6. Where does *Ginkgo* grow natively? Are there any trees in your locality?
7. Where do cycads grow natively? Are any used as ornamentals in your locality?

8. How can one distinguish cycads from ferns and palms?

9. How do the male gametophytes of *Zamia, Ginkgo,* and *Pinus* differ?

10. What is the method of nutrition of the male and female gametophytes of gymnosperms?

11. What plant produces the largest sperms?

12. With the aid of drawings, describe what reproductive structures would be visible on a pine tree in December of any year. Do the same for March to April of any year.

13. What would the ovules of pine contain at the time of pollination? In April of the following spring? In June, a year after pollination? In October of the year after pollination?

14. Define and distinguish the terms polyembryony, simple polyembryony, and cleavage polyembryony.

15. Name the conifers growing in your locality. Which are monoecious and which dioecious?

16. How do the female gametophytes of *Welwitschia* and *Gnetum* differ from those of *Ephedra*?

17. Where do *Ephedra, Gnetum,* and *Welwitschia* grow natively?

CHAPTER NINE

Seed Plants II:
Angiosperms

INTRODUCTION

The second great group of seed-producing plants, the Angiosperms—commonly known as flowering plants (see Table 1.1)—is both the largest group in number of genera, species, and individuals, and the most recent to develop on the earth, its origins being in the Cretaceous (see Table 6.1). The angiosperms, which comprise the Division Anthophyta, differ from gymnospermous seed plants in that their ovules and seeds are *enclosed* within the pistil (see p. 174) or megasporophyll(s) (see Figure 8.1a–c), which later becomes a seed-bearing fruit. The structure of the pistil in certain primitive angiosperms suggests that the enclosure of the seeds may have come about by the evolutionary folding of a leaflike, ovule-bearing megasporophyll. Other important differences between the reproduction of gymnosperms and angiosperms are summarized on p. 228.

The angiosperms exceed all other vascular plants in range of diversity of the plant body and habitat, and in their utility to humans. Both woody and herbaceous angiosperms exist, and among the latter especially there is considerable diversity of vegetative structure, exemplified by bulbous hyacinths, onions, lilies, rhizomatous *Iris,* and many grasses. Diversity of habitat is demonstrated by such aquatics as water lilies, *Elodea,* and duckweed, or *Lemna* (see Figure 5.1); such xerophytes as cacti; and such epiphytes as "Spanish moss," orchids, and bromeliads. In some xerophytes and epiphytes, the leaves are much reduced or absent.

Woody angiosperms are used extensively as lumber and fuel and as the source of commercial cork; herbaceous types are important sources of food, beverages, fibers, textiles, drugs, and vegetable oils. Both the vegetative and reproductive portions of angiosperms are used as foods. Sweet potatoes, carrots, turnips, beets, and parsnips are examples of fleshy roots that are important foods; white, or "Irish," potatoes and asparagus are stems. Various greens, such as spinach, turnips, chard, and lettuce, are leaves. The immense terminal buds of cabbages and head lettuce, as well as the fleshy petioles of rhubarb and celery, are also eaten.

Examples of the reproductive organs of angiosperms—flowers, fruits, and seeds—used as food are even more abundant. In both cauliflower and broccoli, groups of flowers, called **inflorescences,** are eaten. National cultures and economies are based on the use for food of such fruits as the grains of corn, rice, wheat, and rye. Indeed, fruits used as food are too numerous to list completely, but among them may be cited citrus fruits, squashes and melons, tomatoes, grapes, bananas, apples, pears, and various berries. The preceding list contains examples, such as tomatoes and squash, of fruits that the layperson frequently classifies as "vegetables." However, structures are truly fruits if they are derived at least in part from the pistil(s) or megasporophyll(s) of the flower; vegetative organs and vegetables, strictly speaking, are nonreproductive parts of plants. The term "vegetable" is much more loosely used otherwise in common idiom.

After the angiosperm seed germinates, an extensive period of somatic or vegetative development of the sporophyte follows. This may be terminated by flowering, as in annuals (for example, corn), or it may continue during and after flowering, as in perennials (for example, lily, magnolia, or maple). **Perennials,** as we know, are plants that continue to grow for an indefinite number of growing seasons. Many perennials are woody, that is, they have active cambiums that add abundant secondary xylem. Others lack secondary xylem and are relatively soft; they are said to be herbaceous perennials.

Chapter 5 briefly summarized some basic facts regarding the vegetative organs of vascular plants, including the flowering plants; therefore, this chapter will emphasize primarily their reproduction.

GROSS MORPHOLOGY OF FLOWERS

Since 1920 it has been known that in many plants the change from the vegetative to the reproductive state is dependent on the daily balance between duration of daylight and darkness, that is, the **photoperiod.** Later it was demonstrated that the initiation of flowering involves a hormonal mechanism. Flowering, therefore, is triggered by chemical changes under the influence of light.

The flower is the reproductive structure of the angiosperms, but it is a difficult structure to define in precise enough terms to distinguish it from aggregations of microsporophylls and megasporophylls, which we have called

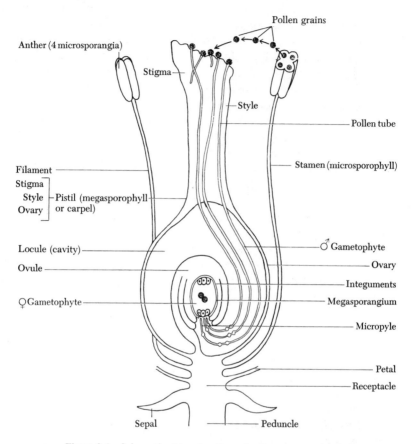

Figure 9.1   Schematized longisection of a flower, parts labeled.

strobili or cones in gymnosperms and vascular cryptogams. A schematic section of a flower is illustrated in Figure 9.1; the parts mentioned in the following discussion of the flower may be located either in this figure or in Figure 9.2.

Flowers, like strobili, are stems in which the apical meristems have dif-

Figure 9.2   (*Opposite page.*) *Ranunculus macranthus,* floral structure. (*a*) Habit of growth. (*b*) Single flower more highly magnified. Note petals and numerous stamens surrounding numerous pistils. (*c*) Single flower showing sepal (at the left), petals, stamens, and pistils. (*d*) Postpollination and postfertilization phase. The sepals, petals, and stamens have fallen, leaving only the numerous enlarging pistils or young fruits on the receptacles. (*e*) Receptacle and maturing fruits (achenes). (*f*) Diagram of bisection of a flower. (*g*) Bisection of a single pistil. [*a–e* courtesy of Dr. William Ruf.]

a

b

c

e

d

Pistil

Stamen

Petal

Sepal

f

Ovule

g

ferentiated completely. In flowers, as in strobili, the axis, or **receptacle,** that bears the sporophylls has short internodes, so that the sporophylls are borne either in a tight spiral or in a seemingly whorled and cyclic arrangement. In the latter case, three, four, or five sporophylls usually arise at a given level of the axis. In addition to the sporophylls, floral axes usually bear sterile appendages called **sepals** (collectively, the **calyx**), which are generally green (but sometimes other colors), and **petals** (collectively, the **corolla**). When petals and sepals are not clearly different from each other, they may be called **tepals.** The sepals and the petals together comprise the **perianth.**

The *essential* parts of the flower are the sporophylls themselves. In angiosperms, the microsporophylls are known as **stamens** and the megasporophylls **(carpels),** or fused groups of them, are known as **pistils.** Stamens produce microspores, and pistils produce megaspores (within their ovules). Stamens and pistils of angiosperms correspond especially in function to the microsporophylls and megasporophylls, respectively, of both gymnosperms and certain seedless vascular plants. This correspondence will facilitate our understanding of the reproductive process in angiosperms.

Three basic patterns of positional relationship of the floral organs occur in flowers. In the first, **hypogyny,** the stamens, petals, and sepals arise below the base of the pistil (Figure 9.3*a*). In a second pattern, **perigyny,** the stamens, petals, and sepals arise from the rim of a cuplike structure that surrounds, but is free from, the pistil (Figure 9.3*b*). Finally, some flowers are **epigynous.** In these the pistil is sunken within a structure probably composed of the united bases of petals, sepals, and stamens so that these three organs arise above the pistil (Figure 9.3*c*).

Pistils (Figures 9.1, 9.2, and 9.16) usually consist of an enlarged basal portion, the **ovary,** which contains one or more ovules, and a receptive surface for pollen, the **stigma.** The stigma and ovary usually are connected by a more or less elongated **style.** Pistils may be either simple or compound. A **simple pistil** is composed of one ovule-bearing megasporophyll, or **carpel;** the carpel, therefore, is the equivalent of the megasporophyll. **Compound pistils** are composed of several simple pistils (or carpels or megasporophylls) that have become united during evolution; in some flowers they even unite in development. Simple pistils (see Figures 8.1*a, b* and 9.1 and 9.2*b, c*) usually have but one

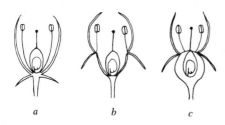

Figure 9.3   Median longitudinal sections of (*a*), a hypogynous, (*b*) a perigynous, (*c*) an epigynous flower diagrammatic. [After H. C. Bold, C. J. Alexopoulos, and T. Delevoryas.]

a   *b*   *c*

locule containing ovules, whereas many compound pistils have ovaries partitioned into two or more chambers (see Figures 8.1*c* and 9.15*b*).[1]

In the vast majority of angiosperms, both stamens and pistils occur on the same individual sporophyte and are usually borne together in single flowers; such flowers are said to be **perfect.** In some species, however, **staminate flowers** bear microsporophylls alone, while **pistillate flowers** have only megasporophylls on their receptacles. Such staminate and pistillate flowers are said to be **imperfect.** Corn (Figure 9.4) is a good example of a **monoecious** plant with imperfect flowers, since both types of flowers are borne on the same individual. In other angiosperms, the staminate and pistillate flowers occur upon different individuals, as in the willow (Figure 9.5), poplar (cottonwood), and mulberry, among others; such plants are, accordingly, **dioecious.**

Flowers may be large, conspicuous, and borne singly, or they may arise on the same axis in various types of **inflorescences** in which the individual flowers may sometimes be smaller and less striking. Of the various types of inflorescences, the head, or **capitulum** (Figure 9.6*a*), is especially frequent and

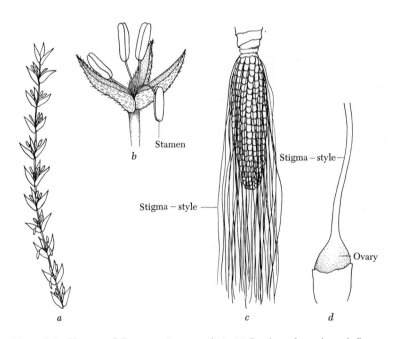

Figure 9.4 Flowers of *Zea mays* (corn, maize). (*a*) Portion of staminate inflorescence. (*b*) Single staminate flower. (*c*) Pistillate inflorescence or young "ear" of corn. (*d*) Single pistillate flower with stigma-style.

[1]However, some compound pistils, like those in the grass, sedge, and aster families, have only one chamber, lacking partitions betwen the parts.

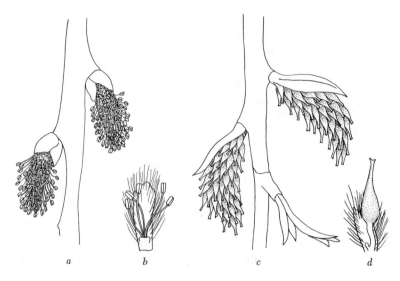

Figure 9.5 *Salix* sp. (willow) inflorescences and flowers. (*a*) Staminate inflorescence. (*b*) Single staminate flower, enlarged. (*c*) Pistillate inflorescence. (*d*) Single pistillate flower.

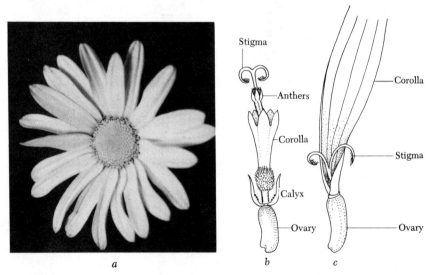

Figure 9.6 *Helianthus* sp. (sunflower). (*a*) Capitulum, or inflorescence. (*b*) Detail of disc floret. (*c*) Detail of ray floret (corolla only partially shown).

characterizes the large family Asteraceae (p. 235). In the type of capitulum illustrated in Figure 9.6, two types of flowers are present: the minute, bell-like, central **disc florets** (Figure 9.6*b*) and the larger, peripheral **ray florets** (Figure 9.6*c*). The disc florets are perfect and complete, with stamens, a pistil, a calyx, and a corolla. In the ray florets, the corolla is split open near the base, and stamens are absent.

THE REPRODUCTIVE PROCESS

To those who have mastered the essential features of reproduction in gymnosperms described in Chapter 8, the reproductive process in angiosperms will not seem unduly complicated. Attempts to abbreviate an account of this process often result in inaccuracies and confusion, so we shall discuss it in some detail in the following paragraphs.

Reproduction in angiosperms, as in gymnosperms, includes the following basic phenomena: (1) sporogenesis; (2) development of the gametophytes and gametogenesis; (3) pollination; (4) fertilization; and (5) embryogeny and development of the seed and fruit (the latter in angiosperms only).

Sporogenesis

The production of the flowers with their sporophylls marks the maturation of the angiosperm sporophyte. In all annuals and in many perennials, the flowers, seeds, and fruit are produced during the first growing season; however, in many other perennials, a number of years of purely vegetative growth precede the appearance of flowers.

Microsporogenesis does not differ in any important way in angiosperms and gymnosperms. Microspores are produced in groups of four from microsporocytes (microspore mother cells) undergoing meiosis within the microsporangia of the stamen (Figures 9.7a–d and 9.8a–c). This occurs when the stamens are still enclosed within the young flower bud. The four eusporangiate microsporangia are collectively called the **anther;** the stalk that elevates them is the **filament.** Stamens in some flowers, like those of the water lily, may be petallike. Like the microspores and pollen grains of gymnosperms, those of angiosperms have walls that are variously sculptured and ornamented in ways that are highly characteristic of a given species; this marking may be quite elaborate (Figure 9.8d). In any case, the pollen grains of individual plants can be identified and assigned with great accuracy to their species; this, in part, is the division of botany known as **palynology.** Identification of pollen grains is important in the diagnosis and treatment of such allergies as hay fever, rose fever, and so forth. Furthermore, through the examination of peat and other deposits containing spores and pollen grains, it has been possible to ascertain the composition of ancient floras and to determine past changes of climate in locations where such deposits occur (see also p. 93).

Megasporogenesis in flowering plants is also like that in gymnosperms. You will recall that the megasporangia of seed plants are permanently enclosed in integuments and are called ovules (Figure 9.1). Recall, too, that in gym-

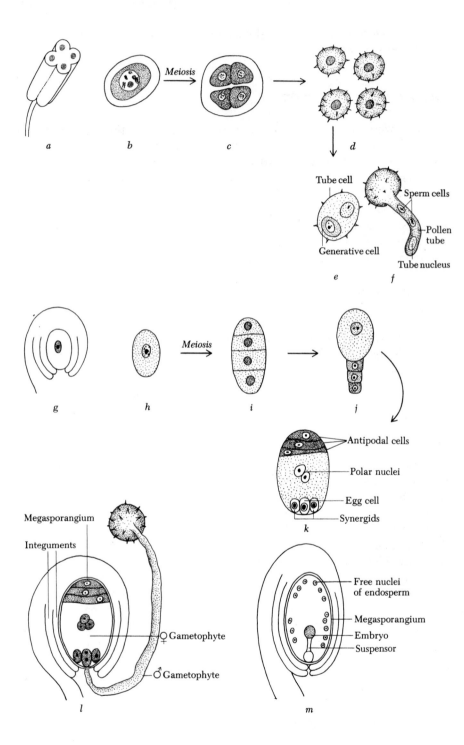

Tube cell
Sperm cells
Generative cell
Pollen tube
Tube nucleus

e *f*

Meiosis

g *h* *i* *j*

Antipodal cells
Polar nuclei
Egg cell
Synergids

k

Megasporangium
Integuments

♀ Gametophyte
♂ Gametophyte

l

Free nuclei of endosperm
Megasporangium
Embryo
Suspensor

m

nosperms, the ovules are produced on the *surface* of appendages of strobili (as in most cycads and conifers, see Figure 8.1*d, e*), or at the ends of stalks (as in *Ginkgo,* see Figure 8.11*b*). In the angiosperms, the ovules always occur *within* the more or less enlarged base of the pistil or megasporophyll, known as the ovary (see Figures 8.1*a–c* and 9.1). The number of ovules within an ovary varies from one to many, as does the place of their attachment, or type of **placentation;** the ovules may occur either on a central axis (axile placentation) or on the ovary wall (parietal placentation). The remainder of the megasporophyll is composed of the style and stigma (Figures 9.1, 9.2, and 9.15*a*); the stigma is a specialized receptive surface to which the pollen grains adhere at pollination. In some flowers, such as those of corn (Figure 9.4), the pollen tube may have to grow parasitically 6 or more inches before it reaches the micropyle of the ovule. As in the gymnosperms, each ovule usually produces only a single megasporocyte; this undergoes meiosis to form a linear tetrad of megaspores (Figures 9.7*i* and 9.9*b, c*) while the flower is in the bud stage. In most angiosperms, as in all other seed plants, only a single functional megaspore normally survives (Figure 9.9*d*), usually the one farthest from the micropyle. Thus, megasporogenesis in angiosperms is not essentially different from that in gymnosperms.

Development of Gametophytes and Gametogenesis

Compared with the time required for the development of the gametophytes in many gymnosperms, the process in most angiosperms is rapid. This

Figure 9.7   (*Opposite page.*) Summary of the reproductive process in angiosperms. (*a*) Lower portion of an anther (four microsporangia). (*b*) Microsporocyte. (*c*) Tetrad of microspores. (*d*) Mature microspores. (*e–f*) Maturation of male gametophyte and formation of pollen tube. (*g*) Median longitudinal section of an ovule containing a megasporocyte. (*h*) Megasporocyte enlarged. (*i*) Linear tetrad of megaspores. (*j*) Functional and three degenerating megaspores. (*k*) Mature female gametophyte developed by functional megaspore. (*l*) M.l.s. of an ovule at moment of double fertilization. (*m*) M.l.s. of an ovule soon after fertilization. (*n*) Dormant seed with dicotyledonous embryo.

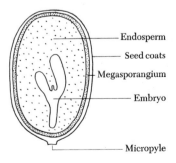

— Endosperm

— Seed coats

— Megasporangium

— Embryo

— Micropyle

n

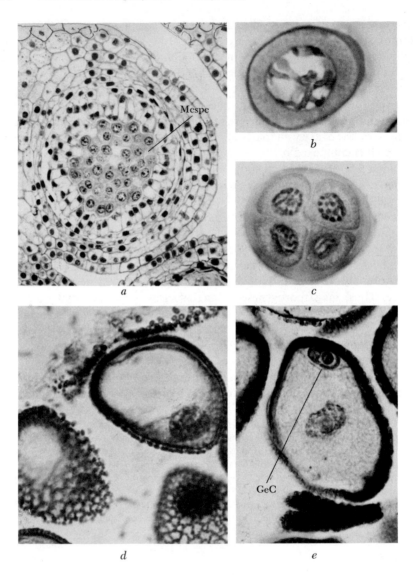

Figure 9.8 *Lilium* sp. (lily). (*a*) Transection, anther lobe or microsporangium; Mcspc, microsporocytes. (*b*) Microsporocyte, prophase of meiosis. (*c*) Tetrad of microspores. (*d*) Microspores with sculptured walls. (*e*) Pollen grain containing immature male gametophyte consisting of large tube cell and generative cell, GeC.

is correlated with the fact that the gametophytes themselves are smaller and less complex in angiosperms. As usual in seed plants, the development of the male gametophyte from the microspore is at first endosporic and is initiated soon after microsporogenesis has been completed (Figures 9.8*e* and 9.10*a*). In angiosperms the male gametophyte is simpler than that of gymnosperms. In

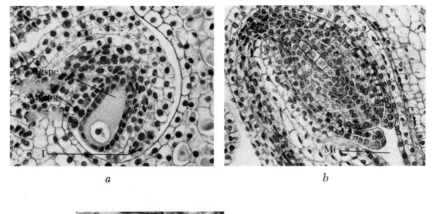

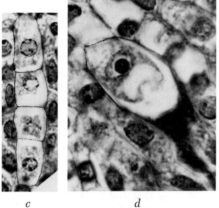

Figure 9.9 Megasporogenesis. (a) Median longitudinal section of young ovule of *Lilium*. (b-d) *Oenothera* sp.: (b) M.l.s. of ovule with linear tetrad of megaspores; (c) the same, enlarged; (d) functional and degenerated megaspores. I, integuments; Mgspc, megasporocyte; Mgspg, megasporangium; Mi, micropyle.

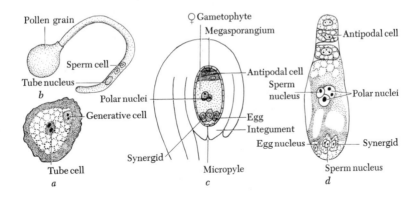

Figure 9.10 The gametophytic phase in flowering plants. (a) Immature male gametophyte within pollen grain consisting of generative cell and tube cell. (b) Pollen germination and mature male gametophyte. (c) Median longitudinal section of ovule with mature female gametophyte. (d) Double fertilization in lily.

development, the microspore nucleus undergoes mitosis followed by cytokinesis to form a generative cell and tube cell (Figure 9.10*a*). The former divides
to form two sperm nuclei either before the pollen has been shed or after it
germinates.

Except for the formation of the pollen tube after pollination (Figure
9.10*b*), development of the male gametophyte may be completed within the
microspore wall before the pollen has been shed from the anther. In some
species, on the other hand, the nuclear division in which the generative cell
produces the two sperm nuclei occurs in the pollen tube during germination
(Figure 9.10*b*). The mature male gametophyte (Figure 9.10*b*) contains only
three nuclei, the tube nucleus and two sperm nuclei; the latter probably are
surrounded by delicate sheaths of specialized cytoplasm delimited from that
of the pollen tube.

In most angiosperms, the nucleus of the functional megaspore undergoes
three successive free-nuclear divisions to form eight haploid nuclei that become somewhat differentiated and characteristically arranged within the mature female gametophyte, which has developed from the functional megaspore
(Figures 9.1, 9.7*l*, and 9.10*c, d*). The megaspore wall does not thicken. Of the
three nuclei nearest the micropylar pole of the female gametophyte, one functions as the **egg nucleus** and the other two are known as **synergid nuclei**. These
three nuclei are delimited from the common cytoplasm by delicate membranes
to form the egg and synergids. At the opposite pole, three **antipodal cells** are
formed. The remaining two nuclei, having previously migrated from the poles
to the center of the female gametophyte, are, because of their migration, called
polar nuclei.

It should be noted that in more than 70 percent of Anthophyta, the female gametophyte arises from a single functional megaspore. In some members of the Anthophyta,[2] for example lily (*Lilium*), frequently used to
demonstrate the reproductive process in flowers, all four megaspore nuclei
(Figure 9.11*a*) resulting from meiosis (not followed by cytokinesis) function
to form the female gametophyte: the genetic significance of this will occur to
the thoughtful reader! An additional complexity in the process in lily is that
before these megaspore nuclei (which are not separated from each other by
cell walls) divide, they move from their linear arrangement (Figure 9.11*b*); one
remains at the micropylar pole of the female gametophyte and three move to
the opposite one. All four nuclei now undergo mitosis, but the spindles of the
three nuclei at the antipodal pole become connected to form one (Figure 9.11*c*).
As a result, two triploid nuclei are formed at one pole and two haploid nuclei
at the other pole of the female gametophyte (Figure 9.11*d, e*). These cells divide
once more, and an eight-nucleate, seven-celled female gametophyte is organized. Note that the antipodal and one of the polar nuclei are triploid, while

---

[2]And probably also in *Gnetum* and *Welwitschia*.

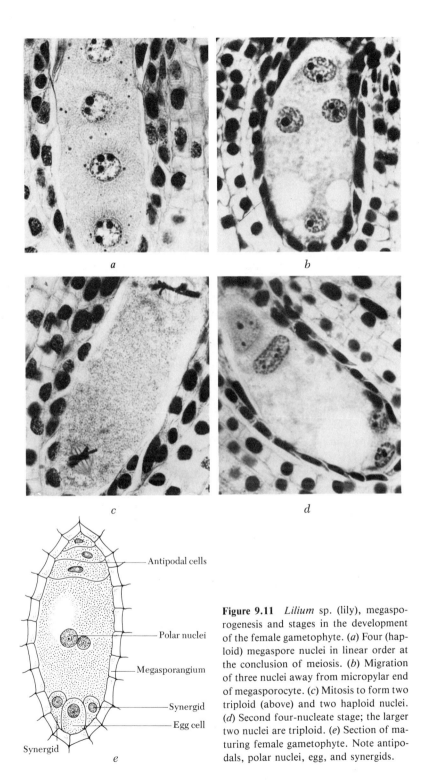

Antipodal cells

Polar nuclei

Megasporangium

Synergid

Egg cell

Synergid

e

Figure 9.11 *Lilium* sp. (lily), megasporogenesis and stages in the development of the female gametophyte. (*a*) Four (haploid) megaspore nuclei in linear order at the conclusion of meiosis. (*b*) Migration of three nuclei away from micropylar end of megasporocyte. (*c*) Mitosis to form two triploid (above) and two haploid nuclei. (*d*) Second four-nucleate stage; the larger two nuclei are triploid. (*e*) Section of maturing female gametophyte. Note antipodals, polar nuclei, egg, and synergids.

the other polar nucleus, egg and synergid nuclei are haploid. Whatever their mode of development, the female gametophytes of angiosperms are parasitic on the sporophyte.

Compared with the female gametophyte of most gymnosperms, the female gametophyte of angiosperms has a short existence and little internal differentiation, but both arise by free-nuclear division. A female gametangium, or archegonium, is absent; only an egg cell is present. As the flower opens, and as the stigmas become receptive to pollen, the ovule (or ovules) within the ovary contains mature or maturing female gametophytes.

Pollination and Fertilization

When the flowers open and afterward, the microsporangia, which may coalesce internally to form two "**pollen sacs**," open by fissures or pores and begin to shed the pollen grains and their enclosed male gametophytes. Some of these pollen grains are transferred to various forces, such as gravity, wind, insects, and other animals, and even by water (in certain aquatics), to the receptive surface of the stigma (Figure 9.1). A number of special relationships between insects and the pollination of flowers are well known; they are indicative of close correlations between the evolution of the flowering plants and that of the insects involved. Thus, pollination of the female inflorescence of figs, resulting in the edible fruit, is accomplished by a small wasp, *Blastophaga;* when these wasps are absent, edible fruits do not develop. Humming birds and long-tongued insects such as certain bees, wasps, and butterflies, in search of **nectar**[3] (which may contain up to 25 percent glucose) and pollen, are the agents of pollination in many plants. One of the most interesting examples of a seemingly obligate relationship is that between the Spanish bayonet, *Yucca,* and the yucca moth, *Tegeticula yuccasella.* This moth lays its eggs in the ovary of the *Yucca* flower and simultaneously pollinates it. The larvae developing from the eggs eat a few of the seeds, but large numbers of seeds survive and maintain the species of *Yucca.*

In the process of pollination, a great difference between angiospermous and gymnospermous seed plants is apparent. In angiosperms, pollination is the transfer of pollen grains from the microsporangia of the stamen to the stigma of the megasporophyll, but not directly to the micropyle of the ovule (as in gymnosperms). Once on the stigma surface, the pollen grains germinate rapidly to form pollen tubes, which penetrate the tissues of the stigma and style, enter the ovary, and, finally, enter the micropyles of ovules. The male gametophyte of angiosperms, as well as the female, is parasitic on the sporophyte. If pollination has been heavy enough, there is sufficient pollen for one pollen tube to grow toward the micropyle of every ovule, enter it, and make contact with the female gametophyte. Probably because of differences

---

[3]A secretion of plant glands that may occur anywhere on the plant but especially in flowers.

in turgor pressure, the pollen tubes burst and discharge their nuclei into the cytoplasm of the female gametophyte upon making contact within the ovule. In at least 15 genera of angiosperms, in which fertilization has been carefully investigated, the sperms are discharged into one of the synergids as it degenerates. From there, one sperm migrates into the egg cell and the other into the central cell containing the polar nuclei.

At this point, another important difference between angiosperms and gymnosperms becomes apparent, that is, the occurrence of **double fertilization,** a phenomenon known only in flowering plants. This involves two sperms: one sperm nucleus unites with the egg nucleus, and the other with the two polar nuclei (which may unite before fertilization by the second sperm) of the female gametophyte to form a triploid nucleus (Figure 9.10d). The functioning of both sperm suggested the term "double fertilization." Here again, although fertilization is accompanied by a number of attendant secondary phenomena, we see that sexual reproduction involves the union of cells and nuclei, and the association of chromosomes—in this case, forming both a zygote nucleus and a triploid nucleus, the **primary endosperm nucleus.** In lily, of course, the primary endosperm nucleus is pentaploid. In the postfertilization processes, now to be considered, these two nuclei play leading roles.

Embryogeny and Development of the Seed and Fruit

The occurrence of pollination and double fertilization stimulates nuclear and cell division in the ovule and pistil (and often in such closely associated structures as the receptacle and **hypanthium** or floral tube [Figure 9.23c], in flowers that have such a structure); accordingly, these enlarge greatly. Their enlargement is controlled by formation of hormones. It will be recalled that the gymnosperm ovule reaches its maximum size approximately at the time of fertilization, but in angiosperms, ovule enlargement follows fertilization. The stamens and petals gradually disintegrate or are shed. These changes eventually become noticeable to the unaided eye as the ovary enlarges to form the **fruit** and ovules enlarge to form the seeds.

Soon after double fertilization, the primary endosperm nucleus initiates a series of nuclear divisions to form triploid endosperm nuclei (Figure 9.12a), which, in most cases, are sooner or later separated from one another by cell walls. Thus, a cellular **endosperm** is formed. This tissue is rich in stored food that has been transported from the parent sporophyte; hence the cellular endosperm serves as a source of nutrition for the developing embryo. Here we have another difference between the angiosperms and gymnosperms. In angiosperms, the embryonic sporophyte is nourished by a special nutritive tissue, the **endosperm,** which is formed after fertilization. By contrast, the gymnosperm embryo obtains its metabolites from the haploid vegetative tissues of the female gametophyte (see Figure 8.24c) formed before fertilization.

Sometime after the initiation of endosperm development, the zygote, by

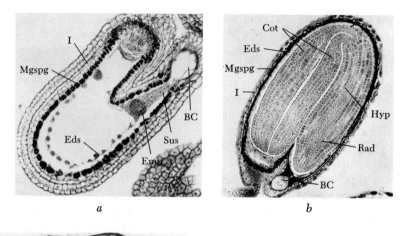

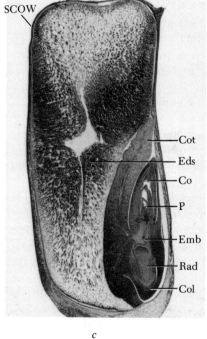

Figure 9.12 Embryogeny of flowering plants. (*a, b*) *Capsella* sp., shepherd's purse. (*c*) *Zea mays* (corn). [After J. E. Sass.] BC, basal cell; Co, coleoptile; Col, coleorhiza; Cot, cotyledons; Emb, embryo; Eds, endosperm; Hyp, hypocotyl; I, integument; Mgspg, megasporangium; P, plumule; Rad, radicle or embryonic root; SCOW, seed coats and ovary wall, Sus, suspensor.

a series of nuclear and cell divisions, forms a mass of cells that varies in extent and degree of organization, depending upon the particular genus of flowering plant. This mass of cells is the young embryonic sporophyte of the next generation, the so-called germ of the seed. In some angiosperms, such as many orchids, the embryo enters a period of dormancy after only a few cells have developed. In most others, the embryo consists of an axis, the **hypocotyl**, bear-

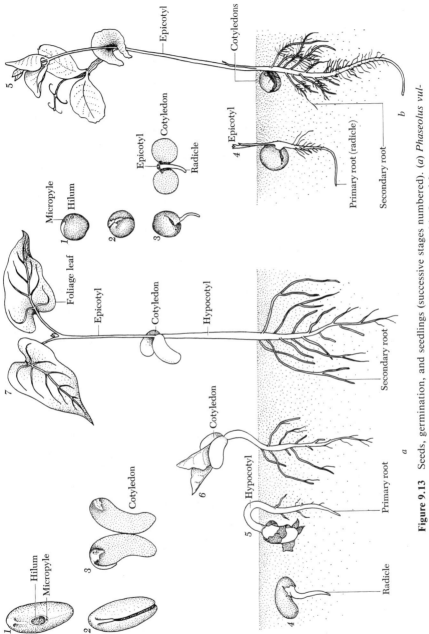

Figure 9.13 Seeds, germination, and seedlings (successive stages numbered). (*a*) *Phaseolus vulgaris* (garden bean). (*b*) *Pisum sativum* (pea), seed coats removed in 2 and 3.

ing the **cotyledons,** between which (in dicotyledons) is a terminal bud, the **plumule** or **epicotyl,** and below which is an embryonic root, the **radicle** (Figure 9.12*b, c*). As the development of the embryo nears completion, the tissues of the ovule become somewhat dehydrated, and the integuments become impervious and dark in color; by this time, the ovules have matured into seeds. As Figure 9.12*b, c* illustrates, an angiosperm **seed** consists of an embryonic sporophyte (a "germ") in a dormant condition; this is embedded within the endosperm and the remaining megasporangial tissues and integuments. These integuments are now called **seed coats.** In some angiosperms, the embryo does not become dormant until it has digested most of the endosperm and absorbed into itself (usually into cotyledons, which, accordingly, become fleshy) the metabolites stored in the endosperm; as a result, the embryo is massive. Beans

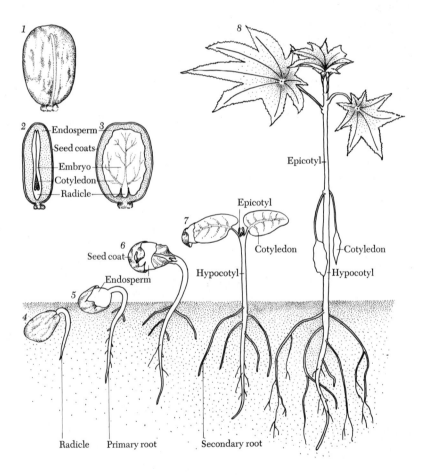

a

(Figure 9.13*a*), peas (Figure 9.13*b*), peanuts, and many other leguminous plants have seeds of this type. In such seeds as corn (Figure 9.12*c*), wheat, barley, rye, and the castor bean (Figure 9.14*a*), an extensive endosperm persists. The starch grains from the endosperm of wheat constitute flour; those from corn are cornstarch. The endosperm of some seeds, such as that of castor bean, is rich in lipids, while protein is abundant in the fleshy cotyledons of beans and peas, among other leguminous plants.

In addition to enlarging, the ovary of the flower (and in some cases associated structures) may undergo considerable change of shape and differentiation of tissues during embryogeny. This is clear in such a familiar example as the tomato (Figures 8.1*c* and 9.15), in which the ovary in the flower bud is a minute, rather firm, whitish green structure composed largely of meristematic cells and some vascular tissues. After fertilization, the ovary enlarges tremendously, passing through the familiar "green tomato" stage, until it finally ripens. As the tomato is ripening, the green plastids become reddish, because breakdown of the chlorophylls reveals the carotenoid pigments, and complex cellular changes occur to form the skinlike, firm, fleshy layer and the juicy layer of the fully ripened fruit. Different changes occur in fruit formation in other angiosperms, giving rise, with various modifications, to the great diversity of fruits characteristic of that group.

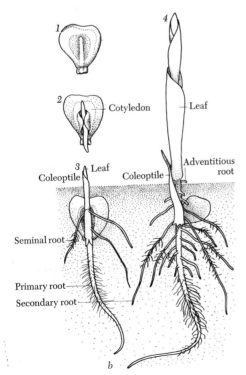

Figure 9.14 Seeds, germination, and seedlings (successive stages numbered). (*a*) *Ricinus communis* (castor bean), seed bisected, in two different aspects in 2 and 3. (*b*) *Zea mays* (corn).

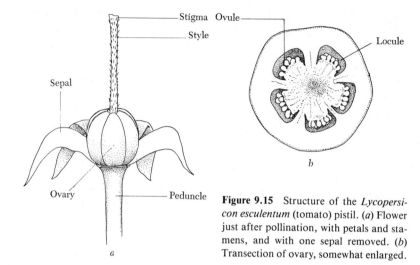

Figure 9.15 Structure of the *Lycopersicon esculentum* (tomato) pistil. (*a*) Flower just after pollination, with petals and stamens, and with one sepal removed. (*b*) Transection of ovary, somewhat enlarged.

Fruits.   The fruit consists of the ripened pistil or pistils of one or more flowers and sometimes of accessory components. Fruits are often divided in three classes—simple, aggregate, and multiple.

Simple fruits arise from single pistils (which may be simple or compound) of a single flower. Simple fruits may be dry, either dehiscent (Figure 9.16*a, b*) or indehiscent (Figures 9.12*c* or 9.16*c, d*) or fleshy. This depends on

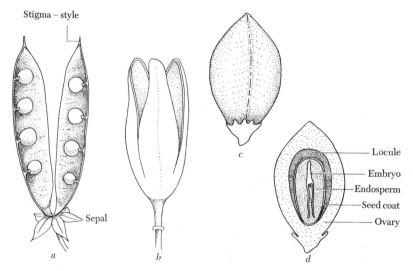

Figure 9.16   Simple dry fruits. (*a*) *Pisum sativum* (pea), pod. (*b*) *Iris* sp., capsule. (*c, d*) *Fagopyrum esculentum* (buckwheat): (*c*) external view and (*d*) bisection of achene.

the behavior of the ovary wall, called the **pericarp,** during the development of the fruit. It may remain thin, as in dry fruits, or become fleshy and composed of several layers, designated centripetally, the **exocarp, mesocarp,** and **endocarp.** The simple fruit of tomato, for example, develops from a compound pistil; that of the avocado from a simple pistil.

Simple dry fruits may be dehiscent or indehiscent at maturity. Thus, **legumes** or **pods** (Figure 9.16a), which develop from simple pistils, and **capsules** (Figure 9.16b), which develop from compound pistils, are dehiscent. By contrast the dry fruit of corn (Figure 9.12c), called a **grain** or **caryopsis,** or that of buckwheat (Figure 9.16c, d), called an **achene,** are indehiscent. In the corn grain, the integument of the seed is united completely with the pericarp of the fruit. In the achene of buckwheat, the seed is attached to the pericarp at just one place.

Simple fleshy fruits may be classified on the basis of pericarp organization. In **berries,** such as those of grape and tomato, the exocarp is skinlike, the mesocarp fleshy, and the endocarp often slimy or juicy. In **drupes,** or stone fruits, like those of peaches, plums, and cherries (Figure 9.17a), by contrast, the endocarp is stony. **Pomes,** such as those of pear, quince, and apple (Figure 9.17b), are somewhat more complex. Here the bases of the petals form a fleshy "floral tube," which encloses the compound ovary that consists of five carpels. It is the floral tube that forms the fleshy, edible portion of the apple fruit.

Aggregate fruits, which include numerous pistils from a single flower and its receptacle, are exemplified by strawberries (Figure 9.18), raspberries, and blackberries. After pollination and fertilization of the strawberry flower,

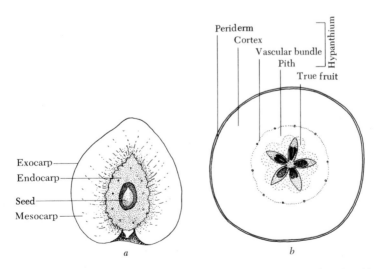

Figure 9.17 Simple fleshy fruits, sectional views. (a) *Prunus armeniaca* (peach). (b) *Pyrus malus* (apple).

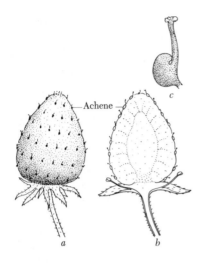

Figure 9.18 *Fragaria* sp. (strawberry), aggregate fruit. (*a*) External view. (*b*) Longisection. (*c*) Single fruit (achene).

the receptacle enlarges and becomes fleshy and red. Cultivated strawberries have been bred and selected for this characteristic. The true fruits of strawberry, often called "seeds" by laypeople, are achenes attached to the receptacle. In both rasberries and blackberries, in contrast to strawberries, the true fruits are small drupes or druplets.

Multiple fruits include numerous mature pistils from more than one flower attached to the axis of the inflorescence. Pineapple (Figure 9.19*a*) and mulberries (Figure 9.19*b*) exemplify multiple fruits, and even a mature ear of corn may be considered as one.

Seed Germination and Seedlings.   As the seeds and the fruits mature in various plants, the seeds may be ejected by the splitting of the drying fruits, or they may be freed only after the fleshy and stony layers of the enclosing fruits have rotted. If the seeds are planted, or if they happen to come to rest in a suitable environment, they sooner or later germinate. Germination is merely a continuation of embryogenesis involving the emergence of the embryonic sporophyte into an external environment.

The monocotyledonous (Figure 9.14*b*) or dicotyledonous (Figures 9.13 and 9.14*a*) organization of an angiosperm is obvious in its seed and seedling, in addition to other differences in the adults (p. 231). The single cotyledon of cereal grains, such as corn (Figure 9.12*c*), functions in digestion and absorption of the endosperm and remains within the seed during germination; the engorged, fleshy cotyledons of the pea (Figure 9.13*b*) also remain below the soil. In contrast, the two cotyledons of the garden bean (Figure 9.13*a*) are raised above the ground by the elongation of the hypocotyl, as are those of the castor bean (Figure 9.14*a*), after the latter have digested the nutriments of the endosperm and transferred them into the developing seedling. The cotyledons of castor beans function later as photosynthetic leaves.

Fruitlet

a   *b*

Figure 9.19 Multiple fruits. (*a*) *Ananas sativa* (pineapple). (*b*) *Morus* sp. (mulberry).

Various types of seed dormancy occur among angiosperms. They may be either morphological or physiological. In some plants the embryos are rudimentary and require time to grow. In other cases the seed coats may be impervious to water or oxygen, or to both, or the seed coats may offer resistance to the expansion of the embryo. In still other seeds chemical inhibitors are present that inhibit germination; these must be leached away or dissipated for germination to occur.

Most seeds are viable for only a few years or decades at the most, but there are exceptions. Storage of seeds at low temperatures and at lower concentrations of oxygen retards loss of viability by slowing down the rate of respiration. Apparently the longest record for seed viability is that of the lotus (*Nelumbo nucifera*), the seeds of which—about 1000 years old and buried in a peat bog—germinated.

Summary of the Reproductive Process

Reproduction of angiosperms, although similar in many ways to that of gymnosperms, differs in a number of important respects:

1. The ovules, and hence the seeds, are borne *within* megasporophylls (angiospermy) instead of being exposed on their surfaces (gymnospermy) (see Figure 8.1).
2. Development of the gametophytes is a much more abbreviated process in angiosperms than it is in gymnosperms.
3. The gametophytes themselves are smaller and simpler in angiosperms.
4. Pollination in angiosperms involves the transfer of pollen grains from the microsporangia (anther) to the receptive surface (stigma) of the megasporophyll, rather than to the micropyle of the ovule, as in gymnosperms.
5. Double fertilization occurs only in angiosperms.
6. The embryo of angiosperms is nourished by the endosperm, a special tissue that arises after fertilization, rather than by the female gametophyte, as in gymnosperms.
7. The angiosperm ovule does not enlarge to seed size until after fertilization, in contrast to that of gymnosperms.
8. The seeds of angiosperms are enclosed within fruits, which are enlarged megasporophylls (pistils), sometimes with associated parts of the flower; in gymnosperms, fruits of this type are absent, as the megasporophyll does not enclose the seed.

EVOLUTION OF ANTHOPHYTA

A number of evolutionary developments are apparent in the organization of Anthophyta, as compared with their predecessors on earth and many of their contemporaries. One of these involved the development of a different type of conducting system in the xylem called a vessel. Vessels, it will be recalled (p. 104), are composed of systems of vessel elements or cells, presumably derived from tracheids, in which the terminal walls have become perforated so that continuous water-conducting systems are developed. Although vessels occur only among a few vascular cryptogams (*Selaginella, Equisetum,* the fern *Pteridium,* and *Marsilea*) and in the *Gnetophyta,* they are present and highly developed in most angiosperms.

The development of seeds both by angiosperms and gymnosperms was a highly significant evolutionary innovation, but all the steps by which it occurred have not been elucidated. One of them must certainly have been covering the megasporangium by an integument to form the ovule; a second was reduction of the number of functional megaspores to one. A third was the permanent retention of the functional megaspore, and consequently the female gametophyte and embryo within the megasporangium. A fourth, and related, evolutionary development must have been the phenomena of pollination and development of the pollen tube and of all the adaptations ensuring the success of pollination in relation to various agents, including air currents, insects, birds, and in few cases, water.

There is good evidence from the fossil record that woody, treelike forms were among the first Anthophyta to develop. Woodiness, it will be recalled, is a reflection of continued secondary growth through the activity of a cambium. Phylogenetic reduction in the amount of cambial activity has been suggested as the explanation for the appearance on earth of at least some of the herbaceous flowering plants. It is also possible that some of the herbaceous angiosperms were primitively so, having been derived from herbaceous precursors.

The fossil record has not provided conclusive information about the origin of angiosperms. Although absent in earlier Mesozoic strata, diverse and abundant angiosperms first appear in Cretaceous deposits in the form of leaves, flowers, pollen, seeds, and fruits. In these specimens, angiospermy is clearly well established, so no insight regarding its origin has been supplied by such fossil remains. Various groups of gymnosperms have been suggested as angiosperm precursors, but these hypothetical ancestors have not been universally accepted as authentic. Angiospermy, it has been suggested, may have arisen from cuplike structures (Figure 9.20) that loosely surrounded the seeds of certain seed ferns. An alternate hypothesis, supported by the evidence of ontogeny and the study of certain supposedly primitive living genera, suggests that angiospermy developed by the phylogenetic unfolding and fusion of leaves that bore marginal ovules (Figure 9.21). Charles Darwin's statement, [4] "The rapid development as far as we can judge of all the higher plants within recent geological times is an abominable mystery," aptly characterizes the present state of our knowledge, or the lack of it, regarding the origin of the angiosperms.

REPRESENTATIVE FLORAL TYPES

Space and the nature of this text do not permit an extensive treatment of the classification of the more than 300,000 species of flowering plants into orders and families. However, the organization of several different types of flowers is discussed in the following paragraphs. The morphology of the flower is the most significant criterion in the taxonomy of flowering plants.

[4]The authors are grateful to Professor Herbert G. Baker of the University of California at Berkeley for providing them with an accurate quotation from Charles Darwin's letter (395) to J. D. Hooker.

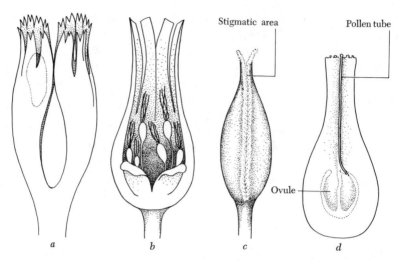

Figure 9.20   Seed-bearing structures of primitive plants. (*a, b*) Extinct seed ferns: (*a*) *Stamnostoma huttonense* [after A. G. Long. Reprinted with permission of The Royal Society of Edinburgh from the original figure in *Transactions,* Vol. 64, pp. 201–215.]; (*b*) *Calathospermum scoticum* [after J. Walton]. (*c, d*) Primitive angiosperm carpel (pistil): (*c*) ventral view showing paired stigmatic areas; (*d*) transection. [*c* and *d* after I. W. Bailey and B. G. L. Swamy.]

The Anthophyta are often subdivided into two groups on the basis of the organization of their seeds, namely, the dicotyledons and monocotyledons. In view of the prevalence of two or more cotyledons in the seeds of gymnosperms, monocotyledony is often considered to have been derived from dicotyledony by phylogenetic suppression of one cotyledon. The two groups of flowering plants differ in other respects, as follows:

Figure 9.21 *Drimys winteri* var. *chilensis.* Ontogenetic closure of carpels (pistils) in transection, three with margins appressed and two with margins still open. [Modified from S. Tucker, "Ontogeny of the Inflorescence and the Flower in *Drimys Winteri* var. *Chilensis,*" *Botany,* Vol. 30. Published in 1959 by The Regents of the University of California; reprinted by permission of The University of California Press.]

Dicotyledons	*Monocotyledons*
1. Leaves most often with reticulate venation.	1. Leaves most often with striate venation.
2. Vascular tissue eustelic, that is, a ring of vascular bundles surrounding the pith.	2. Vascular tissue atactostelic, that is, vascular bundles scattered.
3. Secondary growth widespread, the cambium between the secondary xylem and phloem.	3. Secondary growth rare, but if present, the cambium adding groups of both xylem and phloem internally to itself.
4. Floral organs, if definite in number, in groups of 5 or 4, sometimes 3, and rarely 2 or 1, carpels often fewer.	4. Floral organs, usually in 3s, sometimes 2 or 1, rarely in 4s.

Selected Dicotyledons

Ranunculus.   Figure 9.2 illustrates floral organization in *Ranunculus,* the "buttercup." Note the radial symmetry of the flowers. They are borne singly and consist of an elongate receptacle from which emerge, in acropetal order, the pistils and stamens (both indefinite in number) individually attached to the receptacle and spirally arranged; yellow petals (five or sometimes more), and five green sepals. The flowers are **hypogynous,** that is, the pistils are at the apex of the receptacle, while the other floral organs arise below them. The ovary of each pistil contains a single ovule and matures as an achene.

Brassica.   The sepals and petals of *Brassica* (cabbage and turnip, Figure 9.22, and a number of wild species) are in fours; the sepals alternate with the petals, which are arranged as a cross; this suggested the earlier family name Cruciferae, currently the Brassicaceae. The petals are elongated at their bases and clawlike. The stamens are in whorls, an inner whorl of four and an outer composed of two short members. The flower of *Brassica* is also radially symmetrical and hypogynous. The pistil is compound and composed of two carpels and matures as a dry fruit, **a silique,** which opens in two parts with a central partition (Figure 9.22).

A number of members of the Brassicaceae have been domesticated and selected for use as vegetables. Some of these are biennial, forming a rosette of leaves during one growing season and flowers and fruit in the second. An example is cabbage, in which the elongate stem of the wild ancestor has been shortened by selection to form a large bud, or "head." In Brussels sprouts, the axis is elongated and bears small "heads," which are axillary buds. Cauliflower is a variety of cabbage with an aberrant, fleshy inflorescence; kales are

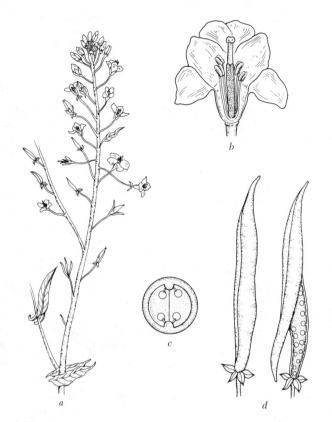

Figure 9.22 *Brassica* sp., organization of the flower and fruit. (*a*) Inflorescence. (*b*) Bisection of single flower. (*c*) Transection of ovary. (*d*) Fruits.

cabbages with leaves less compactly arranged. Turnips, radishes, cress, and horseradish are members of the Brassicaceae, and spices and types of oils are derived from various members of the family.

    Rosa.   Figure 9.23 illustrates floral organization of a wild rose, also a radially symmetrical flower. Here the flowers are *Ranunculus*-like in that the pistils and stamens are indefinite in number, and there is a cuplike modification of the receptacle. The sepals are present at the rim of the receptacle and the pistils are at the base. Flowers with such a cuplike receptacle are said to be perigynous. In the fruit, the receptacle becomes scarlet and fleshy to form the so-called rose hip. The pistils become hard and bony in the fruit. Cultivated roses have been bred and selected for the production of numerous petals. They are most often grafted on to wild rose stocks and propagated vegetatively.

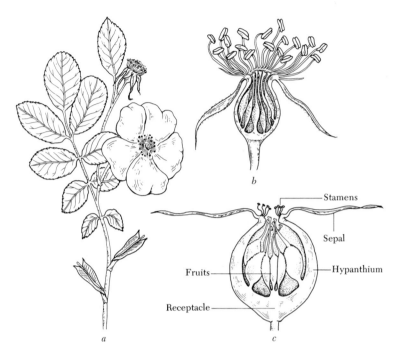

Figure 9.23 *Rosa* sp., organization of the flower and fruit. (*a*) Branchlet with pinnately compound leaf and flower. (*b*) Bisection of floral tube enclosing pistils, stamens on rim of tube. (*c*) Longisection of rose "hip" with fruits.

Lathyrus.   A flower of *Lathyrus,* the sweet pea, and its organization are illustrated in Figure 9.24. It is apparent that these flowers, also hypogynous, are not radially symmetrical. In addition to five green sepals, the flowers have five rather showy petals of somewhat different form. Two of them are united to form a keellike structure, which is partly concealed by two lateral petals sometimes spoken of as wings. The largest, uppermost petal is called the standard. When these are carefully removed one can observe that there are 10 stamens; the filaments of nine stamens are partially united to form a sheath around the pistil, while the uppermost, tenth, stamen is entirely free. When this filament sheath is removed, the simple pistil, consisting of stigma, style, and elongate ovary, becomes visible. The ovary enlarges greatly in the fruit to form the pod or legume, which splits into two parts at maturity.

Sweet peas (*Lathyrus odoratus*), locust (*Robinia pseudacacia*), and peas (*Pisum sativum*) have essentially similar floral organization and are members of the large family Fabaceae, formerly called the Leguminosae. This family contains many nutritious food plants, such as various beans, peas, and lentils, and also forage plants, such as clover, alfalfa, and vetches.

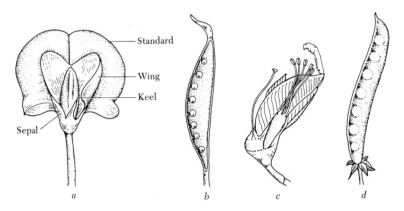

Figure 9.24 *Lathyrus odoratus* (sweet pea), organization of the flower and fruit. (*a*) Single flower. Note standard, wings and keel formed by petals. (*b*) Dissection to show ovules in podlike ovary. (*c*) Pistil enlarging to form fruit; stamens and sepals still present. (*d*) Maturing fruit.

Ipomoea.   The flowers of *Ipomoea* (Figure 9.25), the commonly cultivated morning glory, are radially symmetrical and hypogynous. Here, however, the petals are united into the trumpetlike, tubular structure that characterizes many Anthophyta. The five stamens are **epipetalous,** that is, attached to the corolla. The pistil is compound with two to four carpels. It matures as a one to several-seeded, dehiscent, dry fruit.

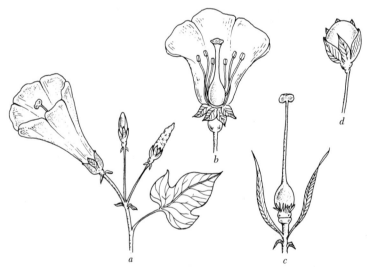

Figure 9.25 *Ipomea* sp. (morning glory), organization of the flower. (*a*) Branch with open flower, bud, and faded flower. (*b*) Dissection of open flower. Note sepals, corolla, stamens, style, and stigma. (*c*) Young fruit; corolla and stamens have disappeared. (*d*) Maturing fruit.

Antirrhinum.   *Antirrhinum majus,* or snapdragon flowers, are borne in spicate inflorescences (Figure 9.26). The flowers here are bilaterally symmetrical and the petals united to form a five-membered corolla subtended by five sepals. Four stamens are present. The pistil is compound and composed of two carpels, which comprise the dry, dehiscent capsule in the fruit.

Campanula.   The flowers of *Campanula,* the bellflower (Figure 9.27), occur on elongate inflorescences. The radially symmetric flowers are epigynous; the ovary is below the level of insertion of the sepals, petals, and stamens. The pistil is compound, of three carpels, and ripens as a capsule containing many seeds. The anthers of the stamens form a cylinder through which the style and stigma emerge.

Composites.   Daisies, sunflowers (Figure 9.6, p. 210), marigolds, and many other dicotyledons are members of the enormous family Asteraceae (about 15,000 species, formerly the Compositae), in which the flowers are grouped in compact inflorescences called **capitula,** or heads. Because of their small size, the individual flowers are called **florets.** They are all epigynous, and the five stamens have their anthers united around the style and stigma in

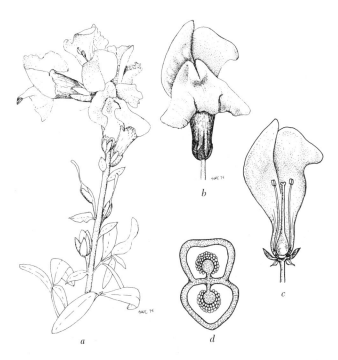

Figure 9.26   *Antirrhinum majus* (snapdragon), organization of the flower and fruit. (*a*) Inflorescence. (*b*) Single flower. (*c*) Dissection of flower showing two (of four) stamens and pistil. (*d*) Transection of compound ovary.

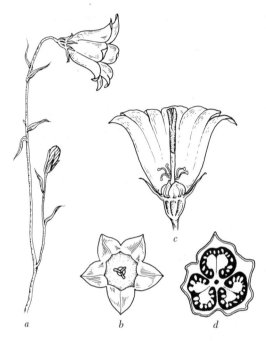

Figure 9.27 *Campanula* sp. (bellflower), organization of the flower and fruit. (*a*) Stem with flowers. (*b*) Frontal view of single flower. (*c*) Bisection of flower; note epigyny. (*d*) Transection of compound ovary.

a sort of piston-cylinder arrangement. The pistils are compound, composed of two carpels, and mature in the fruit as achenes. The petals are united to form tubelike corollas, or they may be elongate and split longitudinally to form ligulate ray florets. In some members of the family, such as dandelion, the heads are composed entirely of ligulate florets, while in others, such as daisy (*Chrysanthemum leucanthemum*) and sunflower (*Helianthus annuus,* Figure 9.6*b*), both ligulate ray florets and tubular disc florets occur in the same head. In all these the calyx may be absent or represented by tufts of hairs or bristles, the pappus, on the fruit.

Amentiferous Flowers. A number of angiosperms have inconspicuous flowers united in erect or pendulous inflorescences known as aments or catkins. *Salix (willow),* already discussed on p. 209 and illustrated in Figure 9.5, is an example of these, as are poplars or cottonwoods (*Populus*), oaks (*Quercus,* Figure 9.28), beeches (*Fagus*), birches (*Betula*), walnuts (*Juglans*), and hickory (*Carya*). In oak, the individuals are monoecious, but the flowers imperfect (Figure 9.28). The staminate flowers occur in pendulous catkins, while several pistillate flowers are borne at the tips of young branches. The staminate flowers contain 3 to 12 stamens; the pistillate flowers are simple, consisting of inconspicuous perianth parts and overlapping bracts around the

a

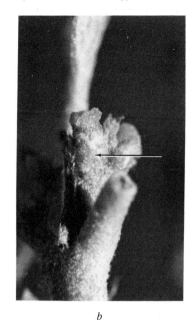

b

c

Figure 9.28 *Quercus virginiana* (live oak). (*a*) Branchlet with staminate inflorescences (aments). (*b*) Branchlet tip with single pistillate flowers (arrow). (*c*) Early enlargement of pistils and bracts to form fruit (acorn).

receptacle. The pistils are compound (tricarpellary) with two ovules in each cell, but only one survives as a seed in the fruit. The bracts form the cup of the acorn in the fruit, often a nut.

In the past some botanists have postulated that the simple, dioecious flowers of the Amentiferae represent the most primitive angiosperms, but this view is no longer supported by most investigators.

Selected Monocotyledons

Hesperaloe.   The flowers of *Hesperaloe,* a lily (Figure 9.29), and of such related plants as onion (*Allium*), tulip (*Tulipa*), and Spanish bayonet (*Yucca*), are radially symmetrical and hypogynous. The perianth is undifferentiated into sepals and petals, but consists of two whorls of petallike mem-

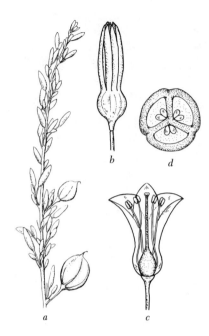

Figure 9.29 *Hesperaloe breviflora* (a lily), organization of the flower and fruit. (*a*) Inflorescence with buds and two fruits. (*b*) Single flower. (*c*) Single flower, part of perianth removed showing stamens and pistil. (*d*) Transection of compound ovary (three carpels).

bers. These may be separately inserted on the receptacle or united at their bases to form a perianth tube. The six stamens are in two whorls of three, and the pistils are compound and composed of three carpels. They mature in the fruit as dehiscent capsules. The flowers of amaryllis (*Hippeastrum*) are similar to those of lily but are epigynous.

Grass Flowers.   The flowers of grasses, like those of the dicotyledonous ament-producing types, are inconspicuous because they are small and lack colored petals. The grass family (Gramineae or Poaceae) is an enormous group (about 4500 species), which contains such economically important plants as the forage grasses, oats (*Avena*), wheat (*Triticum*), barley (*Hordeum*), rye (*Secale*), corn or maize (*Zea*), and rice (*Oryza*). The flowers usually occur in inflorescences, which may be complex. The ultimate branches of the inflorescences, are called spikelets and each one of the axes of the spikelets is called the *rachilla*. In most grasses, the flowers are perfect, corn (Figure 9.4, p. 209) being a familiar exception. At the base of the rachilla are a pair of bracts, although they may be absent. The individual flowers occur between other pairs of bracts (the **lemma** and **palea**); these, too, may be absent. In most grass flowers two small, supposed perianth vestiges, the **lodicules** (Figure 9.30), are present. The flowers of most grasses have three stamens and a compound ovary, only one carpel of which is functional. A generalized drawing of a grass flower is illustrated in Figure 9.30. Note the feathery, much-branched stigmas,

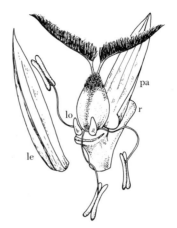

Figure 9.30 Organization of a grass flower, diagrammatic, le, lemma; lo, lodicule; pa, palea; r, rachilla, Note two feathery stigmas and three stamens. [After A. M. Johnson.]

an adaptation to wind pollination. The pistils of grasses mature as grains or caryopses (Figure 9.12c).

RELATIONSHIP OF ANGIOSPERMS

In the absence of evidence from the fossil record, botanists, on the basis of their studies of living angiosperms, have speculated regarding their relationships.

According to one hypothesis (no longer supported by many botanists), the amentiferous flowering plants are the most primitive. This is because of the simplicity of their flowers, their lack of colored petals, and their wind pollination. The stamens are also considered to be quite similar to the microsporophylls of gymnosperms. However, many other botanists consider the simplicity of these flowers to be the result of reduction and specialization.

A second hypothesis is based on the supposed strobiloid nature of certain angiosperm flowers, such as those of *Ranunculus* (Figure 9.2) and *Magnolia,* in which an indefinite number of microsporophylls (stamens) and of megasporophylls (pistils) is spirally arranged on an axis with short internodes. From such a supposedly primitive type of flower, more specialized types were postulated to have been derived through shortening and crowding on the receptacle, so that sepals, petals, stamens, and pistils became definite in number, and in some instances, as in the formation of compound pistils, union of parts occurred. Although this second hypothesis, albeit continually modified, has more support at present, it also has the basic difficulty that the strobilus of gymnosperms, except in cycadeoids (p. 199), produced only one type of reproductive structure, *either* microsporophylls or megasporophylls.

A third point of view is that the Anthophyta are polyphyletic, that is, they had multiple origins in evolution.

QUESTIONS FOR REVIEW

1. Define the term "flower" and with the aid of labeled drawings discuss its gross morphology and variations in its floral organs.

2. Discuss the importance to humans of flowering plants.

3. Distinguish between the terms "vegetable" and "fruit" from the botanical viewpoint.

4. Define or explain annual, perennial, sepal, calyx, petal, corolla, stamen, pistil, carpel, simple pistil, compound pistil, stigma, style, ovary, anther, filament, perfect flower, imperfect flower, inflorescence, capitulum, antipodal cell, polar nuclei, synergid, endosperm, primary endosperm nucleus, double fertilization, pollination in angiosperms, angiosperm seed, fruit, pollen, hypocotyl, radicle, plumule, dehiscent, and indehiscent.

5. With the aid of labeled diagrams, discuss the reproductive process in Anthophyta. How does *Pinus* differ from most Anthophyta in this respect?

6. List the respects in which reproduction in angiosperms differs from that in gymnosperms.

7. Define or explain and give examples of simple, aggregate, and multiple fruits; pod or legume; achene; caryopsis or grain; drupe; berry; pome; pericarp.

8. How does the fate of the hypocotyl and cotyledons differ in the germination of seeds of garden bean, pea, castor bean, and corn?

9. What types of seed dormancy occur?

10. What steps probably occurred in the evolutionary development of seeds?

11. How many angiospermy have evolved?

12. In what respects do monocotyledonous and dicotyledonous flowering plants differ?

CHAPTER TEN

Slime Molds, Fungi, and Lichens

INTRODUCTION

Although the organisms slime molds, fungi, and lichens, discussed in this chapter, are no longer considered to be plants by most biologists, they were first studied by plant scientists and, in spite of their lack of chlorophyll and consequent lack of photosynthetic nutrition, they were classified with plants (Table 1.1, columns 1 and 2) and studied in plant science courses. This classification was because of similarities in the structure and reproduction of some of them to those of certain algae. Their classification at present is still based on the International Code of Botanical Nomenclature.

The nutrition of slime molds and fungi, in the absence of chlorophyll, is **saprobic** or **parasitic.** Bacteria are similar in their nutrition (Chapter 2). The nutrition of saprobic organisms is based on the metabolic products of living protoplasms or on nonliving protoplasm itself. By contrast, parasitic organisms require living protoplasm in their nutrition.

Slime molds and fungi are still studied by many plant scientists (mycologists) and, accordingly, are included in the present volume. The slime molds are classified by some as fungi (*sensu lato*), while others consider them to have affinities with the protozoa. In this book they are classified (Table 1.1) in the Kingdom Mycetae (Fungi), as distinct from the Kingdom Phyta (Plants). They are, of course, not classified with the achlorophyllous bacteria because slime molds and fungi are eukaryotic. Slime molds are usually classified in two distinct groups, the cellular slime molds (Acrasiomycota) and plasmodial slime molds (Myxomycota). Representatives of both of these will be discussed in the following account.

SLIME MOLDS (DIVISIONS MYXOMYCOTA AND ACRASIOMYCOTA)

Although they are fundamentally different types of organisms, the Myxomycota and Acrasiomycota have in common the characteristic of phagotrophic nutrition in the vegetative or somatic phases of their life cycles. By phagotrophic, it will be recalled, is meant the ingestion or engulfment of food particles as a basis for nutrition. A few of these organisms, however, can be grown in laboratory culture as facultative saprobes, absorbing organic nutrients (**osmotrophic**). In the Acrasiomycota, the vegetative or somatic phase consists of amoeboid cells (Figure 10.4*d*), while in the Myxomycota it is a multinucleate protoplasmic structure called a **plasmodium** (Figure 10.1*a*). Hence, the Myxomycota are known as the plasmodial slime molds and the Acrasiomycota as the cellular slime molds. The slimy nature of the migrating plasmodial phases and their slimy tracks suggested the name "slime molds."

Plasmodial Slime Molds (Division Myxomycota)

The plasmodial slime molds (Figures 10.1 to 10.3) have been considered as either "animallike plants" or "plantlike animals," depending on whether a botanist or a zoologist was discussing them. The modern biologist finds such questions of less critical interest, in view of the remarkable uniformity of organization and function of living systems at the molecular level, although the

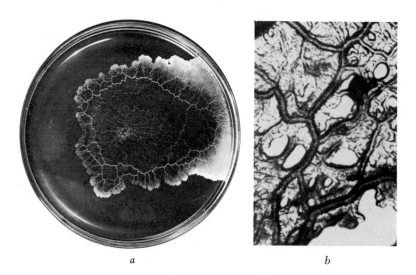

a   b

Figure 10.1 Slime mold. (*a*) Plasmodium of *Physarum polycephalum* on agar in a Petri dish. [Courtesy of C. J. Alexopoulos.] (*b*) Portion of plasmodium magnified showing streams of unwalled protoplasm.

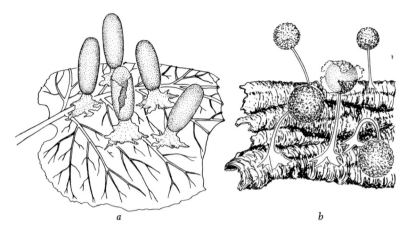

Figure 10.2 Spore-bearing structures of slime molds. (*a*) *Diachea* sp. (*b*) *Lamproderma* sp.

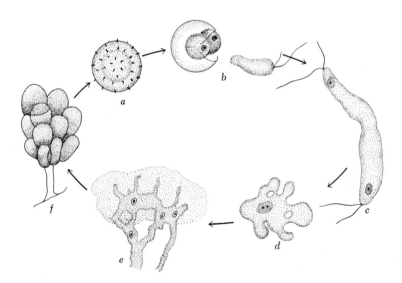

Figure 10.3 Life history of a plasmodial slime mold. (*a*) Dormant spore. (*b*) Spore germination to form motile gametes. (*c*) Gamete union. (*d*) Zygote. (*e*) Portion of plasmodium (compare with Figure 10.6). (*f*) Sporangium. [Modified from C. J. Alexopoulos.]

question has meaning from an evolutionary perspective. Because slime molds have been classified both as fungi and as protozoa, we shall consider them in this book as a division separate from other fungi (see Table 1.1).

However classified, slime molds are inhabitants of decaying plant materials such as moist logs, twigs, or leaves. In many of the Myxomycota, two biflagellated[1] isogametes unite to produce a motile, diploid zygote (Figure 10.3*c, d*). In many others the isogametes are amoeboid. The zygote sooner or later loses its flagella and becomes amoeboid as it moves over the substrate, engulfing bacteria and organic particles that are then digested in vacuoles. As this occurs, more protoplasm is synthesized, and the zygote nucleus divides mitotically. Repeated synchronous nuclear divisions of the resulting diploid nuclei, without accompanying cytoplasmic division, result in the development of a more or less extensive amoeboid mass of multinucleate protoplasm, the plasmodium (Figures 10.1*a, b* and 10.3*e*). This is considered to be the somatic, vegetative, or feeding phase of the life cycle.

Under suitable conditions of moisture and nutrition, plasmodia several square feet in area may arise. Sooner or later, with dehydration and simultaneous light, upwellings of the plasmodium give rise to a spore-producing reproductive phase (Figures 10.2 and 10.3*f*); this varies in form in the different genera of slime molds. As the spore-bearing structures mature, the protoplasm cleaves into uninucleate spores, which become walled; meiosis occurs in the young spores. Therefore, the mature spores (Figure 10.3*a*) contain haploid nuclei; in most cases only one nucleus survives in the mature spore. Upon dissemination, these spores germinate (on a suitably moist substrate) to form motile, flagellated gametes (Figure 10.3*b*) or amoeboid cells. These cells apparently do not function as gametes until a period of multiplication has intervened. The flagellated cells withdraw their flagella before division; flagellate and amoeboid cells are interconvertible, probably depending on the presence of water in their environment. The nutrition of the flagellated cells, amoebae and plasmodia, is phagotrophic. Inasmuch as the plasmodium is diploid and the products of spore germination, which may persist and multiply, are haploid, the life cycle may be considered dibiontic with sporic meiosis.

The stationary sporogenous phase, in contrast with the plasmodial one, is more typically plantlike. The nonwalled, multinucleate plasmodia of some slime molds, which can readily be maintained and increased in the laboratory, have long been a favorite experimental material of biochemists and biophysicists, because they provide protoplasm for immediate chemical analysis without the complication of nonliving cellulose walls; they are also excellent for the study of stimulus, response, and protoplasmic synthesis and for studies of the nuclear cycle because the mitoses are synchronous.

Cellular Slime Molds (Division Acrasiomycota)

Superficially similar to Myxomycota are the cellular slime molds, exemplified by *Dictyostelium* (Figure 10.4), which has been a frequent and fruitful subject of biological investigation. The similar genus *Polysphondylium* is also of interest. Although they apparently have the same type of life cycle,

---

[1]One of the flagella may be shorter than the other.

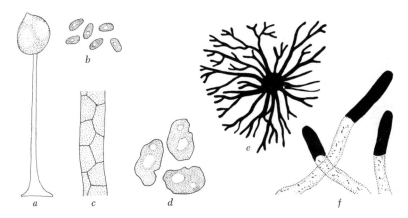

Figure 10.4 *Dictyostelium* sp. (*a*) Stalked spore-bearing structure. (*b*) Spores. (*c*) Portion of stalk of (*a*) showing component cells. (*d*) Amoeboid stage. (*e*) Streams of aggregating amoebae. (*f*) Migrating pseudoplasmodia, or slugs, with slime trails behind. [After John Tyler Bonner, *The Cellular Slime Molds.* Copyright © 1959, rev. ed. © 1967 by Princeton University Press. Plates I, II, III adapted with permission of Princeton University Press. Reprinted by permission of Princeton University Press.]

except for the site of meiosis, cellular slime molds differ from plasmodial slime molds in forming a **pseudoplasmodium,** a mass of individual, uninucleate amoebae that have aggregated after leading an individual existence.

Their aggregation is a response to the secretion of acrasin (cyclic AMP), secreted by a primary cell, and by amoebae in an aggregating stream and also by the forming pseudoplasmodium. This group of aggregated amoebae, called the slug, builds a spore-producing structure, the **sporophore,** composed of amoebae, some of which then function as walled spores (Figure 10.4*a*, *b*). These continue the cycle at germination by forming amoebae. The pseudoplasmodium is preceded by a nutritive phase in which individual amoebae feed and multiply independently. These amoebae are the main feeding phase of the cellular slime molds. Later, when they gather together to form the slug and, finally, spores with cellulosic walls, the amoebae abandon their completely independent existence. Thus, the formation of a "republic" or a "federation" by free-living individuals occurs in the ontogeny of these organisms. This developmental pattern exemplifies a possible transition from unicellular to multicellular organisms, as suggested by some biologists.

Evidence that sexual reproduction occurs in these organisms has recently been uncovered. In certain populations of *Dictyostelium* and *Polysphondylium,* sexually compatible amoebae have been reported to unite in pairs to form "*giant cells,*" which are probably zygotes. These become centers of aggregation for other amoebae, which later become enclosed, with the zygote at the center, to form a structure called a **macrocyst** (Figure 10.5*a-c*). During the process, the giant cell engulfs surrounding amoebae, whereupon the enlarged

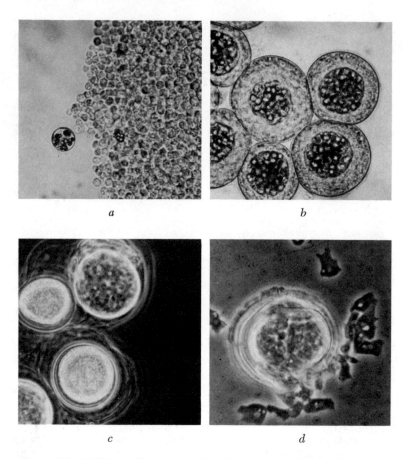

a   *b*

c   *d*

Figure 10.5   (*a*) *Dictyostelium mucoroides:* giant cell expressed from the center of a premacrocyst-forming mass of amoebae. (*b*) *D. discoideum:* macrocyst formation; the well-defined central area represents the giant cell; the granules are the engulfed amoebae. (*c*) *D. mucoroides:* macrocyst at upper center near germination, dormant mature cysts below. (*d*) *D. mucoroides:* germinating macrocyst. [Courtesy of Professor K. B. Raper.]

giant cell lays down a heavy cellulose wall. An inner wall is subsequently deposited at the surface of the cyst protoplast. Over a considerable period of maturation, the zygote ingests and digests the amoebae that have been incorporated to form the macrocyst, so that the protoplasmic content of the zygote increases and becomes more homogeneous. The zygote nucleus finally undergoes what seem to be meiotic divisions, and the products of these undergo further mitoses (and cytokineses) to form a number of amoebae within the macrocyst. These are liberated (Figure 10.5*d*) through a fissure in the macrocyst wall and reinitiate the life cycle, which is summarized in Figure 10.6.

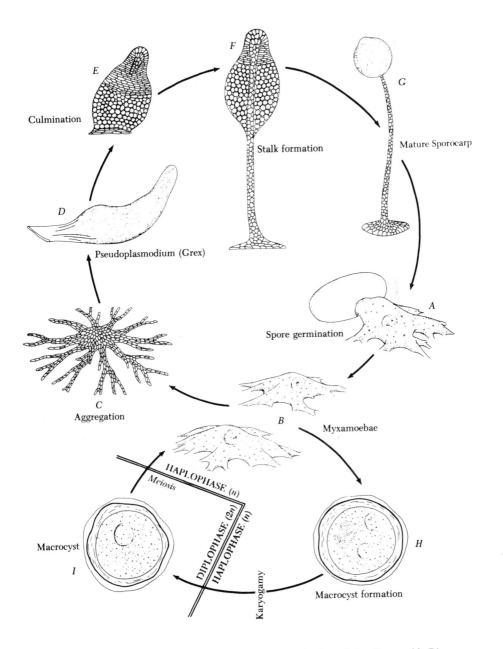

Figure 10.6 Diagrammatic summary of the life cycle of a cellular slime mold, *Dictyostelium discoideum*. [After C. J. Alexopoulos and C. Mims, *Introductory Mycology* (New York: John Wiley & Sons, Inc. 1979). Reprinted by permission of John Wiley & Sons, Inc.]

FUNGI

Fungi differ from the slime molds in lacking plasmodial stages and phago-trophic nutrition; they differ from the bacteria, of course, in being eukaryotic, in which respect they more closely resemble algae (not blue-green algae) and other green plants. The plant bodies of fungi are among the simplest in the plant kingdom, being either unicellular or filamentous. In the latter case, the plant body is called the **mycelium**; the individual filaments are called **hyphae** (sing., *hypha*). These hyphae may be composed of cells with one, two, or many nuclei, or they may be tubular, with no transverse walls (coenocytic), like certain algae (see page 44). The cell walls of most fungi contain chitin, whereas a few others contain cellulose and other polysaccharides. The mycelium spreads over and through the substrate or host, absorbing nutrients for growth by secreting extracellular enzymes that digest some of the components of the substrate (the soluble products then diffuse into the hyphae). Some fungi develop special absorptive branches, called **rhizoids** in saprobic species and **haustoria** in parasitic ones. In many fungi, the spore-producing filaments are raised above the remainder of the mycelium.

Aquatic fungi with zoospores are considered primitive, and nonaquatic types with airborne spores are presumed to have arisen from them. Both saprobic and parasitic organisms occur. The type of parasitism varies from superficial and facultative to systemic and obligate. These types of parasitism may be defined as follows: In **superficial parasitism** the parasite is on the surface of the host and does not pervade the host as it does in systemic parasitism. In **obligate parasitism** no nutritive substitute can replace the living host; **facultative parasites** can grow on nonliving substrates and also on living hosts.

In some cases, parasitic fungi enter into relationships with their hosts that may be termed *mutualistic,* because nutritional and/or other advantages accrue to both members of the partnership. This seems to be true in lichens (p. 264) and probably in the relationship between certain mycorrhizal fungi and their host plants.

In striking contrast with the relatively simple and unspectacular vegetative mycelium of fungi is the spore-bearing phase, or "fruiting body," which arises in some of the sac and club fungi such as the familiar morels, mushrooms (toadstools), puffballs, and shelf fungi. It is important to remember, however, that the fruiting body of a fungus has been preceded by an extensive vegetative mycelium that has sometimes grown for months or years.

Classification of Fungi

Like that of algae, the classification of fungi has undergone modification (see Table 1.1) with an increased tendency toward a polyphyletic, as opposed to monophyletic, system. The most recent change has been in the dismemberment of a single taxon that formerly included so-called algalike fungi (Phycomycetes, Phycomycota) and the elevation of its components to higher categories of classification. This abbreviated account of the fungi will discuss representatives of only the Chytridiomycota, Oomycota, Zygomycota, Ascomycota, and Basidiomycota, and briefly mention the Deuteromycota and lichens.

Chytrids (Division Chytridiomycota).   The Chytridiomycota are mostly aquatic organisms that occur in muds and on decaying plants and animals. They may parasitize aquatic plants and animals and even other fungi.

Among the simplest members of this group are the chytrids, here represented by *Rhizophydium globosum* (Figure 10.7), which lives saprobically on decaying algae and pollen grains that have fallen into the water. This unicellular organism begins life as a posteriorly uniflagellate zoospore that settles on the surface of the host cell and, at germination, produces a globose vegetative cell with rhizoidal appendages. At maturity, the vegetative cell becomes transformed into a zoosporangium from which released zoospores start new infections. Sexual reproduction has been observed in several species of *Rhizophydium*.

Allomyces (Figure 10.8), a widely distributed genus of Chytridiomycota, is of interest for a number of reasons. It is a mycelial organism that grows saprobically on plant debris in aquatic habitats; it may be readily isolated from this debris by using small, boiled, split seeds (often hempseed), as "bait." The mycelium is coenocytic and only incompletely septate, except at the sites of gametangial and sporangial origin, where complete septa occur. Absorptive rhizoidal hyphae penetrate the substrate, functioning in anchorage. After a period of growth, the plants mature and produce reproductive organs.

The life cycle of *Allomyces macrogynus,* summarized in Figure 10.9, is dibiontic with sporic meiosis. Thick-walled, rust-colored **meiosporangia,** as well as thin-walled **mitosporangia,** are produced by the diploid plants (Figures 10.8 and 10.9). Both types of sporangia produce posteriorly uniflagellate zoospores. Those from the mitosporangia are diploid and grow into new diploid

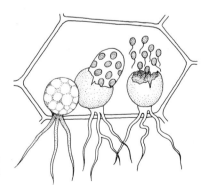

Figure 10.7 *Rhizophydium globosum,* a chytrid, growing on the leaf cell of an aquatic plant. Note release of zoospores.

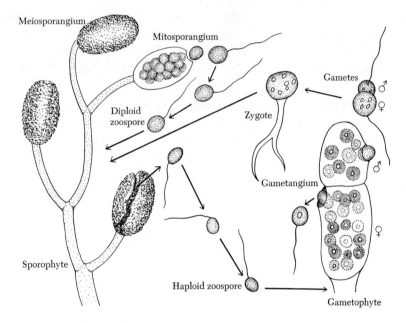

Figure 10.8 *Allomyces macrogynus*, organization and reproduction.

mycelia if a suitable substrate is available, whereas haploid zoospores from the meiosporangia develop into mycelia which produce gametangia (Figures 10.8 and 10.9). The male gametangia appear to be orange at maturity because of the color of the male gametes within them. Anisogametes pair and undergo plasmogamy and karyogamy to form zygotes that develop directly into diploid mycelia. It has been demonstrated that a sexual hormone, **sirenin,** attracts the free-swimming male gametes to the female gametangia and gametes. The thick-walled, resistant meiosporangia may become detached from the mycelium and serve to preserve the fungus through periods of desiccation.

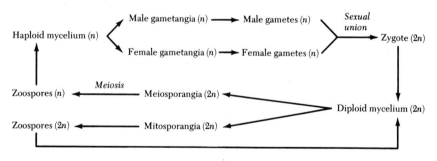

Figure 10.9 Diagrammatic summary of the life cycle of *Allomyces macrogynus*.

Water Molds (Division Oomycota).   The Oomycota are so called because their sexual reproduction is oogamous, involving the fertilization of large eggs by nuclei from a male hypha that functions like an antheridium. A few Oomycota are parasitic, causing economically important diseases such as grape and potato blights. They seemingly differ from other fungi in having cellulose in their hyphal walls, and most lack chitin.

Achlya (Figure 10.10), one of the water molds, is chosen here as a representative of the Oomycota. The numerous species of *Achlya* may be isolated readily from pond water and from soil submerged in water. The substrate in nature is often a dead insect, but boiled, split hempseeds and other small seeds are favorite laboratory substrates. Most species of *Achlya* are saprobic. The mycelium of *Achlya* forms a radiating mass of branching, tubular, multinucleate, nonseptate filaments surrounding the substrate (Figure 10.10*a*), evidence of the efficiency of the absorptive rhizoids and the enzymes they produce. After a short period of development, the tips of certain hyphae are delimited by septa and function as zoosporangia (Figure 10.10*b*), each of which produces a large number of zoospores (Figure 10.10*c*). These encyst at the apex of the sporangium and biflagellate zoospores later emerge from the cysts, migrate to other available substrates, and there form new mycelia and zoosporangia.

Sexual reproduction is apparently initiated when growth depletes certain substances. Particularly interesting investigations have been made of this process as it occurs in the species *Achlya ambisexualis*. In this organism, in which the male and female sex organs (Figure 10.10*d*) are produced on separate individuals, the formation and functioning of the sex organs are controlled by chemical substances from the sterile male and female mycelium and later from their differentiated sexual branches themselves. The rather complex process is summarized in Figure 10.10 *e-j,* which illustrates the orderly, progressive, and correlated steps in the production and union of sex organs. The chemicals that evoke these steps are termed **hormones.** It has been shown that female hyphae produce a substance, called **antheridiol,** which stimulates the production of male branches and antheridia. The chemical structure of antheridiol is depicted in Figure 10.11.

The mycelium of the Oomycota is diploid, and meiosis probably occurs during gametogenesis. The young eggs are multinucleate, but before fertilization, all but one of the nuclei degenerate. The eggs and sperms are the only haploid structures in these fungi. The life cycle is thus like that of *Acetabularia* and *Fucus*.

The related genus *Saprolegnia* differs from *Achlya* in that its zoospores move directly out of the zoosporangia. *Saprolegnia* often occurs as a parasite on fish.

Black Molds (Division Zygomycota).   The sexual reproduction of the coenocytic Zygomycota is by a conjugation process (Figure 10.12*d*) that is in

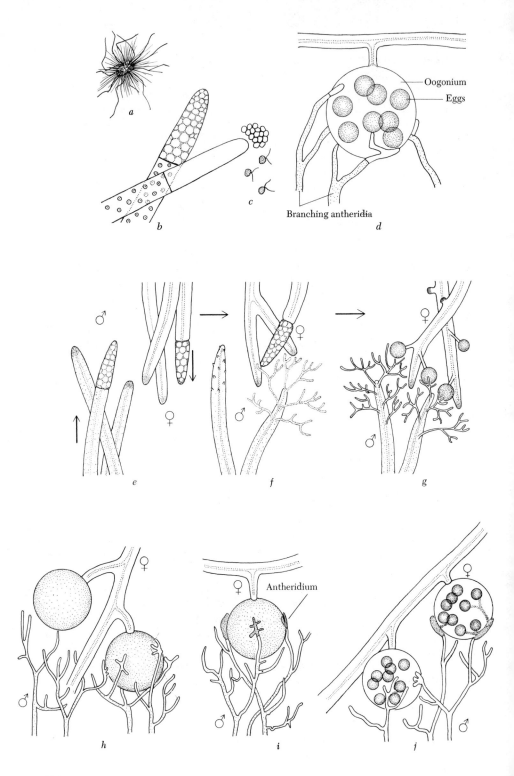

Oogonium

Eggs

Branching antheridia

Antheridium

OH

O

O

Figure 10.11 Structure of antheridiol.
[After Edwards et al.]

HO   O

some respects similar to, but in others different from, that of the alga *Spirogyra*. *Rhizopus stolonifer* (Figure 10.12), often called "black mold of bread" (here chosen to represent the Zygomycota), consists of tubular, multinucleate hyphae differentiated into prostrate branches, absorptive rhizoids, and erect **sporangiophores**. The blackness of the walls of the myriad spores is responsible for the color of the mature fungus. If the spores chance to fall upon a suitable substrate, they germinate and produce mature, spore-bearing mycelia within 72 hours under favorable conditions. It was in *Rhizopus* that self-incompatibility, or heterothallism, of fungi was first demonstrated, early in the twentieth century. When compatible mating types grow close together, the sexual process results; it is clearly affected by secretions of trisporic acids, which are hormonelike. Closely growing compatible + and − hyphae, indistinguishable as male and female, develop lateral branches that become contiguous. The ends of these, after contact, are delimited by septa and unite in conjugation to form a black, dormant zygote, the compatible pairs (+ and −) of nuclei within it uniting. Unless both mating types are present, only asexual reproduction occurs. Meiosis is probably zygotic in *Rhizopus;* if so, its life cycle is monobiontic and the fungus, haploid. The germinating zygote forms a sporangiophore with a sporangium as its apex.

Sac Fungi (Division Ascomycota).   The Ascomycota include several largely saprobic groups—the yeasts; the brown, green, and pink molds; the

---

Figure 10.10 (*Opposite page.*) *Achlya,* a water mold. (*a*) Habit of growth on a hemp seed. (*b*) Zoosporangia, one shedding its spores. (*c*) Zoospores. (*d*) Sex organs in union; male nuclei from antheridia are transported by tubes to the eggs. (*e–j*) Hormonal control of sexual maturation in *Achlya:* (*e*) male and female branches grow close; both have only asexual zoosporangia; (*f*) proximity causes proliferation of hyphae to form slender antheridial hyphae; (*g*) formation of antheridial hyphae stimulates the mycelium to form oogonial branches; (*h, i*) formation of these branches causes growth of antheridial hyphae directly toward the oogonia; upon making contact, the antheridial hyphae branch and their tips become antheridia. (*j*) Contact of the antheridial hyphae and antheridia with the oogonium stimulates cleavage of the latter into eggs, and fertilization occurs. Each of the stages from (*e*) to (*j*) is brought about by the secretion and diffusion of sexually active substances sometimes called hormones. [After J. Raper.]

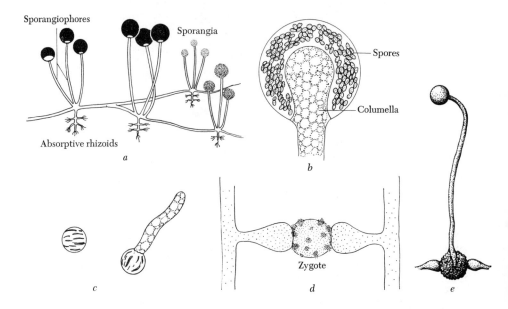

Figure 10.12   *Rhizopus stolonifer,* "black mold of bread." (*a*) Habit of growth. (*b*) Median longitudinal section of sporangium with sterile, central columella covered by spores. (*c*) Spore germination. (*d*) Sexual stage with zygote. (*e*) Germinating zygote. [*e* after R. M. Holman and W. W. Robbins, *Textbook on General Botany* (New York: John Wiley & Sons, Inc., © 1927). Reprinted by permission of John Wiley & Sons, Inc.]

morels and cup fungi; and the parasitic powdery mildews. The **ascus** is a sac-like cell within which eight (sometimes four or fewer) **ascospores** are formed. These spores arise as a result of meiosis of the ascus nucleus and are thus meiospores; in the formation of the latter, residual cytoplasm surrounds the ascospores. The asci may be formed directly, as in the yeasts and their relatives, or in a special fruiting body, the **ascocarp.**

Sexual reproduction in the Ascomycota is variable in its mechanisms. In the yeasts, for example, two compatible haploid cells may unite in pairs and their nuclei unite immediately. In others there may be differentiated sex organs, the female called an **ascogonium** and the male an **antheridium.** In yet others, differentiated sex organs are absent, and compatible nuclei are brought together by the union of hyphae, **somatogamy.** Finally, antheridia may be absent, nuclei in the ascogonium pairing, and their descendants ultimately uniting in the ascus, a saclike sporangial structure. In mycelial Ascomycota, the asci develop at the tips of hyphae, **ascogenous hyphae,** with binucleate cells. The binucleate ($n + n$), or **dikaryotic,** condition arises because compatible nuclei, brought together by fusion of cells, fail to unite immediately but, instead, continue dividing synchronously. Thus, plasmogamy and karyogamy are separated in time and site, as in the Basidiomycota (p. 258). The union of nuclei in the young ascus is the culmination of sexuality. Young asci are binucleate and become uninucleate by fusion of the nuclei. This is followed by meiosis, and often by mitosis, so that four or eight haploid nuclei are formed. These are the nuclei of the four or eight ascospores. When the latter are organized in the ascus, residual cytoplasm, called **epiplasm,** remains, the ascospores being delimited from the ascus cytoplasm like cookies are cut out from flattened cookie dough. In a number of Ascomycota, the mechanism of sexual reproduction is still unknown, and in still others, as in some species of *Aspergillus* and *Penicillium,* it seems to be absent.

Yeasts. Among the simplest Ascomycota are the yeasts, here exemplified by the brewer's yeast, *Saccharomyces cerevisiae* (Figure 10.13). Yeasts, which occur commonly in nature on ripening fruits, are simple unicellular organisms. Cellular multiplication by an unequal partition known as **budding** (Figure 10.13*a-c*) rapidly increases the population in suitable environments containing sugar. That *Saccharomyces* is an ascomycete is apparent by its production under certain conditions of ascospores in groups of four (Figure 10.13*d*). The cells which function as asci are, of course, diploid, and meiosis occurs in the formation of the four ascospores. If the ascospores of a single ascus are isolated singly into cultures, they multiply by budding, producing populations of haploid cells. It has been demonstrated that the ascospores from a single ascus are of two different mating types. Hence, if populations of two different mating types are mixed, diploid cells (zygotes) arise which reproduce by budding, forming diploid populations. The life cycle of *Saccharomyces,* accordingly, is dibiontic as in the algae *Ulva, Cladophora,* and *Ectocarpus,* among others.

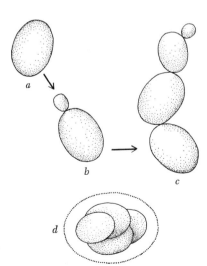

Figure 10.13 *Saccharomyces cerevisiae,* brewer's yeast, highly magnified. (*a-c*) Reproduction by budding. (*d*) Ascus containing ascospores.

The yeast organism, of course, has been the servant of human beings from antiquity, both as a leavening agent by production of carbon dioxide, prized by bakers, and as a producer of ethyl alcohol from sugars, prized by brewers. The degradation of sugar, known as **fermentation,** is catalyzed by an enzyme complex called zymase; the process is intracellular and occurs under anaerobic conditions. The low energy yield is evidence of the incomplete breakdown of sugar; much more energy still remains in the alcohol produced. Some yeastlike fungi are pathogenic and parasitize human beings. The life cycle of yeast is essentially dibiontic with sporic meiosis.

Ascomycetous Molds. Several genera of ascomycetous molds, for example, *Aspergillus* and *Penicillium*[2] (Figure 10.14), are significant for a variety of reasons. Most species are saprobic and widespread on organic substrates; their airborne spores are everywhere. Flagellated motile cells do not occur in the life cycles of these fungi or other Ascomycota. Colonies of these genera often will grow on a piece of moistened bread exposed to the atmosphere and then covered by a glass tumbler, or on overripe fruit.

Aspergillus and *Penicillium* belong to a group of brown and blue-green molds. Here again the color resides in the spore walls, although certain species such as *Penicillium chrysogenum* secrete a golden yellow pigment into the culture medium. The asexual spores, called **conidia,** are borne in chains on erect branches of the mycelium (Figure 10.14*b, c*). Some species produce closed ascocarps called **cleistocarps,** containing the asci and ascospores (Figure 10.14*e*), presumably after sexual fusions. *Penicillium* is an especially important genus, since it affects human welfare in several ways. On the adverse side, certain species may cause respiratory infections, mildew of cloth, and food spoilage (especially of citrus fruits and apples). Favorably, other species have important roles in the manufacture of such cheeses as Roquefort and Camembert. Far overshadowing all other useful activities, however, is the production of the lifesaving antibiotic **penicillin** by *Penicillium chrysogenum.*

Fleshy Ascomycota. The morels (Figure 10.15*a*) and cup fungi (Figure 10.15*b, c*) are Ascomycota that produce fleshy ascocarps in which asci are borne. The shallow cups of *Peziza* and other cup fungi are common on moist wood, in which the vegetative portion of the fungus ramifies as it digests the cellulose and lignin. The inner surface of the cup is lined with sterile hyphae, called **paraphyses,** and columnar asci containing ascospores (Figure 10.15*c*). Morels have not been grown in laboratory culture, and the details of their life history are unknown.

Powdery Mildews. The powdery mildews of the Ascomycota are widespread as obligate parasites upon many flowering plants. Their hyphae, which

---

[2]Strictly speaking, *Aspergillus* and *Penicillium* are Deuteromycota (see p. 263); however, some ascomycetous genera such as *Eurotium* and *Eupenicillium* have *Aspergillus* and *Penicillium* stages in their life cycles.

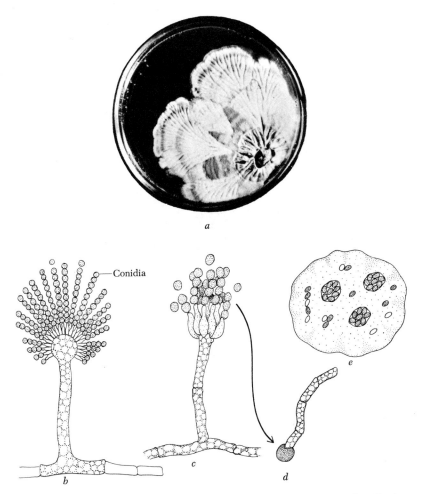

Figure 10.14 Brown and blue-green molds. (*a*) *Penicillium* sp., culture in a Petri dish of potato dextrose agar. (*b*) *Aspergillus* sp. (*c–e*) *Penicillium* sp.: (*c*) spore chains; (*d*) germinating spore; (*e*) section of ascocarp containing asci and ascospores.

absorb food from the leaf cells, produce both asexual spores and ascocarps (Figure 10.16) containing asci and ascospores. Powdery mildews are common on plantain, roses, cereal grains, and lilacs, among others. Additional plant diseases are caused by Ascomycota. Of these, Dutch elm disease is an example, as is chestnut blight, which has decimated that tree in the forests of the eastern United States. Few, if any, mature chestnut trees have been left growing by the pathogenic fungus involved. Oak wilt threatens the oaks in many sections of the country, while a disease of apples, called scab, is prevalent worldwide.

a

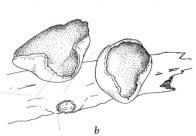

b

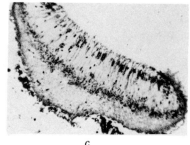

c

Figure 10.15 Fungi. (*a*) *Morchella* sp., the morel. (*b*) *Peziza* sp., a cup fungus; (*c*) *Pyronema* sp., a cup fungus; section of ascocarp. Note vertical asci on upper surface.

Brown rot of stone fruits, also caused by one of the Ascomycota, plays havoc with the peach industry.

 Club Fungi (Division Basidiomycota).   Fungi that produce basidia and basidiospores freely on the mycelium or in various types of fruiting structures,

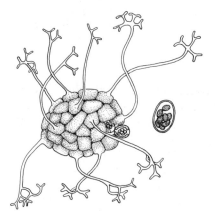

Figure 10.16 *Microsphaera* sp., a powdery mildew. Ascocarp (fruiting body) with appendages, slightly crushed, with detail of single ascus.

or **basidiocarps,** belong to the Basidiomycota. **Basidia** are either clublike hyphae, each (usually) with the four **basidiospores** borne at its apex, or septate hyphae arising upon germination of thick-walled spores. The Basidiomycota include economically important parasitic rusts and smuts of cereal grains and other plants, the mushrooms, and the puffballs and pored shelf fungi, some of which destroy timber and lumber.

Mushrooms. Most mushrooms (Figure 10.17), the inedible and poisonous species of which are called "toadstools" by the layperson, are saprobes; they depend for their nutrition on decaying wood and on soils rich in organic matter. The mushroom itself is the basidiocarp, or spore-bearing body, of the

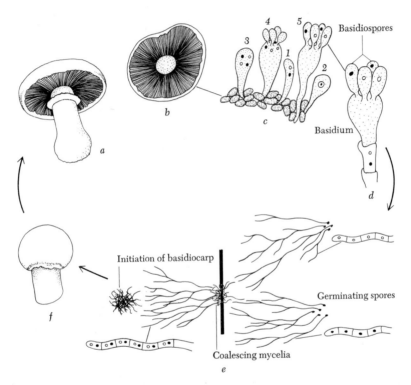

Figure 10.17 Life cycle of a mushroom. (*a, b*) Fruiting structure, or basidiocarp, showing gills. (*c*) Portion of a gill: (1) binucleate basidium; (2) basidium after nuclear fusion; (3) basidium after meiosis; (4) early stage in formation of basidiospores; (5) mature basidiospores. (*d*) Basidium and basidiospores enlarged. (*e*) Spore germination and formation of young mushroom; the spores of two mating types germinating and the resulting primary mycelia coalescing to form the secondary mycelium from which a new basidiocarp will arise. Note enlargements showing both primary mycelia containing nuclei of the opposite mating types (shown as white and black) and segment of secondary mycelium with compatible nuclei brought together in the same mycelium. (*f*) Immature basidiocarp.

organism. It is preceded by and develops upon an extensive vegetative mycelium. Unlike most plants and animals, in which cells divide and redivide to form the tissues of the body, the mushroom is built up by complicated interwoven hyphae of the filamentous mycelium. The mushroom cap bears **gills** on its lower surface. The gills (Figure 10.17*a, b*), also composed of interwoven hyphae, produce the basidia and basidiospores (Figure 10.17). Meiosis occurs in the basidium, so the basidiospores are haploid (*n*); these, upon germination, produce a **primary mycelium,** the cells of which are also uninucleate. When compatible pairs of such mycelia are grown together, fusions of hyphae (**somatogamy**) occur between certain compatible cells, but nuclear union is delayed until basidia are formed. This plasmogamy initiates the **secondary mycelium,** with binucleate (*n* + *n*) cells from which the basidiocarp is formed. The common edible mushroom, a species of *Agaricus*, is grown commercially from **spawn,** a mass of soil, manure, and rotting leaves that contains the mycelium of the fungus. When the spawn has been planted in properly prepared beds, the basidiocarps—that is, the mushrooms—develop after a period of vegetative growth of the mycelium.

Two additional features of mushrooms are of special interest—namely, the bioluminescence of some species and the hallucinogenic properties of others. The mycelium of certain mushrooms, both in laboratory cultures and in nature, is luminescent. This luminescence is mediated by the enzyme **luciferase** in the presence of **luciferin** as substrate. Substances bearing a similar name are also functional in the firefly, but evidence to date indicates that these are of a different chemical nature.

The mushroom *Psilocybe*[3] *mexicana* and related species were and are valued for the ecstatic effects they generate when eaten. The chemical nature of the active substances is being investigated, and one of the hallucinogenic substances synthesized, **psilocybin,** is being used in the study of certain mental aberrations.

In this brief discussion of mushrooms it is important to emphasize that there is no way of determining whether a mushroom is edible or poisonous except by having an "expert" identify it and/or by profiting from the experience of others who have eaten a given species and lived or died! It is also important to understand that different people react differently to the same species and that it is dangerous to pick and eat mushrooms indiscriminately. The commercially cultivated mushroom is perfectly safe, but mushrooms gathered in the field and offered for sale by amateurs should be avoided.

Puffballs and Shelf Fungi. Puffballs (Figure 10.18*a*) are the fleshy (later dry) basidiocarps of fungi whose mycelium ramifies through rich soil and decaying stumps and lumber. The inside of the developing puffball contains many minute chambers lined with basidia, which form myriad spores. These spores are liberated by decay or compression of the dried basidiocarps.

---

[3]Pronounced "sigh-*los*-i-bee."

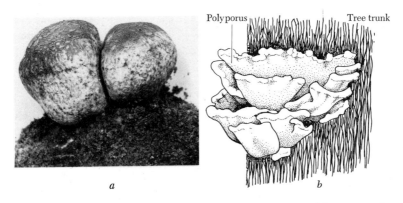

Figure 10.18   Basidiomycota. (*a*) *Scleroderma cepa,* a puffball; basidiocarp on soil. (*b*) *Polyporus* sp., a shelflike pore fungus; basidiocarp on tree trunk.

Shelf and bracket fungi (Figure 10.18*b*) are the basidiocarps of wood-destroying fungi whose mycelia are within the host tree or the lumber that serves as substrate. Basidia line the numerous pores of these basidiocarps and are discharged from their cavities over long periods.

It is significant that in the majority of Basidiomycota, although a sexual process occurs, differentiated gametangia and gametes do not develop. It should be emphasized that the union of nuclei in the young basidium of Basidiomycota, like the union of nuclei in the young ascus, is preceded by a dikaryotic phase. The initial two divisions of the fusion nucleus are meiotic in both cases, and the spores that are produced are, accordingly, haploid meiospores. This is perhaps but one step from isogamy (or just as primitive), in which the gametes, although specially differentiated, are not morphologically distinguishable. These sexual processes of the algae and fungi are instructive with respect to the sexual process in general, because they are not obscured by secondary and supplementary phenomena.

Rusts.   Among the Basidiomycota, the rusts are worth consideration for two reasons: Economically they cause decreased yields in grains and other plants, and biologically they represent classic examples of several striking phenomena to be discussed below. The wheat rust (Figure 10.19), a strain of *Puccinia graminis,* grows parasitically in the leaves and stems of wheat (other strains occur on other grains), absorbing materials from the wheat protoplasm.

At maturity the hyphae of *P. graminis* erupt in localized lesions on host leaves and stems. These lesions are known as **uredinia** and consist of erect hyphae-bearing spores with rust-colored cell walls at their tips (Figure 10.19*b*); these spores are called **urediniospores.** They may be blown to other host plants of the species on which they are produced, thus spreading the infection. Toward the end of the growing season of the host, the uredinial hyphae begin to pro-

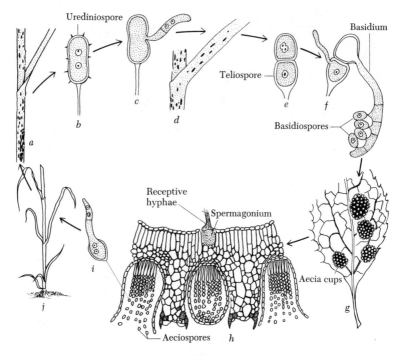

Figure 10.19 Life cycle of wheat rust, *Puccinia graminis tritici*. (*a*) Portion of infected wheat plant. Small, streaklike areas release binucleate urediniospores, as at (*b*). These germinate (*c*) and infect other wheat plants (*d*). Ultimately, two-celled teliospores (*e*), each cell binucleate, are produced on the wheat plants. These thick-walled spores germinate after a period of dormancy during which the two nuclei in each cell unite (*f*) to form a septate basidium from which four basidiospores are explosively discharged. If these land on a barberry leaf, they infect it upon germination and form a cuplike structure (aecium) full of spores (*g*). Sections of the barberry leaf (*h*) show the binucleate aeciospores being released (below) and flask-like spermagonia. Aeciospores, upon germination (*i*), infect young wheat plants (*j*), and the cycle is thus completed.

duce two-celled, black-walled **teliospores,** and these are finally produced in lesions called **telia** (Figure 10.19*d, e*). After a period of dormancy, the teliospores may germinate on the soil or on host stubble, forming delicate, septate hyphae, the **basidia** (Figure 10.19*f*), which produce four thin-walled **basidiospores.** These are projected from the basidia and, if they chance to be carried by air currents to a suitable alternate host, which in the case of *Puccinia graminis* is the common barberry (*Berberis vulgaris*), they germinate to produce an intercellular mycelium, which forms two additional types of reproductive structures—the **spermagonia** and **aecia.** The former are flasklike, most often on the upper surface of the leaf; the latter are bell-like and most often on the lower surface.

The spermagonia produce minute cells called **spermatia**, which are carried, sometimes by insects, to compatible **receptive hyphae** that protrude through the leaf surface. This is the stimulus that causes the aecial rudiments to produce aeciospores (Figure 10.19h), explained as follows: a nucleus from the spermatium enters a cell of the receptive hypha and it or its descendants migrate to the cells of the mycelium in the aecial rudiment, transforming them into binucleate cells. When this has occurred, they are stimulated to produce **aeciospores** in enormous numbers. If air currents chance to carry aeciospores to the leaves or stems of wheat plants (Figure 10.19i, j), they germinate and form an intercellular mycelium there, which again begins the cycle with urediniospores.

The aeciospores and the hyphal cells they produce in the wheat plant are binucleate as are the urediniospores (Figure 10.19b) and young teliospores. The nuclei unite (Figure 10.19e, upper cell) as these mature, and meiosis then occurs as the diploid nuclei divide later to form the basidial and basidiospore nuclei (Figure 10.19f). Accordingly, the spermatia, receptive hyphae, and those of the aecial rudiment are also uninucleate and haploid until the spermatium unites with a receptive hypha and reinitiates the binucleate condition. The latter is referred to as **dikaryotic**, or $n + n$. Thus, six types of reproductive cells are produced by *Puccinia graminis*, namely, urediniospores, teliospores, basidiospores, and aeciospores, along with receptive hyphae and spermatia, which are gametelike in function.

Puccinia graminis, like the powdery mildews of the Ascomycota, is a specialized parasite; it has only recently been cultivated apart from its wheat host or its alternate host. Apparently in nature the hosts supply it, during most of its life cycle, with the substances it requires to build its protoplasm. How this and similar host-parasite relationships have been initiated in the course of evolution is by no means clear. The specific requirement of wheat rust for wheat protoplasm is the more remarkable because in another phase of its life cycle (Figure 10.19g, h) the parasite is dependent on another host plant, the native American barberry, *Berberis vulgaris*, which is not closely related to wheat.

Imperfect Fungi (Division Deuteromycota).   In Deuteromycota are classified a vast number of fungal species for which no sexual stages are known and which reproduce only by asexual spores. Their mycelia are septate, like those of Ascomycota and Basidiomycota. Both saprobic and parasitic species are known; the latter are of economic importance as the etiological agents of diseases of cultivated plants such as celery, beans, onions, and apples. Figure 10.20 illustrates one member of this vast assemblage.

Most Deuteromycota resemble the asexual (conidial) stages of Ascomycota, or, more rarely, of Basidiomycota, and they are, therefore, believed to be Asco- or Basidiomycota that have lost their sexual stages in evolution. In evidence of this may be cited the fact that powdery mildews in the tropics

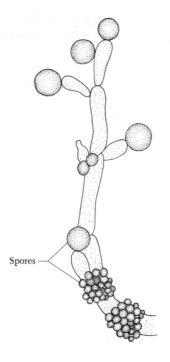

Spores

Figure 10.20 *Candida albicans,* a member of the Deuteromycota. Note spores of two different types. [After C. J. Alexopoulos, *Introductory Mycology, 2nd ed.* (New York: John Wiley & Sons, Inc. 1952). Reprinted by permission of the publisher.]

produce only conidia and omit the sexual phase that culminates in the production of asci and ascospores.

Lichens

Lichens (Figure 10.21) are dual organisms composed of an alga (green or blue-green) and a fungus. They are classified with Ascomycota or Basidiomycota, depending on their fungal component; in most lichens the fungus is a member of the Ascomycota. The nutritive relationships between the components have inspired much uncritical speculation, and the real relationships are only now being investigated by the techniques of pure culture. Recent work has shown that both the algal and fungal components of a lichen may lead independent existences in the same culture medium, even when placed in contact. Only when nutrition is minimal or subminimal and moisture is at a low level can the intimate association of fungus and alga be reestablished, forming a lichen.

These dual organisms may be encrusted on rocks or wood (**crustose**), or branched and emergent from the substrate (**fruticose**), or membranous and leaflike (**foliose**). The dual organism often is able to flourish in habitats where neither component could exist alone.

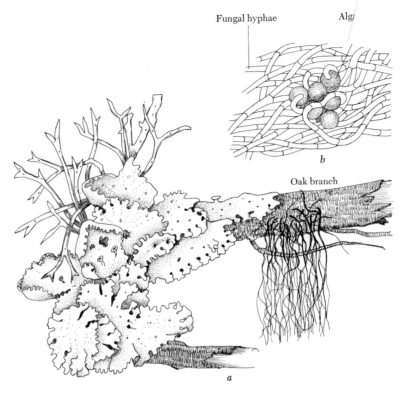

Fungal hyphae   Alg

b

Oak branch

a

Figure 10.21 Lichens. (*a*) Several species on an oak branch; the fibrous, pendulous form at the right is a species of *Usnea* called "the old man's beard." (*b*) Algal cells (phycobiont) among fungal hyphae (mycobiont) of a lichen.

Lichens grow, albeit very slowly, in a wide variety of habitats, including soil and rocks, and as epiphytes on other vegetation, especially tree bark. They can survive extreme desiccation and when moist may increase 100 to 300 percent in weight because of their water-holding capacity. Because of their secretions, lichens are important agents in initiating soil formation by playing a role in disintegration of rock.

Propagated by windborne fragments that contain both alga and fungus, each partner may also reproduce independently, liberating its reproductive cells from the lichen thallus; however, it is doubtful that the new lichens are often synthesized from these in nature. The ascomycetous fungus may develop ascocarps (**apothecia**), or little cups, the surface of which is covered with asci, which discharge their ascospores. Furthermore, reproductive agents of the algae (for example, hormogonia of *Nostoc* or zoospores of green algae) may disseminate the alga.

Fossil Record and Importance of Fungi

The fossil record of the fungi is not as clear as that of algae, but mycelial fungi were probably coexistent with algae and bacteria in the Precambrian (see Table 6.1). Figure 10.22 illustrates a fossilized fungus from Carboniferous strata; well-preserved fossil fungi that parasitized Devonian plants have also been found. Putative Ascomycota are known from the Silurian (Figure 10.23).

The fungi, like the bacteria and slime molds, are of fundamental importance in medicine, industry, and other aspects of human welfare. The role of saprobic fungi (and bacteria) in causing decay in moist habitats is of ines-

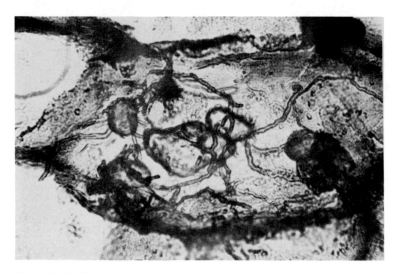

Figure 10.22 Fossilized fungus in a rhizome of a Carboniferous plant. [After H. N. Andrews and L. W. Lenz, "A Mycorhizome from the Carboniferous of Illinois," *Bull. Torrey Bot. Club,* Vol. 70, pp. 120–125. Figure 4. Reprinted by permission of the publisher.]

Figure 10.23 Fungal hyphae from Silurian strata. [Courtesy of Professor Jane Gray.]

timable importance. On the one hand, were it not for their degradative activities in such habitats, vast quantities of nutrient materials would remain "locked up" in dead organisms and organic products, unavailable for recycling to living organisms. On the other hand, these same degradative processes are of serious import in the preservation of cloth, insulation, lumber, and similar materials in moist environments.

Certain fungi have been of paramount importance in the development of the science of biochemical genetics. When subjected to mutagenic agents, these organisms have undergone a variety of genetic changes. The changes have been manifested in the chemical activities of the organisms, providing fundamental knowledge regarding the pathways of metabolism. Especially fruitful in this connection have been researches on the mold *Neurospora*, among others. Furthermore, parasitic fungi have directly inspired the genetic research that has provided humans with many fungus-immune races of economically important plants. The fungi have been important, too, in the elucidation of the nature of specificity in host-parasite relationships. Finally, it should be noted that most plant diseases are caused by parasitic fungi.

QUESTIONS FOR REVIEW

1. List the respects in which the divisions Myxomycota and Acrasiomycota differ. What, if any, characteristics do they have in common?
2. Describe, with the aid of drawings, the life cycle of one of the plasmodial slime molds.
3. Describe, with the aid of labeled drawings, the life cycle of a cellular slime mold.
4. When and where does meiosis occur in plasmodial slime molds?
5. When and where does meiosis occur in cellular slime molds?
6. Where would you look for plasmodial slime molds in nature?
7. How do both the Myxomycota and Acrasiomycota differ from fungi? From bacteria?
8. Define or explain plasmodium, pseudoplasmodium, "slug."
9. What method of nutrition is used by slime molds?
10. In what respects do fungi differ from bacteria and slime molds?
11. Define or explain mycelium, hypha, zoospore, coenocytic, haustorium, rhizoid, meiospore, meiosporangium, mitosporangium, zoosporangium, self-incompatability, sporangiophore, somatogamy, heterothallism.
12. Describe the life cycle and reproduction in *Allomyces macrogynus*. Is it dibiontic? Give the reason for your answer.
13. How do Oomycota differ from other fungi?
14. Describe the life cycle of *Rhizopus stolonifer*. To what type of algal life cycle does it correspond?
15. Define or explain ascus, ascospore, ascocarp, epiplasm, paraphysis.

16. Cite two activities of *Saccharomyces cerevisiae* that are of value to humans.

17. In what respects is *Penicillium* important to humans?

18. Define or explain basidium, basidiospore, basidiocarp, primary mycelium, and secondary mycelium.

19. Describe the life cycle, including nuclear condition, of the rust *Puccinia graminis*.

20. Give the chromosome condition in terms of n, $n + n$, or $2n$ of the following: urediniospore, young teliospore, teliospore just prior to germination, basidiospore, spermatium, aeciospore, mycelium in wheat plant, and mycelium in the barberry plant.

21. Describe the structure and reproduction of mushrooms.

22. List some harmful and some beneficial activities of fungi.

23. What are lichens and where do they grow?

24. How do lichens reproduce?

25. What are the Deuteromycota?

CHAPTER ELEVEN

Conclusion

It seems appropriate at this point to consider the various types of organisms described in some detail in earlier chapters, in order to consolidate our understanding of the plants themselves and the groups they represent, and to emphasize some of the important principles they illustrate. We are now in a better position than at the outset to consider the diversity of the plant kingdom, the causes for this diversity, and the problems of the relationships and classification of plants. Let us begin by summarizing some of the more important phenomena described in the preceding chapters.

ORGANIZATION OF THE PLANT BODY

Our discussion of the diversity of the plant kingdom (*sensu lato*) has included reference to such groups of organisms as bacteria, algae, fungi, mosses and liverworts, seedless vascular plants (psilotophytes, club mosses, arthrophytes, and ferns), and seed-bearing vascular plants, including gymnosperms and angiosperms. Was there any important reason for studying them in that particular order? Could we have started as well at the other end of the series, or perhaps with any intermediate group, and have proceeded in a different sequence? The order of study is indeed significant for it reflects to a great degree both an increasing complexity and the order of appearance of the earth's flora.[1] There is evidence that this increasing complexity was built up over several

[1]The fungi, in this edition, were considered last, because they are classified in a separate kingdom by many biologists.

billion years, starting from relative simplicity. Diversities of structure and function, both vegetative and reproductive, are best explained as manifestations of gradual change, or evolution. We must be cautious, however, in our appraisal of supposed simplicity and complexity. In the first place, apparent simplicity, as in the case of the many aquatic plants that have little differentiated xylem, may well be a secondary simplicity through loss of complexity, a phenomenon known as **reduction.** The absence of xylem and phloem from algae (except for the phloemlike tubes in certain kelps), liverworts, and mosses, on the other hand, is usually interpreted as true simplicity and as a primitive condition.

Some further words of caution are appropriate. In spite of their manifest complexity, the so-called higher plants are performing essentially the same biological functions that go on even in unicellular organisms, which are often spoken of as the "lower" or "simple" plants. These manifold chemical and physical processes are elegantly complex, interrelated, and coordinated in all living organisms; thus the terms "lower," "higher," "primitive," and "advanced" are often misleading and illusory, as are "simple" and "complex." The following terms might be used more appropriately in some of these comparisons: "alternate" or "different"; "ancient," and "recent"; and "similar" and "dissimilar."

On the other hand, when one considers unicellular, colonial, and multicellular organisms, it becomes clear that an organism is more than the sum of its individual cells. This is evidenced by the movement through the plant body of hormones that evoke different responses from different descendants of the initial reproductive cell (usually a spore or zygote). The evidence of modern electron microscopy shows clearly that multicellular plants are not made of isolated cells stacked together like bricks or boxes (see Figure 1.2). An extensive, netlike system passes through the walls from cell to cell, so the original unity of the zygote probably is partially preserved as it gives rise to the multicellular organism. Furthermore, development of the multicellular organism involves coordinated responses to the environment. Multicellular plants and animals are considered by some biologists to be cell republics that have evolved from the aggregation of unicellular organisms. Others look upon unicellular organisms as complex and acellular, not strictly comparable to single tissue cells. These theorists regard multicellular organisms as having arisen by secondary subdivision of the organisms into cells.

Since all organisms start as single cells, ontogeny (the development of an individual organism) suggests that multicellular organisms probably arose by the failure of cells to separate after the completion of cell division. Growth in multicellular plants may be generalized, as in such filamentous blue-green algae as *Oscillatoria* (see Figure 2.8a); but in most cases, it is restricted to tips of stems and roots or to certain other definite regions. Such apical growth occurs in a number of algae and fungi, and is the rule in almost all of the remaining types of plants, although in many plants lateral growth is also pronounced. Some exceptions occur, as in *Equisetum,* members of the grass family and other monocotyledons, in which intercalary meristems are also present.

A survey of the plant kingdom indicates that when the component cells of a plant are essentially uniform in structure and function, as in the sea lettuce, *Ulva* (Figure 3.18), and a number of other algae and liverworts, the size of the plant is limited, especially when the plants are not aquatic. Although internal differentiation is apparent to a limited degree in such algae as certain kelps, in which even phloemlike tissues are present, the stimulus for internal complexity seems to have been the land habitat. This is apparent to some degree in such liverworts as *Ricciocarpus* (see Figure 4.2b, d), in the stems and leaves of certain mosses, and, finally, to the greatest degree in the vascular plants.

In the vascular plants, with the exception of the Psilotophyta, the plant body consists of an axis composed of stem, root, and leaves. There are two fundamentally different types of leaves. Of these, microphylls (with simple, unbranched veins) characterize only the Microphyllophyta (*Selaginella* and so forth), whereas the remaining vascular plants are probably all megaphyllous. It has been suggested, on the basis of the fossil record, that megaphylls represent branching axes that have become flattened and bladelike through extension of the nonvascular tissues by a sort of webbing.

REPRODUCTION

We have alluded in earlier chapters to various methods of reproduction, both asexual and sexual, the latter involving cellular and nuclear union, the association of parental chromosomes, and meiosis. The simplest and most direct method of asexual reproduction is by **fragmentation** of a plant itself. This is exemplified by **binary fission** (cell division) in unicellular organisms, as well as by various cases in which fragments of a plant regenerate complete new individuals: dissociation of such colonial algae as *Merismopedia* (Figure 2.7); dissociation of such truly multicellular organisms as branching liverworts, mosses, ferns, and other rhizomes; and *cuttings* of leaves, stems, and roots. Special agents of reproduction, **spores** (unicellular and multicellular spores such as the airborne spores of fungi, liverworts, hornworts, mosses, and ferns, and the zoospores of certain algae and fungi) and **gemmae** (buds or fragments) are also produced. All these are asexual in that they develop into new individuals without uniting with another spore or gemma.

Sexual reproduction throughout the plant kingdom almost always involves a union of cells; it always involves a union of nuclei, the consequent association of chromosomes and, ultimately, meiosis. The origin of sexual reproduction remains unknown, but evidence in unicellular algae suggests that union of cells may have resulted from inadequate supplies of certain metabolites.

Less complex organisms, such as unicellular algae and fungi, are only apparently and deceptively simple, for they carry on both vegetative (somatic) and reproductive functions within a single cell. The gamete of *Chlamydomonas* (see p. 32) is merely an immature individual that is sexually active. It is capable of union with another compatible individual as a result of certain chemical changes within it and on its surface. In certain colonial and filamentous algae and fungi, and in all plants of other groups, the vegetative function is more clearly segregated from the reproductive, as indicated by the formation of special fertile areas containing reproductive cells, often in gametangia and sporangia. The gametees of *Chlamydomonas,* on the contrary, are both vegetative and reproductive in function, and are primitive in this respect. This is evidenced by the fact that gametes failing to unite will, under suitable conditions, produce large populations by cell division. In most multicellular organisms, these powers of rejuvenation and asexual reproduction no longer characterize the differentiated reproductive cells, and those reproductive cells that do not unite die, except in parthenogenesis, for example, as in *Ulva* (p. 44).

From the preceding chapters, it is clear that, with respect to the distribution of the compatible gametes (+ and −, male and female), individuals may be either bisexual (hermaphroditic) or unisexual. Individuals of a number of species of *Volvox,* liverworts, mosses, and the gametophytes of *Psilotum, Lycopodium, Equisetum,* and of many ferns are bisexual. In contrast, the individuals of certain species of *Chlamydomonas* and those of *Pandorina, Achlya ambisexualis, Rhizopus,* and *Polytrichum,* as well as the gametophytes of *Selaginella* and of all the seed plants, are genetically unisexual, either + or −, or male or female.

It should also be apparent that gametes may or may not be differentiated *morphologically.* Thus, we have seen that among the algae and fungi various degrees of gametic differentiation exist, from morphological **isogamy** (*Chlamydomonas moewusii, Rhizopus*) through **anisogamy** (*Chlamydomonas* spp.), culminating in oogamy. **Oogamy,** in which the minute male gametes are called sperms and the large female gametes are called eggs, occurs in some algae (*Volvox, Fucus*) and fungi (*Achlya*), and in all liverworts, mosses, and vascular plants. It should be evident that in defining isogamy as the condition that produces undifferentiated gametes, we are saying that the lack of difference between uniting gametes is more apparent than real. The term "isogamy" is founded upon morphology; from ingenious genetical and biochemical experiments, it is clear that even isogametes are physiologically and chemically different from each other, and these differences are apparently the basis for the compatible unions in which zygotes are formed.

From a survey of the various reproductive phenomena in plants and fungi, the following generalizations may be stated:

1. Some plants may be *haploid,* with a single, basic complement of chromosomes in their nuclei, throughout their existence. The *diploid* condition prevails only temporarily in the zygote of such species, which divides meiotically at germination to form a new generation of haploid individuals. This occurs only among algae and fungi and is exemplified by *Chlamydomonas, Rhizopus,* and *Achlya,* among others. Meiosis in such organisms is zygotic; that is, it occurs in the germinating zygote.

2. In a few algae (*Fucus,* for one), the individual plant is diploid throughout its existence and only its gametes, which arise by meiosis, are haploid. The gametic union, forming a zygote, initiates a new diploid individual. Meiosis here is gametic, occurring during gametogenesis.

3. Certain algae (for example, *Ulva,* the sea lettuce) and a few fungi, and all the liverworts, mosses, and vascular plants (therefore, the great majority of plants) have both haploid and diploid phases, which are designated as gametophytes and sporophytes, respectively. These alternate in regular sequence, so that the haploid, sexual gametophyte forms gametes that unite to produce zygotes, which, in turn, give rise to diploid sporophytes that undergo meiosis and produce spores (meiospores). The sporophytes and gametophytes may be physically connected, either sporophyte upon gametophyte (as in mosses) or gametophyte upon sporophyte (as in seed plants), or they may be independent of each other, that is, dibiontic (as in ferns). In the liverworts, hornworts, and mosses, the gametophytic phase is dominant in duration and stature, whereas in vascular plants the sporophyte is dominant and the gametophyte is ephemeral.

It should not be construed that there is a sort of antagonism between sporophyte and gametophyte; both are merely different phases of the same organism. Inasmuch as meiosis, with its reassortment of parental genes, is the culmination of sexual reproduction, spores are "asexual" only in the sense that they undergo further development without union with each other. Actually, since they are products of meiosis, they themselves are an ultimate result of sexual union.

Finally, the land plants may be divided into those that are homosporous (producing similar spores) and those that are heterosporous (producing dimorphic spores). The most pronounced types of heterospory we have discussed are present in *Selaginella* (in some species the megaspores are hundreds of times larger than microspores), and in *Isoetes, Marsilea, Salvinia,* and *Azolla.* The inevitable consequence of heterospory, it will be recalled, is the production of unisexual gametophytes (although these sometimes also arise from homosporous sporophytes, as in *Polytrichum*). The seed plants are usually interpreted as heterosporous; the similar size of microspores and megaspores is regarded as the result of the permanent retention of the megaspore and female gametophyte within the megasporangium. Megaspores of seed plants enlarge *after* their contained female gametophytes have developed, rather than *before,* as in *Selaginella* (p. 135).

The seed is apparently a highly efficient mechanism for perpetuating and disseminating the species. Furthermore, the habit of producing seeds must account in large part for the dominance of the angiosperms in our present flora.

CLASSIFICATION AND EVOLUTIONARY DEVELOPMENT OF PLANTS

In Chapter 1, we stated that most current classifications of the plant kingdom are phylogenetic, in that they attempt to group organisms in categories that indicate real, genetic relationships. Now that we have surveyed representative types of plants, we can discuss the possible relationships of currently living plant groups to one another and to extinct members of the plant kingdom, known to us only through fossils. Phylogenetic systems of classification of higher taxa, such as families, orders, classes, and divisions, necessarily are increasingly speculative regarding real relationships, as one progresses to the higher categories of classification. This is in contrast to evidence of evolutionary change in individuals and species, where experimental procedures are possible. Thus, the changes in individuals that may be transmitted to their offspring, or **mutations,** produced by irradiation, chemicals such as nitrogen mustard gas, and other agents, are a direct and incontrovertible indication of change and of relationship by descent, or **evolution.** The occurrence of such mutations in nature and their segregation and recombination in sexual reproduction are undoubtedly responsible for changes in individuals, species, and populations. These changes are effected by natural selection of mutations.

From such evidence, we infer that the operation of mutation and natural selection over millions of years has brought about the diversity now apparent in our flora and fauna. Although the adequacy of such mechanisms in evoking the present manifold diversities among plants and animals has from time to time been questioned, no satisfactory alternative has yet been proposed. No experimental evidence is available to confirm relationships among plants of the past and their supposed descendants now living. Recent identification of amino acids from fossil material, however, suggests that comparative chemical analyses of fossils might well contribute to our knowledge of plant relationships. The evidences that support speculations regarding the origin and putative relationships among the groups of plants in our present flora and those of the past result from studies of comparative morphology of living plants, of their geographical distribution, of their comparative biochemistry, and of extinct plants as revealed in the fossil record, to mention a few. Examples of these several lines of evidence will be presented in the following paragraphs.

The comparative study of plants (and animals) reveals certain common attributes cited previously. Among these are similarities of cellular organization, metabolism, reproductive phenomena (including sexuality, meiosis, and life cycles), inheritance, and the capacity for adaptation. The occurrence of the same active, photosynthetic pigment, chlorophyll *a,* throughout the plant kingdom and of the storage product, starch, in a great majority of green plants, provides two examples of a widely distributed characteristic. In a word, there are a number of attributes common to species, genera, families, orders, classes, and, finally, to divisions of plants—both living and fossil—that indicate continuity. These are most satisfactorily explained on the basis of kinship.

The fossil record presents us with important information regarding the course of evolution and the relationships of various forms of plant life. As the original, igneous rocks of the earth's crust weathered, particles were washed away and deposited as sediments in bodies of water. Among these particles, various organic remains were deposited. Later, when compression transformed these mixed sediments into sedimentary rocks, the organic remains sometimes were preserved as fossils. They are of various types and different in the perfection of their preservation. The most perfectly preserved are petrifactions (fossil plant remains themselves embedded in a rocky matrix), in which details of microscopic structure are remarkably clear upon sectioning.

The older strata of sedimentary rocks obviously contain fossil remains of the most ancient organisms, whereas strata deposited subsequently contain increasingly more recent organic remains, culminating in those of extant plants. Although this "rock record of plants" is remarkably long and uninterrupted in such localities as the Grand Canyon, there are few places where such a great series of strata is exposed. Paleobotanists are forced, therefore, to rely on the exposure of fossil-bearing strata by landslides, washouts, road and rail construction, and, especially, mining and drilling operations.

In spite of the incompleteness of the fossil record, considerable information has been obtained about plants of the past (see Table 6.1). Paleobotany has not shed direct light on the earliest forms of life, but indirect evidence of their existence—for example, calcareous sediments (limestones) and iron ores—is available. Algalike organisms have been discovered in Precambrian rocks in Africa over three billion years old and in similar rocks in Canada about one and three-quarter billion years old. The earliest organisms were aquatic—algal, bacterial, and probably fungal. Many calcareous algae occur in the lower Ordovician strata of the Paleozoic era. Rock from the Devonian period of the Paleozoic is strikingly different from earlier strata in that it contains the remains of truly terrestrial plants, including liverworts and representatives of four (or more) lines of seedless vascular plants (see Chapters 6 and 7). The gradual development of terrestrial plants with vascular tissue indicates the correlation between the migration of plant life to land and the evolution of xylem and phloem. In spite of the rise of the land plants, however, aquatic algae, bacteria, and fungi have continued to flourish until the present, apparently with little change.

Sedimentary rocks of nonmarine origin from the late Paleozoic (Mississippian and Pennsylvanian) contain a wealth of fossils, some of which have been referred to briefly in earlier chapters. The occurrence of extensive deposits of coal from the Pennsylvanian is indirect evidence of the abundance of photosynthetic plants in that period. The Pennsylvanian often is called the "Age of Ferns" because of the abundance of fossilized fern leaves in its strata. Many of these, however, were seed ferns (now extinct), considered by some to be the precursors of the flowering plants. In addition, tree-size, *Equisetum*-like plants (Figure 7.21) and others of similar dimensions, somewhat resembling our modern *Lycopodium* and *Selaginella*, flourished in swamps in Pennsylvanian times. Furthermore, fossilized mosses, liverworts, and the remains of treelike gymnosperms (in addition to seed ferns) are preserved in Pennsylvanian strata. Many of these are still well represented as fossils in Mesozoic strata, but in the Cretaceous, angiosperms appeared and became dominant as the number and diversity of other plants waned.

We can make several important generalizations on the basis of this brief survey of the fossil record and by inspection of Table 6.1.

1. Indirect and direct evidence indicates that algae, fungi, and bacteria are probably among the most ancient organisms, the presence of some on the earth extending back into Precambrian, 3 billion years ago, and possibly even longer. Similar organisms, with slight modifications, are represented in our flora at the present time; thus, algae have evolved little and slowly.

2. Land plants, probably derived from algae that gradually colonized muddy shores and finally drier habitats, had evolved and become abundant by the Devonian (395 million years ago). The number, complexity, and diversity of fossilized vascular plants in the Devonian strongly suggest that they must have evolved considerably earlier, although unequivocal evidence of this before the Silurian is lacking.

3. The widespread occurrence of vascular tissues (xylem and phloem) probably coincided with colonization of the land. Colonizers that lack vascular tissues, such as mosses and liverworts, have remained small on land.

4. Successively more recent strata reveal an apparent orderliness of development of representative divisions from ancient to recent: the algae, bacteria, and fungi; seedless vascular plants; and, finally, seed plants. Of the seed plants, the flowering plants are the most recent.

5. A number of organisms prominent in ancient floras are no longer extant. In most cases, the reasons for their extinction are not clear.

Plant fossils, then, indicate that our present flora is changed in composition from floras of earlier periods of the earth's history. Since we know that living organisms are descendants of living precursors, we conclude from the fossil record that our present plants (and animals, of course) are modified descendants of more ancient ones. This, in essence, is what is meant by organic evolution. All modern biologists accept this point of view. It is when individual biologists attempt to outline the *course* of evolution, and thus to draw up actual phylogenetic lines of descent (especially among the taxa that are more comprehensive than genera), that they often disagree, because they interpret evidences differently.

Anyone who surveys the comparative morphology of living plants in the light of the paleobotanical record usually becomes convinced that terrestrial plants have evolved from aquatic green algal precursors, and that the primitive, spore-bearing, seedless vascular plants growing upon the earth from the Devonian through the late Paleozoic periods have now themselves been crowded into near oblivion by the flowering plants that have been dominant since the Cretaceous. What will occur in plant life in the millions of years ahead is open to speculation. The changes are occurring inexorably at present, but the limited framework of the human life span clouds our perception of long-range events yet to transpire in the evolutionary process.

Glossary

Abaxial   The surface of an appendage away from the axis or stem.

Abscission Layer   A zone of cells at the base of an appendage (petiole, fruit stalk, and so forth) that causes the separation of that appendage from another organ.

Achene   A simple, dry, indehiscent one-seeded fruit, the seed being attached to the ovary wall at only one point.

Adaxial   The surface of an appendage toward the axis or stem.

Adventitious Root   A root that is neither primary nor secondary, nor one that arises therefrom; a root usually arising from a stem or leaf.

Agar   A gel-forming polysaccharide, a polymer of galactose, derived from certain red algae and used in microbiology as a solidifying agent in culture media.

Aggregate Fruit   A receptacle bearing a number of matured pistils (fruits) of a single flower.

Akinete   A vegetative cell that has been transformed by wall thickening into a non-motile spore.

Alginic Acid   A polyuronic acid located in the middle lamella and the primary walls of brown algae.

Ament   An inflorescence (spike) of sepal- and petalless flowers, as in willow.

Amphiphloic   Having phloem on both sides of the xylem.

Angiosperm   A seed plant with ovules and seeds enclosed in a carpel, pistil, or fruit.

Anisogamous   Flagellate gametes unequal in size, the larger called female and the smaller male.

Annual A plant that develops, reproduces, and dies in a single growing season, usually within a year.

Annual Ring The cylinder of secondary xylem added to a woody plant stem by the cambium in any one year.

Annulus A specialized or differentiated ringlike layer of cells in the moss capsule or in the sporangial wall of ferns.

Anther The apex of the stamen, composed of microsporangia and containing pollen at maturity.

Antheridiophore A fertile branch that bears antheridia.

Antheridium In plants other than algae or fungi, a multicellular, sperm-producing organ consisting of spermatogenous tissue and a sterile jacket; in algae and fungi, a unicellular sperm-forming organ.

Antipodal Cell Any of three cells of the mature female gametophyte of angiosperms that are located at the opposite end from the micropyle and usually degenerate after fertilization.

Apical Meristem The cells at the apex of a root or stem that are actively dividing.

Apogamy Formation of a sporophyte from a gametophyte without gametic union.

Apospory Formation of a gametophyte from a part of the sporophyte other than a spore.

Archegoniophore A fertile branch that bears archegonia.

Archegonium A multicellular, egg-producing gametangium with a jacket of sterile cells.

Ascocarp The ascus-containing body of Ascomycota.

Ascospore A spore produced by free-cell formation following meiosis in an ascus.

Ascus A saclike cell of Ascomycota in which karyogamy is followed immediately by meiosis and in which ascospores of a definite number arise by free-cell formation.

Asexual Not involving cellular or nuclear union.

Atactostele A scattered arrangement of xylem and phloem groups or vascular bundles.

Autotrophic Requiring only inorganic compounds for nutrition; see also *heterotrophic*.

Axillary Bud A bud borne in the axil of the leaf.

Bacillus A rod-shaped bacterium.

Bacteriophage A virus that is parasitic on bacteria.

Basidiocarp The basidiospore-containing structure of certain Basidiomycota.

Basidiospore A spore attached to a basidium and arising after meiosis.

Basidium   A nonseptate or septate hypha bearing (usually) four basidiospores exogenously following karyogamy and meiosis.

Berry   A simple fleshy fruit in which the exocarp is skinlike, the mesocarp fleshy, and the endocarp shiny or juicy.

Bud   A minute stem with short internodes, bearing the primordia of vegetative leaves or sporophylls.

Budding   Multiplication by abscission of a cellular protuberance, as in certain yeasts.

Bud Scale   A modified basal leaf that encloses the more delicate leaf primordia or sporophyll primordia.

Bud Scale Scar   A scar on a woody stem that marks the former site of attachment of a bud scale.

Bulb   A short, vertical, subterranean stem covered by fleshy leaf bases or scales, as in lily and onion.

Calyptra   The enlarged and modified archegonium that for awhile encloses the embryonic sporophyte of liverworts, mosses, and seedless plants.

Calyx   The collective term for the sepals of a flower.

Cambium   A zone of meristematic cells located between the primary xylem and phloem, the division products of which differentiate into secondary xylem and phloem.

Capitulum   A headlike inflorescence of composite flowers, as in daisy.

Capsule   (1) The sporangium of liverworts and mosses. (2) The colloidal sheath of algae and bacteria. (3) A simple, dry, dehiscent fruit arising from a compound ovary.

Carpel   The enclosing structure of angiospermous ovules, often considered to represent a folded megasporophyll.

Carpogonium   The female gametangium of red algae.

Carposporophyte   In red algae, a group of carpospores, which arise directly or indirectly from the zygote.

Carrageenan   A substance composed of D-galactose units and sulfate groups, formed by extracting polysaccharides by hot water from certain red algae.

Caryopsis   A simple, dry, indehiscent fruit whose one seed is fused all over its surface to the ovary wall.

Casparian Strip   A suberin thickening on the walls of endodermal cells.

Chemoautotrophic   Using chemical energy to synthesize protoplasm from inorganic sources.

Chemosynthetic   Utilization of chemical energy for the production of complex organic compounds from simple inorganic ones (= chemoautotrophic).

Chloroplast   A membrane-bounded area of cytoplasm, containing photosynthetic lamellae.

Cilium Like a flagellum, but short and stiff through the power stroke.

Circinate Vernation The curled arrangement of leaves and leaflets in the bud resulting from their more rapid growth on one surface than on the other.

Cleistocarp An ascocarp which does not open, as in the powdery mildews.

Closed Bud A bud covered by bud scales and dormant except during the growing season.

Coccus A spherical bacterium.

Coenobium (adj. coenobic) A colony in which the number of cells is fixed at origin and not subsequently augmented.

Coenocytic Multinucleate and nonseptate.

Columella A sterile region surrounded by spores in certain molds and mosses, as well as in *Anthoceros* and Mosses.

Companion Cell A small, nucleated cell associated with some sieve cells.

Compound Leaf A leaf with a divided blade.

Conceptacle A chamber in which gametangia are produced, as in certain brown algae.

Conidium(a) An asexual, nonmotile, airborne fungal spore borne at the tip of a hypha.

Conifer A cone-bearing tree or shrub with nonciliate sperms, such as pine or hemlock.

Contractile Vacuole A vacuole that dilates as it accumulates liquid, and subsequently contracts to excrete the liquid.

Cork Tissue, the component cells of which have walls thickened with suberin.

Corm A short, vertical, fleshy, subterranean stem.

Corolla A collective term for petals.

Cortex The region between the stele and the epidermis in stems and roots.

Corticating Cells Those surrounding an axial filament or filaments as in Charophyta and Rhodophyta.

Cotyledon A primary embryonic leaf.

Covered Bud See *closed bud*.

Cryptogam Refers to plants other than seed-producing plants.

Cuticle An impermeable surface layer on the epidermis of plant organs.

Cutin A waxy substance composing the cuticle.

Cyanophycean Starch An amylopectin fraction of starch produced by blue-green algae; resembles glycogen.

Cystocarp   The carpospores and their associated sterile covering cells, in Rhodophyta.

Cytokinesis   Division of the cytoplasm.

Deciduous   Shedding all leaves periodically (usually annually).

Dehiscent   Opening or splitting.

Diatomaceous Earth   The siliceous remains (cell walls) of fossilized diatoms.

Dibiontic   Having two free-living organisms in the life cycle.

Dichotomous   Branching into two equal parts.

Differentiation   The change from homogeneous tissue to heterogeneous tissues, for example, from meristem to primary tissues.

Dikaryon   Having two nuclei, as in the hyphal cells of certain phases in Ascomycota and Basidiomycota.

Dioecious   Producing microspores and megaspores on separate individuals; producing sperms and eggs on separate individuals.

Diploid   Having two complements or sets of haploid chromosomes.

DNA   Deoxyribonucleic acid.

Double Fertilization   In fertilization of angiosperms, the union of one sperm with the egg and of the other sperm with two polar nuclei or a secondary nucleus.

Drupe   A simple fleshy fruit in which the exocarp is skinlike, the mesocarp fleshy, and the endocarp stony.

Ectophloic   Having phloem located external to the xylem.

Egg   A large, nonflagellate female gamete.

Elater   (1) A sterile, hygroscopic cell in the capsule of certain liverworts. (2) The appendages formed from the outer spore wall in *Equisetum*.

Endocarp   The innermost layer of the ovary wall in the fruit.

Endodermis   The innermost, differentiated layer of the cortex, present in roots, rhizomes, and in the stems of certain cryptogams.

Endoplasmic Reticulum   The lamellar or tubular system of the colorless cytoplasm in a cell.

Endosperm   The nutritive tissue used by the embryo in angiosperms.

Endospory   The development of gametophytes within spores.

Epicotyl   See *plumule*.

Epidermis   A superficial layer of parenchyma cells with cutinized walls which covers the tissues of leaves, stems, roots, and the reproductive organs of plants.

Epigyny   A condition in flowers in which the ovary is embedded in the receptacle and the stamens arise above the ovary.

Epiphragm   The membranous structure to which the peristome teeth are attached in *Polytrichum* and related mosses.

Epiphytic   Living on another plant that supports it physically but not nutritionally.

Epiplasm   Residual cytoplasm around ascospores in asci.

Eukaryotic   Having membrane-bounded nuclei, plastids, Golgi apparatus, and mitochondria.

Eusporangiate   A method of sporangium development, contrasting with leptosporangiate, in which the sporangium develops from the internal division products of a cell or cells.

Eustele   Arrangement of xylem and phloem, not surrounded by endodermis, in discrete strands separated by parenchymatous tissue.

Evergreen   Never entirely leafless, as in pine or live oak.

Exocarp   The outermost layer of the pericarp in the fruit.

Eyespot   The stigma of certain algae.

Facultative Parasite   An organism which may grow saprobically or on another living organism.

False Indusium   An inrolled leaf margin that covers marginal sporangia; see also *true indusium*.

Fermentation   The anaerobic respiration of substrates.

Fertile   Reproductive, as contrasted with somatic.

Fertile spike   Designates the spikelike structure bearing sporangia in the *Ophioglossum* group of ferns.

Fertilization   The union of an egg and a sperm in oogamous sexual reproduction.

Filament   (1) A chain of cells. (2) The stalk of the angiosperm stamen.

Flagellum   An extension of the protoplasm, the beating of which propels the cell (plural, flagella).

Flora   The population of plants on part or all of the earth.

Floret   One of the small flowers composing a composite type of inflorescence.

Floridean Starch   A substance composed of extraplastid polysaccharides of red algae similar to the branched amylopectin fractions of other plant starches.

Flower   The reproductive region of angiosperms consisting of stamens, pistils, petals, and sepals, although one or more of these may be absent.

Foliose   Leaflike.

Foot   The absorbing organ of the embryonic sporophyte in liverworts, mosses, and seedless vascular plants.

Free-Nuclear Division   Successive mitoses not followed by cytoplasmic divisions.

Fruit   The matured ovary or ovaries of one or more flowers and their associated structures.

Frustule   The siliceous cell wall of diatoms.

Functional Megaspore   The surviving megaspore of the linear tetrad in seed plants, which produces the female gametophyte.

Gametangium   A structure containing gametes.

Gamete   A sex cell that unites with another to form a zygote.

Gametophore   A branch bearing gametangia and gametes.

Gametophyte   A plant or phase that produces gametes.

Gemma   A bud or fragment of an organism that functions in asexual reproduction (plural, gemmae).

Germination   Renewal of growth.

Golgi Apparatus   A cellular organelle consisting of stacks of sacs or cisternae that are secretory in function.

Gonidium(a)   The asexual cellular initials in algae like *Volvox*.

Ground Meristem   The primary meristematic tissue other than protoderm and procambium.

Growth   An irreversible increase in volume, with or without differentiation.

Guard Cells   Specialized epidermal cells that contain chloroplasts and surround a stoma.

Gymnosperm   A seed plant with seeds not enclosed by a megasporophyll or pistil.

Haploid   Having a single chromosome complement (set).

Haustorium   An absorptive hypha that penetrates a host cell (plural, haustoria).

Herbaceous   Soft rather than woody.

Heterocyst   A transparent, thick-walled blue-green algal cell.

Heteromorphic   Sporophytes and gametophytes that differ morphologically.

Heterospory   The production of microspores that grow into male gametophytes and of megaspores that develop into female gametophytes; the two kinds of spores may or may not differ in size.

Heterothallism   Being sexually self-incompatible, thus requiring two compatible strains or organisms for sexual reproduction.

Heterotrophic   Requiring organic compounds for nutrition; see also *autotrophic*.

Holdfast   An attaching cell or organ in algae.

Holozoic   Phagotrophic, that is, obtaining food by ingesting solid, complex organic particles.

Homoplasy   Parallel evolution.

Hormogonium   In blue-green algae, a trichome segment (usually motile) that can grow into a new trichome.

Hormone   A chemical substance produced by living cells, which has a specific effect on other cells, often remote from the site of production.

Host   An organism on which a parasite is growing.

Hydrophytic   Living in the water or in water-saturated soil.

Hypanthium   The tubular base of a corolla.

Hypha   One branch of mycelium in a fungus.

Hypocotyl   The portion of the plant axis between the cotyledonary node and the primary root.

Hypogyny   A condition in flowers in which the pistil or pistils originate above the other floral organs at the apex of the receptacle.

Imperfect   Flowers lacking either stamens or pistils.

Indehiscent   Not opening or splitting.

Indusium   See *false indusium* and *true indusium*.

Inflorescence   An axis bearing flowers, or a flower cluster.

Integument   The tissues covering the megasporangium in ovules.

Internode   The region of the stem between two nodes.

Isogamous   Having the type of sexual reproduction in which the gametes are morphologically indistinguishable.

Isomorphic   Sporophytes and gametophytes similar in structure.

Karyogamy   Nuclear union.

Kelp   A large seaweed (some of which are more than 100 feet long) of the brown algae.

Leaf Gap   A parenchymatous interruption in a stele, associated with departure of a leaf trace.

Leaf Primordium   A young leaf that will later develop into a mature leaf.

Leaf Scar   A scar at the node of a woody plant that remains after leaf abscission.

Lenticel   A region in the bark of woody stems where gaseous interchange occurs.

Leptosporangiate   A method of sporangium development in which a single superficial cell divides in a plane parallel to the leaf surface and the entire sporangium arises from the outer division product.

Ligule   A small, leaflike appendage at the base of a leaf, as in *Selaginella* and *Isoetes*.

Lip Cells   Thin-walled cells that interrupt the annulus in certain fern sporangia.

Locule   A cavity, like that in the angiosperm ovary, which contains ovules.

Lorica   Term applied to hardened outer covering of certain unicellular algae; it is often darkened with iron and/or manganese compounds.

Megaphyll   A leaf with branching veins, the traces of which are associated with gaps in the stem stele.

Megasporangium   The sporangium in which megaspores are produced.

Megaspore   A spore arising by meiosis in which all four products potentially can grow into female gametophytes; often, but not always, larger than microspores.

Megasporocyte   The megaspore mother cell, which forms megaspores after meiosis.

Megasporophyll   A leaf bearing one or more megasporangia or ovules.

Megastrobilus   The strobilus in which megaspores are produced.

Meiosis   A process involving two successive nuclear divisions, in which the chromosome number is halved and genetic segregation occurs.

Meiosporangium   A sporangium in which meiosis occurs.

Meiospore   A spore that develops immediately following meiosis.

Meristem   Actively reproducing cells or tissues.

Mesocarp   The layer of the pericarp between endocarp and exocarp in the fruit.

Mesophyll   The photosynthetic tissue, interspersed with veins, that is located between the lower and upper epidermis of a leaf.

Mesophytic   Living under moderately moist conditions.

Mesosome   An infolding of the plasma membrane to which the DNA and many enzymes are attached.

Metabolism   The normal, functional chemical processes occurring in living organisms.

Microphyll   A leaf with an unbranched vein, the trace of which leaves no gap in the stem stele.

Micropyle   A passageway between the apices of the integument or integuments of an ovule.

Microsporangium   A sporangium that produces microspores.

Microspore   A product of a microsporocyte, often, but not always, smaller than the megaspore of the particular species; the spore that produces a male gametophyte.

Microsporophyll   A leaf bearing one or more microsporangia.

Microstrobilus   A strobilus that produces microspores.

Mitochondrion   A double-membrane-bounded cytoplasmic organelle, the site of energy release in cellular respiration.

Mitosis   Nuclear division involving chromosomes that are replicated and distributed equally between the daughter nuclei.

Mitosporangium   A sporangium in which the spores arise by mitotic, rather than meiotic, nuclear divisions.

Monobiontic   Having only one free-living organism in the life cycle.

Monoecious   Producing both microspores and megaspores on one individual; having both male and female gametes on one individual.

Monopodial   Plant form in which there is one leaf-bearing major axis with minor leafy branches.

Multiple Fruit   A fruit developing from the maturing ovaries of more than one flower.

Mutation   A sudden change in an organism, morphological or biochemical, that is transmitted to offspring.

Mycelium   The collective term for the hyphae of a fungus; the somatic or vegetative thallus of a fungus.

Mycorrhiza   An either superficial or internal association of a root or rhizome with a fungus.

Nectar   A secretion from plant glands, which may contain amino acids and sugars.

Nitrogen Fixation   The use of gaseous nitrogen as the source of the nitrogen required in metabolism.

Node   Point of attachment of a leaf to a stem; also point of branch emergence.

Obligate Parasite   An organism that cannot exist apart from a host.

Ontogeny   The development of an individual.

Oogamous   Having the type of sexual reproduction that involves a large, nonmotile egg and a small sperm.

Oogonium   A unicellular gametangium that contains an egg.

Open Bud   A bud without bud scales that is continually unfolding.

Operculum   The coverlike apex of a moss capsule, freed by rupture at the annulus.

Osmotrophic   A form of nutrition involving the absorption into cells of soluble nutriments.

Ovary   The ovule-bearing region of a pistil.

Ovule   A megasporangium covered by an integument.

Palynology   The study of spores and pollen grains.

Paramylon   A β-1,3–linked glucan.

Paraphysis   A sterile structure among reproductive cells or organs (plural, paraphyses).

Parasite   An organism living in, upon, or at the expense of another.

Parenchyma   Thin-walled living cells with large vacuoles, that are active in either photosynthesis, storage, or secretion.

Parthenogenesis   The development of an embryo from a gamete without gametic union.

Pathogenic   Disease-causing.

Penicillin   An antibiotic produced by *Penicillium chrysogenum*.

Perennial   A plant that grows and reproduces during more than one growing season.

Perfect   Flowers having both stamens and pistils.

Perianth   (1) In flowering plants, the collective term for sepals and petals. (2) In liverworts, the leaves or other tissue surrounding a group of archegonia.

Pericarp   The ovary wall in the fruit.

Pericycle   A thin zone of living cells just within the endodermis.

Periderm   A corky layer and its generator, the cork cambium, at the surface of organs that are undergoing secondary growth.

Perigyny   A condition in flowers in which the pistil or pistils are sunken within (but free from) a cuplike structure from which the other floral organs arise.

Periplast   A complex and often ornamented plasma membrane.

Peristome   Cellular or acellular structures at the mouth of the capsule in many mosses, involved in spore dissemination.

Perithecium   A type of closed ascocarp with an apical pore.

Petal   A colored, usually sterile appendage of the angiospermous flower; see also *corolla*.

Petiole   The stalk that attaches the leaf blade of a plant to the stem.

Phagotrophic   Obtaining food by ingesting solid organic particles.

Phanerogam   Refers to seed plants.

Phellogen (cork cambium)   A layer of meristematic cells the outer derivatives of which differentiate into cork cells and the inner into parenchyma cells.

Phloem   Living, thin-walled cells, typified by sieve areas in the walls of some of the cells, that function in food-conducting.

Photoautotrophic   Able to use light energy in synthesizing protoplasm from inorganic compounds.

Photoperiod   The light/dark cycle; the relative lengths of daylight and darkness that vary with the seasons.

Phototaxis   Movement stimulated positively or negatively by light.

Phycobilisome   Particulate body attached to the surfaces of photosynthetic membranes in red and blue-green algae that contains the phycobilin pigments.

Phyllotaxy   The pattern of arrangement of appendages (leaves, flower parts, and so forth) upon an axis.

Phylogeny   The evolutionary history of a structure or species.

Pilus   An extension of a bacterial cell that makes contact with another cell in the exchange of genetic material.

Pistil   A megasporophyll, carpel, or group of united megasporophylls in angiosperms.

Pit Connection   Bilenticular structure deposited in the cell wall between daughter cells in the red algae.

Pith   The parenchyma cells at the center of certain stems and roots, inside the zone of primary xylem.

Placentation   The pattern of ovular attachment.

Plankton   Suspended, free-floating, aquatic microorganisms.

Plasmodium   An unwalled, ameboid, multinucleate mass of protoplasm.

Plasmogamy   Union of sex cells or gametes.

Plastid   Any of a group of photosynthetic lamellae bounded by two membranes.

Plumule   The terminal bud of an embryo; epicotyl.

Plurilocular   Having a multicellular structure, each cubical cell producing a single reproductive cell.

Pod   A simple dry, dehiscent fruit that usually opens along two sutures at maturity.

Polar Nuclei   The nuclei of the angiosperm female gametophyte that migrate to the center from the poles of the gametophyte.

Pollen Chamber   A depression at the apex of the megasporangium, formed by cellular breakdown, in which pollen grains are deposited.

Pollen Grain   A microspore containing a mature or immature male gametophyte.

Pollination   The transfer of pollen from the microsporangium to the micropyle of the ovule (in gymnosperms) or to the stigma of the pistil (in angiosperms).

Pollination Droplet   A droplet of fluid at the micropyle involved in pollination.

Polyembryony   The condition of producing more than in embryo: simple polyembryony, the embryos arise from different zygotes; in cleavage polyembryony they represent cleavage products of one embryo.

Polyphyletic   Arising from separate evolutionary lines.

Polyploid   Having two or more times the basic chromosomal complement.

Pome   A simple, fleshy fruit arising from an epigynous flower and consisting of an ovary (true fruit) enclosed by a fleshy floral tube.

Primary Endosperm Nucleus   The nucleus formed by the union of two polar nuclei (or a secondary nucleus) with a sperm, in angiosperms.

Primary Growth   Growth and differentiation which originate in the apical and primary meristems.

Primary Meristem   The three meristematic derivatives (protoderm, procambium, and ground meristem) of the apical meristem.

Primary Mycelium   The haploid mycelium produced by the germination of a basidiospore, as in a mushroom.

Primary Root   The embryonic root after seed germination.

Primary Tissue   A tissue that has differentiated from a primary meristem.

Procambium   The part of the primary meristem that differentiates into vascular tissue and cambium (if present).

Prokaryotic   Lacking membrane-bounded nuclei, plastids, Golgi apparatus, and mitochondria.

Prothallium or Prothallus   The gametophyte of vascular cryptogams, especially that of ferns.

Protoderm   The part of the primary meristem that differentiates into epidermis.

Protonema   The product of spore germination in mosses and certain liverworts, the precursor of the leafy gametophores.

Protostele   A solid core composed of xylem surrounded by phloem in the plant axis.

Provascular Tissue   The procambium.

Pseudoplasmodium   An aggregate of amoebae in cellular slime molds.

Radicle   The primary or embryonic root.

Receptacle   An area of a plant on which reproductive organs are borne.

Rhizoid   A unicellular or multicellular absorbing organ lacking vascular tissue and a root cap.

Rhizome   An elongate, nonerect stem that is often, but not always, subterranean and often fleshy.

Rhizophore   A root-bearing organ or region.

Root Cap   A covering of parenchymatous cells over the apical meristem of the root.

Root Hair   An absorptive unicellular protuberance of the epidermal cells of the root.

Saprobic   Obtaining food by absorbing soluble nonliving organic matter.

Secondary Growth   Growth and differentiation which originate from the vascular cambium and cork cambium.

Secondary Mycelium   The product of fusion of the hyphae of two compatible primary mycelia, as in mushrooms.

Secondary Root   A branch from the primary root.

Secondary Tissue   Tissue that originates from a secondary meristem (either the cambium or the cork cambium).

Seed   An embryonic sporophyte embedded in the female gametophyte (in gymnosperms) or in the endosperm, or gorged with digested products of the endosperm (in angiosperms), enclosed within the remains of the megasporangium and covered with one or more integuments.

Sepal   Any of the lowermost sterile appendages, usually green, on a floral receptacle.

Seta   The stalklike region between the foot and the capsule in liverwort and moss sporophytes.

Sexual Reproduction   Reproduction involving nuclear union and meiosis, and often plasmogamy.

Sieve Cell   A single cell with sieve plates or areas.

Sieve Tube   A series of sieve cells.

Silique   The simple partitioned fruit in the mustard family.

Simple Fruit   A fruit derived from a single pistil (simple or compound) of a single flower.

Simple Leaf   A leaf with an undivided blade.

Siphonostele   A hollow cylinder composed of xylem and phloem.

Sirenin   A secreted substance that attracts male gametes in sexual reproduction of *Allomyces*.

Somatic   Vegetative; not reproductive or germinal.

Somatogamy   The union of somatic fungal hyphae as in certain Ascomycota and Basidiomycota.

Sorus   A group or cluster of plant reproductive bodies, such as fern sporangia.

Sperm   The motile male gamete or male nucleus.

Spermatium   A minute, nonflagellate male gamete.

Spirillum   A spirally twisted bacterium.

Sporangiophore   (1) In certain molds, a hypha bearing a sporangium at its apex. (2) In seedless vascular plants, a branch bearing sporangia.

Spore   A mitotically or meiotically derived reproductive body capable of producing a new organism or phase.

Spore Mother Cell   See *sporocyte*.

Sporocarp A hard, nutlike structure containing sori of heterosporous sporangia in ferns; also the spore-bearing structure in certain fungi.

Sporocyte That cell which undergoes meiosis and forms spores.

Sporophore A spore-bearing structure as in slime molds and certain fungi.

Sporophyll A leaf bearing one or more sporangia.

Sporophyte The diploid, spore-producing alternate of the alternating generations.

Spur Shoot A lateral, dwarf shoot in certain woody plants.

Stamen The microsporophyll of angiosperms.

Stele The primary vascular tissue and closely associated tissues of axes.

Stigma (1) The red eyespot of algae. (2) In angiosperms, the receptive region of the pistil.

Stolon An elongate, horizontal stem rooting at the nodes as its passes over the soil surface.

Stoma A minute, intercellular fissure in the epidermis, surrounded by guard cells.

Strobilus A stem with short internodes and spore-bearing appendages.

Style The portion of a pistil between the stigma and the ovary.

Suberin Cork.

Synangium A structure composed of fused sporangia.

Synergids Sterile cells associated with the angiosperm egg.

Tapetum The nutritive tissue in sporangia.

Taproot An elongate, deeply growing primary root.

Tepal A segment of the perianth not differentiated as are petals and sepals.

Tetrad A group of four (often used in the term "spore tetrad").

Tetrasporangium In red algae, a sporangium that gives rise to four spores after meiosis.

Tetraspore The product of meiosis in a tetrasporangium.

Tetrasporophyte In the red algae, the diploid plant that produces tetraspores.

Thallose Lacking roots, stems, and leaves.

Thallus The plant body of algae and fungi, and the gametophytic stages of liverworts and sometimes other seedless plants (plural, thalli).

Thylakoid The photosynthetic lamella of a chloroplast.

Tissue A group of cells that perform a common function.

Trace A vascular connection from the stele of an axis to an appendage.

Tracheid   A single-celled, lignified, nonliving, water-conducting element of xylem.

Transduction   Genetic modification (in bacteria) effected by the DNA of viruses (bacteriophages).

Transformation   Genetic recombination involving incorporation of DNA from the environment of a microorganism (bacterium).

Trichome   (1) A chain of cells, in blue-green algae. (2) An epidermal hair, in vascular plants.

True Indusium   A thin layer of epidermal outgrowth covering receptacle and sporangia in certain ferns; see also *false indusium*.

Tube Nucleus   The nucleus of the pollen tube, other than the sperm nuclei.

Tuber   The enlarged tip of a rhizome, filled with stored food (usually starch).

Unilocular   Having a single cavity.

Uredinium   The area of rust mycelium that produces urediniospores.

Vacuole   A cavity filled with fluid (the cell sap) within a cell.

Valve   (1) Half of a diatom frustule. (2) A segment of the capsule wall of liverworts and hornworts at dehiscence.

Vascular Bundle Scar   The scars of vascular bundles, visible within leaf scars.

Vascular Tissue   Xylem and phloem.

Vegetative   Somatic, not usually reproductive.

Vein   The strand of xylem and phloem in a leaf.

Venation   The pattern of vein arrangement in leaves.

Vernation   The pattern of arrangement of embryonic leaves within the bud.

Vessel   A series of perforated, lignified, conducting cells of xylem.

Water Bloom   A dense population of planktonic algae.

Wood   Secondary xylem.

Xerophytic   Living in an extremely dry or arid habitat.

Xylem   Lignified, water-conducting tissue.

Zoosporangium   A sporangium that produces zoospores.

Zoospore   A motile, asexual reproductive cell formed by a nonmotile organism.

Zygote   The cell produced by the union of two gametes.

Zymase   An intracellular enzyme complex that degrades sugar to ethyl alcohol and carbon dioxide.

Selected Readings

ALEXOPOULOS, C. J., and H. C. BOLD. *Algae and Fungi*. New York: The Macmillan Company, 1967. A brief discussion of algae and fungi for the general reader.

ALEXOPOULOS, C. J., and C. W. MIMS. *Introductory Mycology*. New York: John Wiley & Sons, Inc., 1979. A well-illustrated general account of the fungi.

ANDREWS, H. N. *Studies in Paleobotany*. New York: John Wiley & Sons, Inc., 1961. A survey of fossil plants and their relationships to extant forms; includes an introduction to palynology.

BENSON, L. *Plant Classification*. Boston: D. C. Heath & Company, 1957. A comprehensive treatment of the classification of vascular plants and the criteria on which the classification is based. Also includes instructions for identifying plants and preserving specimens. The book closes with a consideration of some aspects of plant ecology and a discussion of the floras of North America.

BIERHORST, D. W. *Morphology of Vascular Plants*. New York: The Macmillan Company, 1971. A comprehensive and in-depth treatment of vascular plants.

BOLD, H. C., C. J. ALEXOPOULOS, and T. DELEVORYAS. *Morphology of Plants and Fungi*. New York: Harper & Row, Publishers, 1980. A summary of plant structure and reproduction with reference to algae, fungi, liverworts, mosses, and vascular plants, both seed-bearing and seedless. Includes discussion of systems of classification and of plants of the past.

BOLD, H. C., and M. J. WYNNE. *Introduction to the Algae. Structure and Reproduction*. Englewood Cliffs, NJ: Prentice-Hall, Inc., 1985. A comprehensive survey of the algal groups, with emphasis on structure and reproduction.

BROCK, T. D., D. W. SMITH, and M. T. MADIGAN. *Biology of Microorganisms*. Englewood Cliffs, NJ: Prentice-Hall, Inc., 1984. A comprehensive account of bacteria and other microorganisms.

DELEVORYAS, T. *Morphology and Evolution of Fossil Plants*. New York: Holt, Rinehart & Winston, Inc., 1962. A brief treatment of the nature of fossil floras.

————. *Plant Diversification*. New York: Holt, Rinehart & Winston, Inc., 1962. Selected topics in the evolution of plants.

EAMES, A. J. *Morphology of the Angiosperms*. New York: McGraw-Hill Book Company, 1961. A comprehensive treatment, at an advanced level, of the anatomy and reproductive process in the flowering plants.

ESAU, K. *Plant Anatomy*. New York: John Wiley & Sons, Inc., 1965. A detailed and comprehensive account of the gross and minute structure of vascular plants, with copious illustrations.

FOSTER, A. S., and E. M. GIFFORD, JR. *Comparative Morphology of Vascular Plants*. San Francisco: W. H. Freeman and Co., Publishers, 1974. A summary, at a somewhat advanced level, of the structure and reproduction of vascular plants, and a discussion of general topics in plant morphology.

GRANT, V. *The Evolutionary Process. A Critical Review of Evolutionary Theory*. New York: Columbia University Press, 1985. Excellent discussion of phylogeny and evolution of plant groups.

MEEUSE, B. J. D. *The Story of Pollination*. New York: The Ronald Press Company, 1961.

PARIHAR, N. S. *An Introduction to Embryophyta,* Vol. I (*Bryophyta*) and Vol. II (*Pteriodophytes*). Allahabad, India: Central Book Depot, 1967.

SCAGEL, R. F., R. J. BANDONI, J. R. MAZE, G. E. ROUSE, W. B. SCHOFIELD, and J. R. STEIN. *Nonvascular Plants. An Evolutionary Survey*. Belmont, CA: Wadsworth Publishing Co., Inc., 1982. A comprehensive account of nonvascular plants emphasizing phylogeny and groups of organisms.

SCAGEL, R. F., R. J. BANDONI, G. E. ROUSE, W. B. SCHOFIELD, J. R. STEIN, and T. C. TAYLOR. *An Evolutionary Survey of the Plant Kingdom*. Belmont, CA: Wadsworth Publishing Co., Inc., 1984. A comprehensive account of the plant kingdom emphasizing phylogeny and groups of organisms.

SMITH, G. M. *Cryptogamic Botany*, Vols. I and II. New York: McGraw-Hill Book Company, 1955. A two-volume, advanced-level treatment of representative algae, fungi, liverworts, mosses, ferns, and other seedless vascular plants.

SPORNE, K. R. *The Morphology of Pteridophytes: The Structure of Ferns and Allied Plants,* 2nd ed. London: Hutchinson & Co. (Publishers) Ltd., 1970.

————. *The Morphology of Angiosperms*. London: Hutchinson & Co. (Publishers) Ltd. 1974.

————. *The Morphology of Gymnosperms: The Structure and Evolution of Primitive Seed-plants*. New York: Hillary House Publisher, Ltd., 1974.

STANIER, R. Y., I. INGRAHAM, M. WHEELIS, and P. PAINTER. *The Microbial World,* 5th ed. Englewood Cliffs, NJ: Prentice-Hall, Inc., 1986. A comprehensive introduction to microbiology.

STEBBINS, G. L. *Processes of Organic Evolution*. Englewood Cliffs, NJ: Prentice-Hall, Inc., 1972.

STEEVES, T. A., and J. M. SUSSEX. *Patterns in Plant Development*. Englewood Cliffs, NJ: Prentice-Hall, Inc., 1972. A consideration of development and differentiation of plant organs.

STEWART, W. H. *Paleobotany and the Evolution of Plants*. Cambridge: Cambridge University Press, 1983. A readable account of the fossil record of plants designed especially for students.

TAYLOR, T. N. *Paleobotany. An Introduction to Fossil Plant Biology*. New York: McGraw-Hill Book Co., 1981. Comprehensive and encyclopedic reference book.

Index

P